The Work & the Gift

The Work & the Gift

Scott Cutler Shershow

THE UNIVERSITY OF CHICAGO PRESS | CHICAGO AND LONDON

SCOTT CUTLER SHERSHOW is professor of English at the University of California, Davis. He is the author of *Puppets and "Popular" Culture* and *Laughing Matters: The Paradox of Comedy*. He is also the coeditor of *Marxist Shakespeares*.

The University of Chicago Press, Chicago 60637
The University of Chicago Press, Ltd., London
© 2005 by The University of Chicago
All rights reserved. Published 2005
Printed in the United States of America

14 13 12 11 10 09 08 07 06 05   5 4 3 2 1

ISBN (cloth): 0-226-75256-9
ISBN (paper): 0-226-75257-7

Library of Congress Cataloging-in-Publication Data

Shershow, Scott Cutler, 1953–
        The work and the gift / Scott Cutler Shershow.
            p.   cm.
        Includes bibliographical references and index.
        ISBN 0-226-75256-9 (cloth : alk. paper) — ISBN 0-226-75257-7 (alk. paper)
        1. Work—Philosophy.   2. Generosity.   I. Title.
    HD4904.S444   2005
    331′.01—dc22

                                                        2004023854

♾ The paper used in this publication meets the minimum requirements of the American National Standard for Information Sciences—Permanence of Paper for Printed Library Materials, ANSI Z39.48-1992.

For Helen Elizabeth Shershow (1913–2000)

&

Albert Shershow (1908–2003)

CONTENTS

ACKNOWLEDGMENTS

Portions of this book were published in the essays "Shakespeare beyond Shakespeare," in *Marxist Shakespeares,* edited by Jean E. Howard and Scott Cutler Shershow (London: Routledge, 2000); "Of Sinking: Marxism and the 'General' Economy," *Critical Inquiry* 27, no. 3 (Spring 2001); and "Work and the Gift: Notes Toward an Investigation," in *Money and the Age of Shakespeare: Essays in New Economic Criticism,* copyright © Edited by Linda Woodbridge (New York: Palgrave, 2004). I'd like to thank the respective publishers for permission to reprint this material. Thanks also to Bill Brown at *Critical Inquiry,* who made some particularly helpful suggestions at a formative stage of this project, to Terence Hawkes and Jean E. Howard, my general editor and coeditor on the Marxist anthology, and to Linda Woodbridge, whose comments and queries helped me sharpen the present book's fundamental arguments. I'm grateful to the two anonymous readers of the draft manuscript, who guided my revisions with their detailed suggestions, and to Alan Thomas and Randolph Petilos at the University of Chicago Press, in particular for making their evaluation of the manuscript a process of intellectual collaboration, and to Pamela J. Bruton for editing the manuscript with care and precision.

Thanks also to the College of Arts and Sciences at Miami University in Oxford, Ohio, for its award of an assigned-research appointment in 2001–2. Many of my colleagues at Miami provided commentary and encouragement at various points in the development of this project, especially Barry Chabot, Britton Harwood, Tim Melley, Susan Morgan, and Peter Rose. Thanks to Crystal Bartolovich and Dympna Callaghan for inviting me to present a portion of the book at Syracuse University and for helping to shape it with their tough questions. My colleagues at the University of California, Davis, raised a variety of illuminating questions and comments when I first shared some of these arguments with them; among many others, I thank in particular Greg Dobbins, Margaret Ferguson, Bishnupriya Gosh, Karen Shimakawa, David Simpson, and Evan Watkins. Thanks also to Neal Larsen and the students in Davis with whom I reread Marx's *Capital* as I was putting the final touches on the manuscript.

I have shared an intense intellectual camaraderie with Scott Michaelsen for many years, and our regular discussions of theory and politics have recently blossomed into ongoing collaboration. Many of the arguments of this book were deeply shaped by our conversations, and although a few particular debts to him are recorded in the notes, I add here that the value of his contribution to the book, like that of his friendship, is strictly incalculable.

Finally, I give thanks, which can only be inadequate, to Frances E. Dolan for her many careful readings of this book, for sharing these ideas with me "from California to the New York island," for her advice and encouragement in all my works and days, and for the boundless generosity and limitless joy that, because of her, are simply *given:* in short, for everything, and more.

When someone works for less pay than she can live on—when, for example, she goes hungry so that you can eat more cheaply and conveniently—then she . . . has made you a gift of some part of her abilities, her health and her life. The "working poor," as they are approvingly termed, are in the fact the major philanthropists of our society.

BARBARA EHRENREICH

I'm taking what they're giving
'Cause I'm working for a living.

HUEY LEWIS AND THE NEWS

INTRODUCTION

To begin with, a reckless generalization: practically everything that one might call art or politics or thought—everything, to adapt the Aristotelian figure, that goes beyond mere living and reaches toward living *well*—has for too long been understood in terms of a fatal conjunction of work and the gift. These two present themselves as the most familiar practices of everyday life and as the most vexed of theoretical questions. In either guise, they confront one another in a pattern of convergence and contradiction, each one figuring the other's aspiration and limit.

In this book, the first of these two central terms designates an imaginary spectrum of ideas and practices whose two poles will be called *work* and *the Work*. On the one side, the daily exertions that are always done and never done, the labors by which one lives or, as it is said, *makes a living*. On the other side, the project or the poem, the *opus*, the *oeuvre*, or the Book: those achieved or imagined totalities in which, as Maurice Blanchot puts it, "all combinations of forms, words and letters are rolled up in volumes," and that remain "still to be read, still to be written, always already written, always already paralyzed by reading" (*Station Hill Reader* 471). There will never be an absolute distinction between the two sides of this opposition, for to consider work in any sense is of course also to rebegin the Work of (theorizing) work: the unfinished labor of thinking its value, its necessity, its purpose, or its end(s).

The second of my titular terms designates another spectrum on which both common practices and formidable intellectual debates must be placed in

1

relation. On the one side, the familiar and literal forms of giving: tokens exchanged on special days and everything known under names such as charity, relief, or welfare—practices still at the center of urgent political struggles, as they have been since at least the dawn of modernity. On the other side, an idea or ideal of the gift that once served, in the discourse of a premodern "moral economy," as the very symbol and epitome of benevolent social practice and that still haunts the human sciences in our own time, where it is often seen as a primal building block of culture itself.

One can see the inescapable connection of working and giving vividly figured in a familiar encounter with the social subject variously named beggar, rogue, bum, panhandler, freeloader, and the like. Such a subject, precisely because he or she neither works nor earns, necessarily signifies, as Derrida suggests, "the absolute demand of the other, the inextinguishable appeal, the unquenchable thirst for the gift" (*Given Time* 137). Here, for example, is the comedian Steve Martin's miniature representation of this encounter:

> I'm so mad at my mother!
> She's a hundred and two years old. She called me up the other day; she wanted to borrow ten dollars for some food.
> I said: "Hey! I *work* for a living!"[1]

In this typically untypical case, the excess of the parody merely crystallizes a logic that is also perfectly familiar: a logic by which, as I shall put it in the pages that follow, one refuses or annuls the gift in the name of work. Why should your idleness command the fruits of my labor? Why don't you get a job? It is difficult or impossible, some will claim, to escape these imprisoning economies of effort and scarcity, economies that always seem to cut toward one or the other of my titular terms. That is, we not only commonly refuse to give in the name of work but also are commanded to work in the name of the gift. "Let him rather labour," preaches Saint Paul, "that he may have to give unto him that needeth" (Ephesians 4:28). God created poverty, it has often been sermonized, so that rich people might have an opportunity to be generous.

Needless to say, it is also worth noticing that the one playing the beggar's part in this miniature comic scene is the other speaker's elderly mother. The scene thus takes place in perhaps the only context (the family) where we might at least imagine it should never take place. It is by no means insignificant that the thought of work always reserves some space outside the implacable law of Value, some place where one allegedly gives without thought and strives without recompense. In this case, however, the comic exaggeration merely high-lights how the idea of work, far more commonly, merely heralds a double re-fusal of the gift.

I say the refusal is double because it is not always made in the name of the particular work, "my" work, through which the money that may or may not be given came to be "mine." Here is another miniature representation of the same scene, from a profile of the contemporary utilitarian philosopher Peter Singer:

I saw him walk past homeless beggars without giving them a glance. When I asked if that was difficult he looked surprised. "Not at all," he said. "Maybe you just help them take themselves into oblivion for a while. I would much rather give where I am con-vinced that the money will be used for good." (Specter 53)

This is the equally familiar situation in which the refusal to give becomes a *project:* an annulment of the gift in the name of *the Work.* Let us be clear: the logic that comes into play in this second case cannot be reduced to mere selfish-ness or indifference, for it involves something more like the reverse of both. Yet I will also claim, here at the beginning, that when I give to a beggar, I try to do it without such thought; because giving without thought, if it were pos-sible, would be the one thing that would make me certain that my gift had reached its destination.

The pages that follow thus join a long tradition of thought—some, though not all, of it identifiable as Marxist—that tries to imagine a world no longer doomed to the curse of endless labor, a world where work is no longer man-dated and the gift, accordingly, no longer isolated from a collective life finally recognized as something that can always and only be shared. Let us go ahead and assume that material existence always in principle requires a certain amount of corporeal and mental effort. Let us further assume that a complex and highly developed society such as ours will, for the foreseeable future, con-tinue to require contributions of time and energy from its members. But after all such assumptions, what will remain in question are the myriad other con-straints and obligations that have been so deeply invested in the idea of work that they now appear as inevitable as material necessity itself.

In part 1 of this book, I consider an emerging contemporary consensus that the evolution of capitalism in our times has brought the practice and idea of work to a moment of fundamental crisis. This debate, I suggest, continues to be profoundly influenced by the Marxist critique of labor under the regime of capital—no less for those on the Right who celebrate the transformative potential of a new so-called information economy than for those on the Left who either lament the loss of work's traditional role in human experience or, on the contrary, envision a world where work no longer presents itself as an absolute social obligation. But what remains largely unquestioned across this entire debate, just as it does in classical Marxism itself, is a kind of ethos, or even an ontology, of production: an assumption that work is not only an indispensable requirement for democratic citizenship but, indeed, the absolute token of our common social being, the very figure of our personal or collective freedom.

Specifically, in the first chapter I consider several disparate examples in order to elucidate what I will call the *double necessity of work*. With this phrase, I refer to the common paradox or double-bind by which we see ourselves both as *working to live* and as *living to work*. That is, we understand human labor, at one and the same time, as an inevitable response to brute material scarcity and yet also as a vehicle for those aesthetic or intellectual or spiritual productions that, in their turn, produce and express a personal or collective Work of self and community. In contemporary Marxist interpretations of the Soviet disaster, in Hannah Arendt's critique of Marxism, and in Tony Kushner's acclaimed epic drama *Angels in America,* one sees repeatedly how even writers engaged in powerful and necessary critiques of work under capitalism cannot give up their faith in creativity and self-development as definitive characteristics of the human condition. In chapters 2–4, I consider in more detail a series of other contemporary writers, on both the Right and the Left, who try to articulate work's contemporary crisis or historical fulfillment. All these, I suggest, have so far been unable to abandon a deep-seated assumption of work's absolute personal, spiritual, or existential necessity. Indeed, all these attempts to address our contemporary crisis of work, despite their radically different political assumptions and goals, finally converge in a shared affirmation of a social subject defined by its productivity and therefore itself constituted *in and as a Work*. Such thought can only lead, I suggest, to a politics of exclusion—because, to put it plainly, any attempt to view common being as something to be produced finally must exclude anyone who fails to produce.

In part 2, I move on to consider the pervasive fascination, across the contemporary human sciences, with the idea of the gift. Specifically, I address the theoretical trajectory extending from the anthropological speculations of Marcel Mauss and others about an archaic "gift economy" alleged to precede (or coexist with) the economy of exchange, to Georges Bataille's theoretical projection of a "general economy" of surplus and loss, and, finally, to Jacques Derrida's rigorous philosophic critique of the gift. Two fundamental points will be at stake throughout part 2: first, the evident continuing appeal of the gift as a rubric or figure of the utopian imagination; and second, a certain theoretical weakness that the idea of the gift seems to retain in any of its intellectual applications. On the one hand, the gift presents itself as a radical Other of the commodity—and therefore also of work, insofar as the latter is understood as an investment of time and energy made in the expectation of wages or profit. On the other hand, the idea of the gift seems constantly to be drawn back under the horizon of rational exchange, and to be thus endlessly re-revealed as a secret ally of both work and the Work.

I sketch the terms of this theoretical dilemma in chapter 5, once again using several disparate examples—including James Cameron's immensely popular film *Titanic* (1996) and readings of Bataille by Jacques Derrida and Jean-Joseph Goux—to suggest how contemporary discourse reveals at once an inextinguishable desire for the absolute gift and a relentless refusal to embrace (as Derrida puts it) *what giving wants to say*. In chapter 6, I consider in more detail the famous hypothesis of an archaic gift economy, suggesting that the fatal vulnerability of the gift as a figure of radical economic critique stems, at least in part, from its reliance on an anthropological narrative of origins.

In chapters 7–8, I go on to consider several specific instances of what will increasingly appear to be this fatal interconnection of my two titular terms. In chapter 7, under the schematic formula *the gift as work,* I consider the ideas and practices of charity and welfare. In discourses ranging from the early-modern period to the present moment, one sees repeatedly what I described above as a double annulment of the gift in the name of work. Not only is it argued that the gift of charitable assistance must be earned with enforced labor, but forcing the individual to work with these conditional gifts is itself envisioned as a collective Work of social amelioration.

In chapter 8, correspondingly, under the symmetrically reverse formula *the Work as gift,* I consider the theology of culture: that is, the persistent figure or habit of thought in which human creativity—the Work in its fully developed sense—is understood to be the expression or manifestation of spiritual or personal "gifts" and "talents." In this case, the Work, precisely insofar as it seems to epitomize self-development and freedom, also reveals itself as inextricably bound up in imperatives of duty and obligation. I discover this implicit figure of the Work as (conditional) gift in a variety of otherwise unrelated discourses: in the so-called culture wars of the contemporary academy, in common tropes of the so-called moral economy, in the Kantian categorical imperative, and in F. A. Hayek's libertarian philosophy. In the latter, perhaps most vividly of all, a so-called liberty is centrally affirmed and yet understood as nothing other than a freedom to *produce:* a freedom, therefore, that is in principle not free and that can therefore lead only to a politics of exclusion.

In part 3, I consider several examples of modern and postmodern art and philosophy in which one at least glimpses a way beyond these fatal and self-defeating unities of work and gift. Chapter 9 begins by considering two aspects of twentieth-century avant-garde art: first, the familiar modernist attempt to destabilize the Work by embracing the imagery or techniques of industrial labor; and second, a parallel attempt to destabilize the Work as a *property* via various tactics of appropriation, *"détournement,"* immateriality, and the like. In effect, plagiarism and potlatch, the Work and the gift, prove to be key conceptual sites for a continuing avant-garde critique that, however, never quite succeeds in the kind of radical negation or displacement of art (what the Situationists call art's *supersession*) at which it aims. At this limit, I interpose Maurice Blanchot's "unworking" (*désoeuvrement*), a term that refers obliquely to a certain principle of incompletion that haunts all forms of labor and, especially, every Work of writing, art, or thought. This enigmatic nonconcept indicates or uncovers something which cannot quite be made present: the fragmentation that remains in all that is finished or coherent, the absence at the heart of mortal being itself. As such, however, it makes possible a radical displacement of the opposition of work and the Work and, even more broadly, dispels the exclusionary politics which such an opposition seems inevitably to bring in its wake.

The final chapter recapitulates a number of the interrelated debates touched on throughout the book. I begin by reconsidering how a fundamental opposition of means and ends seems to underwrite the whole field of "economics" itself, even as it reveals a kind of terminal instability whose limit is reached in a prevailing mode of "free-market" capitalist ideology. To state the point in Bataille's terms, contemporary capitalism tries to cloak itself in the glamour of "general" excess (declaring itself an absolute moral and social end in itself) even as it also grounds itself in the alleged existence of a social subject wholly determined by a restricted economy of scarcity and need. Thus, such an ideology finally consigns us, with absolute paradox, to a world that, as it were, must endlessly be produced and yet cannot ever be remade. At this limit, I follow Derrida and Jean-Luc Nancy in projecting a different possible relation between scarcity and surplus, between the restricted and general economies. Material necessity itself, no longer grasped as an infinite reproach to (mortal) being, reveals itself instead as that which binds us to the community, where energy and value are indeed limitless, and where every kind of calculation undoes itself by being shared. This *communauté désoeuvrée,* this community of unworking (as Nancy has named it), is grounded neither in traditional ideals of production and progress (like either Western capitalism or Soviet communism) nor in an ethic of liberal generosity and mutual obligation, nor even in any conceivable model of identity and common being. Rather, such a community is made or formed in the sharing of finitude itself, by beings who experience their own material neediness as their access to a collective wealth that is, if not precisely infinite, then at least *without limit.* Such beings, as it were, neither work nor give but rather simply *exert themselves:* putting themselves forth in an infinite ex-position that is also an entwining (*ex-serere*), a being-in-common.

But how, one will almost certainly want to ask, do these somewhat abstract formulations, as we like to put it, *work in practice?* Whenever I have presented any of these arguments publicly, I am almost invariably confronted with some version of this question. I am asked, for example: in the coming community for which you argue, who will pick up the garbage? Who will care for the children and nurse the sick? Even in the most extravagant fantasy of a technoparadise, who will mind the machines? I am always at first tempted to reply with equal simplicity and to say merely: *now* you're talking! For such questions, of course, will not *end* but, rather, *begin,* as though for the first time, precisely when we have released ourselves from our self-imposed lives at hard labor, and when work no longer appears without question as the only possible human vocation and the absolute figure of self-fulfillment. One way or the other, obviously enough, we will always have to determine just how we will share the work that we will decide has to be done. A more rigorous way to say the same thing is to stipulate that this argument remains first and last a *negative* one, and that it cannot in principle be specified in advance who (or what) will emerge on the other side of the world of work.[2]

At any rate, it is clear that we already live these questions both in the form of urgent political struggles (over welfare and poverty, or the length and quality of the working day) and also as what one can only call matters of the heart: aesthetic or theoretical or religious questions that seemingly take place as far as might be from the workaday world. I will try to address some of these struggles and questions in more detail in the pages that follow. Let me stipulate, however, that this book is in no sense a history or comprehensive survey of all the practices and ideas that might be referred to under the names "working" and "giving." Rather, it addresses the dilemma of historic proportions which they join to constitute. Throughout the book, I argue, in brief, that the attempt to think either the Work or the gift always seems to make it both unavoidable and yet impossible to think the other. This fatal conjunction continues today to vex our politics and our thought as it has done for centuries. It is high time to begin to think our way through it.

PART ONE | THE END(S) OF WORK

DEFINING A CRISIS

The Double Necessity of Work

In the final decades of the second millennium, a whole range of thinkers, otherwise widely different in their political and theoretical allegiances, began to move toward a consensus that the social existence of work had reached a historical crisis. To cite just a few preliminary examples, as far back as 1966, British economist Robert Theobald was already citing "a growing number of experts" who concluded "that the continuing impact of technological change will make it impossible to provide jobs for all who seek them" (17). In 1985, members of the American Sociological Association, at their annual meeting, devoted to the topic "Working and Not Working," largely agreed that "the nature of work in America is being transformed," that "the values and expectations of those who work . . . are shifting as well," and that "most of the familiar patterns of the world of work are at risk" (1). And in 1995, in a controversial but widely discussed book, Jeremy Rifkin declared that "the century-old dream of a future techno-paradise is within sight. The technologies of the information and communication revolution hold out the long-anticipated promise of a near-workerless world in the coming century" (56). I will soon discuss many other examples from writers in a variety of contexts who suggest that the social existence of work, both as a concrete practice and as a political, theological, and philosophic idea, is at last beginning to transform itself. This crisis of work, still perhaps barely nascent as I write these lines, involves the coming-to-question of some of the most deep-seated assumptions of our civilization:

an event—if it can be called an event—whose epochal importance cannot be overestimated.

To be sure, the vast majority of human beings today still work as hard, or harder, than they have ever done. Our institutions are still founded on the work ethic; our public discourses still celebrate work as a uniquely privileged factor in the formation of an individual human life and the moral health of a democratic citizenry. If anything, globalization is extending the discipline of industrial labor to ever-greater areas of the world, even as workers in the West are facing the rollback of traditional benefits, a lengthening workday, and more and more of the kind of temporary and insecure employment arrangements that used to prevail only in the undeveloped South.[1] Nevertheless, as I suggest in the pages that follow, an unmistakable suspicion haunts our thought not only that there may soon not be enough work to go around but also that the very idea of work "has become an entity without substance," a self-perpetuating ritual, a myth that is finally becoming obsolete (Forrester 1–8). And so it might almost be possible, at long last, for human beings to question what Ulrich Beck aptly calls "the godlike powers of work to provide everything sacred to them: prosperity, social position, personality, meaning in life, democracy, political cohesion" (63).[2]

In roughly the same years, and even as futurists and social scientists were thus beginning to contemplate the end of work, a variety of thinkers in other disciplines were beginning to contemplate the end of the Work. A great many important currents in philosophy and literary theory might be cited here. These would include, among many other possible examples, Martin Heidegger's critique of metaphysics, Georges Bataille's critique of economic reason, Maurice Blanchot's analysis of the "absence" at the heart of writing and the Book, Jean François Lyotard's announcement of the end of "grand narratives," Jean-Luc Nancy's critique of the "work" of community, and Jacques Derrida's critique of "logocentrism" and the metaphysics of self-presence. One also thinks of the repeated attempts to question, parody, and destabilize the idea of the Work in twentieth-century art and literature. I will come back to some of this in part 3 of this book. For the moment, it suffices to observe how these theoretical critiques of the Work provide a necessary supplement and theoretical foundation to the growing awareness in the social sciences of a fundamental historical crisis of work.

I also observe, here at the outset, how both these interrelated debates subdivide into radically contradictory positions. The transformation of work's traditional role in human experience sometimes presents itself as the fulfillment of age-old utopian dreams and sometimes as an unavoidable catastrophe and disaster. Some writers eagerly embrace what they declare to be the impending abolition of work; others remain nostalgic for the purported values and practices—craftsmanship, duty, a fair day's pay for a fair day's work—that may (or may not) be passing away from human experience. In the 1950s, the idea that automation might reduce the burden of labor was often viewed, not as an opportunity to be seized, but as a so-called problem of leisure to be solved.[3] More recently, the accelerating work rhythms and labor dislocations brought about by a so-called postindustrial capitalism evoke fears of a new social divide between knowledge workers and service workers or of a general "corrosion of character" in a world where work no longer provides a crucial source of income, status, and self-respect for all citizens. Even as some writers imagine the new technologies of instant communication (cell phones, laptop computers, the Internet, and so forth) as making possible a technoparadise of leisure and personal self-development, others warn that the same devices merely allow work to saturate all of human experience, turning "all time into work time" (Aronowitz et al. 35).

The same ambiguities haunt the theoretical recognition that philosophic or aesthetic Work may have reached its (historical or conceptual) limit. For some thinkers, the possibility of "no more masterpieces" joins the end of *all* work as the two irreducible foundations of the project of liberation itself. Yet such arguments are also often seen, by commentators at either end of the political spectrum, as mere anarchism, nihilism, or moral relativism—as something presenting itself, in Derrida's words, "in the formless, mute, infant, and terrifying form of monstrosity" ("Structure" 293).

This double crisis of work and the Work corresponds precisely to the common paradox or double-bind by which we see ourselves both as *working to live* and as *living to work:* understanding labor at once as an inescapable obligation (a response to brute material scarcity) and as the definitive essence of our humanity (the very expression of our personal and collective freedom). One might venture so far as to suggest that the whole history of civilization is marked by unending struggles both to *reduce* and to *reimpose* the burden of Necessity that is signified by, and manifest in, our daily toil. To cite only the most obvious example, it remains widely assumed in the West that paid full-time employment is a minimal requirement for responsible adulthood and democratic citizenship. As Judith Shklar argues, the contemporary citizen is compelled to be "a member of two interlocking public orders, one egalitarian, the other entirely unequal. To be a recognized and active citizen at all he must be an equal member of the polity, a voter, but he must also be independent, which has all along meant that he must be an 'earner,' a free remunerated worker, one who is rewarded for the actual work he has done, neither more nor less" (63–64). Indeed, as Nikolas Rose suggests, contemporary social-science discourse often intensifies work's double necessity by asking the individual not merely to make a living by work but also "to be fulfilled *in* work, now construed as an activity through which we produce, discover, and experience our selves" (104).[4]

It is perhaps equally obvious that, just as the individual social subject is understood to be constituted and expressed by his work, so our collective identities are understood to be constituted and expressed by our Works. Indeed, throughout the West, art and politics since the dawn of modernity have been pervaded by what Philippe Lacoue-Labarthe calls a "nationalist-aestheticism": a position (whose nightmare fulfillment was German National Socialism) that sees all community as grounded in the alleged purity and self-presence of a national identity and sees that identity, in its turn, as expressed by the alleged purity and presence of a national culture (see Lacoue-Labarthe 61–76). In other words, as Jean-Luc Nancy suggests in *The Inoperative Community,* the political and aesthetic programs of the West are nearly always characterized by a certain *immanence,* by which the members of a community are constrained to produce their own essence as their work and, moreover, to produce this essence *as community.* The practical and theoretical limits of this implicit paradox and fatal double-bind are finally exposing themselves today in a wide variety of continuing political and philosophic debates.

Marxism and the Soviet Disaster

All such debates about the fate of work remain ineluctably conditioned by the Marxist critique of political economy. After all, the very essence of Marxism might be said to lie in its effort to project a realm of Freedom beyond the realm of Necessity; and all Marx's central concepts—surplus value, exploitation, even class itself—are inseparable from the project of rethinking the social existence of labor. Many of the basic assumptions of the Marxist vision of work continue to be deployed at least implicitly even by thinkers who otherwise declare the historical defeat and irrelevance of Marxist theory. Nevertheless, any contemporary approach to work, and particularly those on the Left, must take account of the series of profound historical disappointments that punctuate the history of Marxism: in particular, the failure of a working-class identity to crystallize as a real alternative to national, ethnic, or religious identities and also, of course, the Soviet Union's disastrous failure to achieve anything like a workers' paradise.

Many writers in the Marxist tradition argue persuasively that Soviet socialism went wrong from the start by grounding itself entirely in an ethos of production. As is well known, Lenin defined the Soviet project as the achievement of industrial parity with the West. Writing in 1918, Lenin argues in a frequently cited passage that to achieve such a goal it will be essential to improve "the working people's discipline, their skill, the effectiveness, the intensity of labour and its better organisation," and that "the task that the Soviet government must set the people in all its scope is—learning to work." To that end, Lenin also suggests, Russia must combine "the Soviet organisation of administration with the up-to-date achievements of capitalism" and "organise in Russia the study and teaching of the Taylor system" (448–49).

Such arguments strike one's ear today with profound irony and compel the conclusion that when Soviet Russia embraced "scientific management . . . the stopwatch and the assembly line," it had already doomed its utopian project to failure (Dyer-Witheford 6; see also Gorz *Farewell* 31 and Braverman 12). It has also been observed, so frequently as to be a kind of truism, that Lenin attempted to realize socialism in an underdeveloped, largely precapitalist economy, whereas Marx usually envisioned socialism as a system that could only follow the full development of society's productive powers under capitalism. Yet in fact the Soviet model was, at least at first, astonishingly successful in its rapid expansion and modernization of the nation's industrial capacity. The failure of the Soviet ethos of production must thus ultimately be grasped in its political, cultural, or ideological aspects rather than, in the strict sense, its practical ones.

The Soviet gospel of work does reflect at least one significant thread in the thought of Marx and Engels themselves. In his 1844 manuscripts, Marx declares in memorable terms that "the *entire so-called history of the world* is nothing but the begetting of man through human labour" (*Collected Works* 3:304); and in the text today published as an appendix to the first volume of *Capital,* Marx declares again: "Work is the eternal natural condition of human existence" (*Capital* 998). Engels similarly argues for a kind of anthropological paradox in which the human capacity for labor must itself be understood as a *product* of labor:

Only by labor, by adaptation to ever new operations, by inheritance of the thus acquired special development of muscles, ligaments and, over longer periods of time, bones as well, and by the ever-renewed employment of this inherited finesse in new, more and more complicated operations, has the human hand attained the high degree of perfection that has enabled it to conjure into being the pictures of a Raphael, the statues of a Thorwaldsen, the music of a Paganini. (9)

Engel's anthropological history seems to be marked by a kind of abyssal involution by which humanity is said to progress from work to the Work by means of work. Work, at once the privileged human vocation and the literal source of corporeal dexterity, is therefore itself its own telos and fulfillment. Soviet discourse would not only frequently cite this passage but also apply Engel's implicit figure to the revolutionary project as a whole, suggesting that the historical liberation *of* work must always be grasped as itself a Work of the highest order. Maxim Gorky, for example, echoes Engels by celebrating the historico-anthropological process by which "man . . . was able to develop his fore-limbs . . . so that his hands, his clever hands, became the force that elevated him from his animal environment, encouraged the rapid growth of his brain, finally organizing him into what we have today—the skillful producer of metals, precision tools, apparatuses and machines, the gifted pianist, the surgeon who works almost miracles, and so on" (216). Correspondingly, in his address to the first All-Union Congress of Soviet Writers (1934), a text considered one of the quintessential statements of so-called socialist realism, Gorky declares: "We must make labour the principal hero of our books, i.e., man as organized by labour processes, one who, in our country, is equipped with the might of modern techniques, and is, in his turn, making labour easier and more productive, and raising it to the level of an art. We must learn to understand labour as a creative act" (254). The task of the Soviet writer, in other words, is to produce the Work *of* work, the Work whose ultimate project can be none other than the re-presentation of human labor to itself.

Nevertheless, there is also ample ammunition, both in Marx's own text and in the long history of Marxist thought, for a critique of these characteristic Soviet themes and tendencies. Marx himself always argues, for example, that a condition of "universal industriousness" must be grasped as a distinctive historical characteristic of "production founded on capital" (*Grundrisse* 409). This too is perhaps a kind of truism today, in the wake of Weber's famous study *The Protestant Ethic and the Spirit of Capitalism* and a whole spectrum of subsequent scholarship on the history of work ranging from E. P. Thompson's study of time-discipline in industrial England to recent studies of the postmodern workforce such as Juliet Schor's *The Overworked American*. And even well before the fall of socialist governments in Eastern Europe, many writers on the Left recognized the fatal errors of the Soviet gospel of work. As far back as the 1960s, Georges Bataille suggested that the Soviets, having assembled "an immense machinery . . . in which individual will was minimized with a view to the greatest output," had merely created "a world in which the only possibility is labor" (*Accursed Share* 1:159–60). In the 1980s, similarly, André Gorz, in his aptly titled *Farewell to the Working Class,* argues that "'Socialist morality'—with its injunction that each individual be completely committed to his or her work and equate it with personal fulfillment—is oppressive and totalitarian at root," for it "rejects the very idea of 'the free development of each individual as the goal and precondition of the free development of all'" (10). As such arguments suggest, the Taylorist and Fordist tendencies of Soviet communism merely reimpose on the worker that very dogma of work that ought to be grasped by contrast as a definitive ideological product of capitalism itself.

In the passage just cited, however, a crucial question also emerges that will continue to be at stake in the rest of this book. Even as Gorz strongly rejects a Soviet model in which individuals must, in working, both fulfill their collective responsibility to the state *and* find a "personal fulfillment," he continues to call for a social system in which, to repeat once more the famous Marxist formula, the free development of each individual is the goal and precondition of the free development of all. But what is the difference between these two rather similar formulations? How is an individual or collective "development" to be envisioned at all on the other side of either capitalism or Soviet socialism? Will it exist in the form of, or be constituted by, something wholly other than work and labor? Does not an obligation to the work of self-development imply the same kind of hierarchical or exclusionary politics that has always pervaded every other system of compulsory labor?

There is no clear answer to such questions in Marx himself, who exhaustively critiques the social existence of work under the regime of capital but retains a crucial status for work (especially in the form of a work of personal or group identity) in his thought as a whole. Marx in effect begins by observing how labor under capitalism has become "merely a means to satisfy needs external to it," and he finally envisions a future in which "labour has become not only a means of life but life's prime want" ("Economic and Philosophic Manuscripts of 1844" and "Critique of the Gotha Program," *Collected Works* 3:274, 24:87). Today, the discourse of work, both on the Left and on the Right, continues to center on this relationship between material production and the production of self. The domain of work is thus typically divided into two parts: (1) work as an instrumentality, a means to an end, and (2) work as an autoteleology, a self-fulfilling freedom, an end in itself. On the one hand, working for the weekend; on the other hand, a labor of love. Both in Marx's own writings and in a range of subsequent thought that, on this subject at least, remains entirely within the same horizons, *work* in some proper or literal sense is always being distinguished from something that one must therefore call *a work that is not work;* and the historical struggle to foster and enable the latter, whatever its other political goals and assumptions, must then somehow be thought of as something even more difficult to name: as, so to speak, a Work that works on work.

Hannah Arendt's Critique

The theoretical difficulties at stake here may be illuminated by briefly considering Hannah Arendt's reading of Marx in *The Human Condition,* a text that identifies but does not resolve questions that remain open as well in more recent attempts to think through this historical crisis of work. As Arendt suggests, economic writers typically divide the field of work in terms of various related oppositions between "skilled" and "unskilled," "manual" and "intellectual," or "productive" and "unproductive" forms of labor. Such distinctions, however, are always imprecise and unstable, for as Arendt acknowledges, "every activity requires a certain amount of skill, the activity of cleaning and cooking no less than the writing of a book or the building of a house" (90). The social status and value accorded to any particular instance of human exertion often appear linked to its material conditions (as when we distinguish, say, between handwork and headwork, between "blue-collar" and "white-collar" workers) and yet, just as often, wholly transcend those conditions. Economist Alfred Marshall cites the example of the sculptor who performs "a large amount of hard, nay, of coarse manual work" and yet "the products of whose chisel add to his country's fame" (102, 105). One also thinks, on the other hand, of the scribe or scrivener or data-entry operator, performing a labor that is at once extraordinarily skilled and yet utterly menial.

Therefore, Arendt herself attempts to subsume these slippery oppositions into a more fundamental distinction between what she calls "Labor" and "Work." For Arendt, Labor is the activity by which "vital necessities" are "produced and fed into the life process," whereas Work "provides an 'artificial' world of things, distinctly different from all natural surroundings" (7).[5] In this schema, Labor refers to the activities of the being Locke calls the *animal laborans* and to the field of what Marx calls Necessity: the basic biological struggle against nature for sustenance and survival. Work, by contrast, refers to the activities of Locke's *homo faber* and to what Marx calls Freedom, a field encompassing all the various spiritual, cultural, or intellectual activities that transcend the struggle for survival and all merely utilitarian value.

Arendt's opposition also broadly corresponds—though, here again, somewhat imprecisely—to the opposition between work as a means to an end and work as an end in itself, or between what I have called work and the Work. The paradigm of Labor is agriculture: the production of ephemeral value intended for consumption. The paradigm of Work is philosophy or art: the production of durable value that transcends its conditions of production. These definitions have a problematic relationship to a celebrated previous division of the field of economics: the Aristotelian distinction between *oikonomia*, household management, and *chrematistike*, business or moneymaking, as two modes for acquiring wealth. In Aristotle's schema, economy refers to the practices of a landed proprietor or householder, who exchanges commodities (such as agricultural produce) for other commodities, typically through barter, or the "just" exchange of like for like, a mode of work that Aristotle considers "natural." Business, conversely, refers to the activities of a merchant or dealer, who "buys cheap to sell dear," exchanging money for commodities that are then exchanged for more money, a mode of work that Aristotle considers "artificial" or "unnatural." (This division also closely corresponds, as Marx acknowledges in a long footnote to *Capital*, to Marx's own distinction between two circuits of exchange: C-M-C, the exchange of commodities for money used to buy more commodities; and M-C-M', the exchange of money for commodities to be sold again at a profit.)[6]

Arendt's opposition may also seem at first to echo Aristotle's distinction between "natural" and "artificial" economic practices, in that Labor refers to humanity's direct corporeal encounter with the natural world, and Work refers to an artifice that transcends nature. Looked at more closely, however, Arendt's schema seems to invert or even to displace Aristotle's. For Arendt, "natural" Labor is merely a means to the end of biological sustenance, and "unnatural" Work is self-fulfilling, a pure autoteleology. In other words, Arendt's Labor remains broadly parallel to *oikonomia*, but her Work has nothing whatever to do with *chrematistike*. Arendt's second term, instead, refers to a field of "culture" that—as Pierre Bourdieu, among others, has argued at length—typically resists commodification and attempts to insulate itself from the sordid practicality of business. (In chapter 10, I will come back to this famous Aristotelian distinction and have more to say about the strange in-stability, within an even broader field of economic discourse, of the basic op-position between means and ends.)

Therefore, in this new map of the economic field, Labor continues to oc-cupy the space of "nature" and denote humanity's endless struggle to pro-duce and reproduce the conditions of biological life. But Work opens up a new conceptual space which is nearly opposite to mere moneymaking or business. What, then, has happened to the displaced Aristotelian term? In Arendt's schema, it would seem to be everywhere and nowhere: people buy and sell the products of Labor (and labor itself), but they also buy and sell aes-thetic and philosophic Works. The aspiration of culture to resist commodifi-cation is, after all, merely an illusion, a pose, or at most an alleged essence tran-scending the unmistakable historical and social conditions that characterize cultural production.

Thus, Arendt's division of the field of work seems not quite to extricate it-self from the instability of all such divisions. This instability is further illumi-nated by the particular critique of Marxism that Arendt goes on to offer in the same text. Arendt suggests that Adam Smith and Marx share the same basic understanding of the distinction between productive and unproductive labor and, indeed, that they base "the whole structure of their argument" upon this distinction (85). Both Smith and Marx, she claims, envision the work of household servants, shop clerks, and the like as *unproductive* labor, which they "despised . . . as parasitical, actually a kind of perversion of labor, as though nothing were worthy of this name which did not enrich the world" (86). And yet, she points out, it was precisely these unproductive workers, "menial servants . . . laboring for mere subsistence," who, by freeing their masters' lives from the drudgery of survival, created "their masters' freedom or, in modern language, their masters' potential productivity" (86–87). In this way, through slave labor in the ancient world, or the mechanism of capitalist exploitation in the modern one, "the labor of some suffices for the life of all" (88). Or, a little more precisely, the unproductive labor of the many makes pos-sible the life of all and the productive Work of the few.

By staging her account of Marxism in this way, however, Arendt is led to conclude that Marx's only solution for this situation is "the unfortunately quite unutopian ideal" of a world in which "all work would have become la-bor" (89). In other words, Arendt suggests that, in the Marxist future, the en-tire human vocation would be the reproduction of its own life process, and every other worldly activity would be, instead of self-fulfilling Work, merely what Arendt later calls a "hobby." Her argument anticipates the critiques of

Soviet socialism mentioned above and also implicitly evokes two visions of the future often represented in science fiction: on the one hand, a collective society envisioned as a kind of beehive or anthill, in which no individuality is possible and, therefore, "all serious activities" have been "level[ed] down . . . to the status of making a living" (127); on the other hand, a society of godlike dilettantes freed by futuristic technology to indulge every caprice of individual desire.[7] Either way, Arendt suggests that a profound historical displacement has occurred in the modern world, in which the opposition of productive and unproductive labor—the opposition, that is, of Labor and Work in her sense—gives way to an opposition of *work* and *play*. In this new economic opposition, Arendt claims, "even the 'work' of the artist . . . is dissolved into play and has lost its worldly meaning" (128).

I suggest, however, that in this critique Arendt misrepresents Marx's thought in small but significant ways, beginning with her starting point: Marx's understanding of the distinction between productive and unproductive labor. Marx does acknowledge that Smith is "essentially correct" about this distinction, but only "from the standpoint of bourgeois economy" (*Grundrisse* 273), a crucial qualification. Marx uses these terms, as he does so often with others, with one foot inside and one foot outside this bourgeois economy. He thus suggests that the productivity of labor has nothing whatsoever to do with its *ends,* with any self-fulfilling moral, aesthetic, or cultural value it might be believed to possess (see also Braverman 411). Indeed, as Marx writes elsewhere, "the Determinate material form of the labour, and consequentially of its product, in itself has nothing whatever to do with this distinction between productive and unproductive labour" (*Theories of Surplus Value* 155). Rather, labor may be considered "productive" insofar as it functions, within the capitalist mode of production, to increase capital, and "unproductive" insofar as it is the "mere performance of services for the satisfaction of immediate needs," so that "capital consumes itself in it" (*Grundrisse* 272). In other words, under the regime of capital, "the only worker who is productive is one who produces surplus-value for the capitalist, or in other words contributes towards the self-valorization of capital" (*Capital* 644). An example of a productive worker, therefore, would be an industrial wage laborer; examples of unproductive workers would be a porter, a valet, or a hairdresser (provided, that is, that the latter work as individuals directly providing services, as opposed to working for a capitalist entrepreneur in return for wages).

Marx also, however, always brackets this rigorous distinction so as to uncover that which remains unseen and unsaid within it. He argues that one of the symptomatic ideological distortions of bourgeois economics is its willingness to construe this coldly practical opposition between labor that increases and labor that consumes capital as an essentially *moral* distinction. For bourgeois economists,

the workers in e.g. luxury shops are productive, although the characters who consume such objects are expressly castigated as unproductive wastrels. The fact is that these workers, indeed, are productive, as to the material result of their labour. In fact, of course, this 'productive' worker cares as much about the crappy shit he has to make as does the capitalist himself who employs him, and who also couldn't give a damn for the junk. But, looked at more precisely, it turns out in fact that the true definition of a productive worker consists in this: A person who needs and demands exactly as much as, and no more than, is required to enable him to gain the greatest possible benefit for his capitalist. (*Grundrisse* 273)

For Marx himself, therefore, it is the *productive* laborer, whatever the specific character or goal of his exertion, who is essentially instrumental: such a worker is always and merely a means to the end of multiplying capital. The *unproductive* laborer, correspondingly, refers both to the category Arendt has in mind, those who perform menial service for the consumption of others (the porter or servant), *and* to the artist or philosopher, insofar as such producers of cultural Work resist total subsumption by capitalist economic relations:

For instance, Milton, who wrote *Paradise Lost,* was an unproductive worker. On the other hand, a writer who turns out work for his publisher in factory style is a productive worker. . . . A singer who sings like a bird is an unproductive worker. If she sells her song for money, she is to that extent a wage-labourer or merchant. But if the same singer is engaged by an entrepreneur who makes her sing to make money, then she becomes a productive worker, since she *produces* capital directly. (*Capital* 1044)

Thus, shopkeepers are unproductive only if they are independent proprietors receiving direct remuneration from the people who consume their wares, whereas servers at McDonald's are productive workers regardless of how one judges the quality of the hamburgers they serve. By the same token, "a writer is a productive worker not because he produces ideas, but in so far as he enriches the publisher who publishes his works" (*Theories of Surplus Value* 154).

One will recall how Arendt claims that Marx points us toward a world in which (using her senses of these terms) all Work will have become mere Labor. Yet it is at least equally faithful to Marx's text to suggest exactly the opposite: that he envisions a world in which all Labor will have become Work. Arendt concedes Marx's hope that "free time eventually will emancipate men from necessity and make the *animal laborans* productive" but faults him for assuming that if labor power "is not spent and exhausted in the drudgery of life it will automatically nourish other, 'higher,' activities" (133). Despite the fact that Arendt places the word "higher" in quotation marks, she is surely not herself questioning the distinction between higher and lower activities, given her own essentially similar opposition between the "serious" artist and the mere hobbyist. Indeed, her ultimate point, immediately following, is that "we" now know Marx's dream was deluded because "the spare time of the *animal laborans* is never spent in anything but consumption, and the more time left to him, the greedier and more craving his appetites" (133).[8] In this striking and uncomfortable moment of her text, Arendt deplores, in the strongest possible terms, what she calls the "fool's paradise" (133) of the contemporary commodity culture and anticipates what some today might call postmodernity: a world in which workers have been politically emancipated, but in which cultural Work, the only thing that truly transcends "the worldly futility of the life process" (131), has itself dissolved into a giddy round of trivial consumption and play.

But, as may perhaps be easier to see half a century after she wrote, Arendt's vision is also simply inaccurate as a description of the affluent society of commodity capitalism. On this point alone I believe one must join relatively more right-wing writers in acknowledging that "free and unregulated markets in culture and commerce" have in fact created an "aesthetic bounty" (see Gillespie et al.; Cowen). Whatever one's ultimate judgment on either contemporary art or on the social value of the aesthetic itself, it is surely impossible to deny that the production of cultural Work thrives today with an abundance never before equaled. A few contemporary observers fret about the imminent death of the written word or lament an alleged decline of serious scholarship and aesthetic taste; yet it is evident that there are today more museums, more books published, more music composed and performed, and more artworks produced and exhibited than at any previous point in history.

It will complicate such observations, however, to also observe how Arendt seems, at the same time, to ignore Marx's displacement of the conceptual oppositions of "bourgeois" economics. After all, what essential difference could there be between the Work and the hobby except for the doomed and spurious aspiration of culture to resist subsumption by the economic? (Here, this aspiration is particularly ironic in that usually the only tangible difference between the hobbyist and the artist is that, in real life, the latter *is* paid for his labors.) In fact, Marx looks toward a world in which "the antithesis between mental and physical labour" has vanished, in which "labour has become not only a means of life but life's prime want," and in which "the productive forces have also increased with the all-round development of the individual, and all the springs of cooperative wealth flow more abundantly." It is *"only then,"* Marx stipulates, only *after* such conditions have been met, that "the narrow horizon of bourgeois right [can] be crossed in its entirety and society inscribe on its banner: From each according to his ability, to each according to his needs!" ("Critique of the Gotha Program," *Collected Works* 24:87; emphasis added). This famous formula, so often erroneously cited as the very truth of Marxism, could, as Marx suggests here, have no meaning except when the very ideas of *ability* and *need* have been emptied of their meaning, just as the distinction between productive and unproductive labor itself could have no meaning (or, at least, only a very different one) outside the regime of capital. One must conclude, therefore, *neither* that a Marxist utopia would diminish all Work into Labor (Arendt's critique) *nor* that it would elevate all labor into Work (the possibility that Marx sometimes intimates). Rather, Marx's fundamental theoretical project has to be grasped as an attempt to overcome and displace such distinctions.

But if Arendt's liberal critique of a Marxist utopia thus seems to miss the final point, one must, by contrast, acknowledge a real force to her more fundamental theoretical critique of the Marxist vision of work. Arendt observes what she claims is a "fundamental contradiction which runs like a red thread through the whole of Marx's thought" (104), a contradiction bound up in his "equivocal" attitude toward labor. Marx seems to associate labor (in the generic sense) both with necessity *and* with freedom, seeing it at once as the curse from which humanity must finally be freed and as the essential human vocation. Here again is the idea (that can be named only with an awkwardness that betrays the theoretical dilemma) of a Work that works on work, a laboring to end labor. What else, after all, can Marx mean by "the all-round development of the individual" that will follow the end of capitalism but a process in which all human beings will be freed to produce cultural Work in the old-fashioned sense and also their own selves as their ultimate Work? But this also means that the very thing Arendt most reproaches Marx for being willing to abandon (the Work) is the one thing that he cannot or will not abandon and that leads him into precisely the contradiction Arendt describes—a contradiction that must, then, finally be grasped as what Jean-Luc Nancy calls "the aporia of Marxism" (*Sense of the World* 96), a kind of limit (or threshold) to which Marx's thought leads us through its rigor. At such a limit, one can only ask, one more time: can there indeed be a *work* freed entirely from necessity, a work that presents itself only as what Marx memorably imagines as a blossoming, an absolutely self-fulfilling freedom, something in itself one of "life's prime wants"? This is the unanswered question in which, as Nancy also suggests, "all of political economy, *including* its critique, is at stake" (*Sense of the World* 97).

"The Great Work Begins"

I conclude this chapter with a final example that illustrates with peculiar vividness the dilemma of work in the contemporary imagination. Tony Kushner's two-part epic drama *Angels in America* (1990–93) presents itself, though only indirectly, as an extended meditation on work and the Work. Explicitly, this celebrated play addresses a whole variety of specific sociopolitical issues, particularly the AIDS epidemic of the 1980s and the resurgence of neoconservative politics during the presidency of Ronald Reagan. If anything, the play initially may seem to treat the question of work only by its notable lack of interest in it. Three of the play's seven major characters have no full-time jobs at all. To cite the authorial summaries in the published version (Kushner *Millennium* 3–4), the play's protagonist Prior Walter "occasionally works as a club designer or caterer, otherwise lives very modestly but with great style off a small trust fund"; Harper Pitt is "an agoraphobic with a mild valium addiction"; and Hannah Pitt, Harper's mother-in-law, lives "off her deceased husband's army pension." Prior's boyfriend, Louis Ironson, does have a job, but only as a "word processor working at the Second Circuit Court of Appeals in Brooklyn," a position that we are repeatedly reminded is more or less "the lowest of the low" as a profession (*Millennium* 28; *Perestroika* 109, 124). Of the three remaining major characters, two are lawyers, but one, the real-life figure Roy M. Cohn, is ill for most of the first play and in the hospital for most of the second. Only two major characters have jobs that figure in the play's action: Belize, "a former drag-queen . . . [and] registered nurse"; and Joe Pitt, "chief clerk for Justice Theodore Wilson of the Federal Court of Appeals." With regard to these two, it is notable that Belize exemplifies a service-based labor that, as we shall see in more detail later, has often been identified as the characteristic mode of labor in a new "postindustrial" economy; and that Joe Pitt is eventually bitterly denounced by Louis for having written a legal opinion denying "that gay men are members of a legitimate minority" (*Perestroika* 109)—in other words, because his intellectual labor has *opposed* a Work of group identity that will prove to be central to the play's vision. In this, the play seems to gesture toward a social world in which work no longer plays a central role in the formation of the social subject and in which, accordingly, as David Savran suggests, *"identity politics comes to substitute for Marxist analysis"* (31).

Over the course of the first play, *Millennium Approaches,* a series of portents and visions appear to Prior, culminating in an Angel crashing through the ceiling of his room and declaring, in the play's final lines:

Greetings, Prophet;
The Great Work begins. (119)

But the "great" and millennial Work so clearly announced here is immediately undercut, both in this scene itself (where Prior pronounces the angelic visitation to be "*Very* Steven Spielberg") and in various ways over the course of the second play. *Perestroika* begins with a monologue by Aleksii Antedilluvianovich Prelapsarianov, "the World's Oldest Living Bolshevik" (13), who speaks of that imminent reform or "restructuring" of Soviet socialism that has already been announced in the play's title:

How are we to proceed without *Theory?* What System of Thought have these Reformers to present to this mad swirling planetary disorganization, to the Inevident Welter of fact, event, phenomenon, calamity? Do they have, as we did, a beautiful Theory, as bold, as Grand, as comprehensive a construct . . . ? . . . Change? Yes, we must change, only show me the Theory, and I will be at the barricades, show me the book of the next Beautiful Theory, and I promise you these blind eyes will see again, just to read it, to devour that text. Show me the words that will reorder the world, or else keep silent. (13–14)

This speech, and the myriad other millennial figures that pervade the text unmistakably situate this play in the aftermath of the Work: in a "Sour Little Age" in which we must somehow "move ahead" with no comprehensive construct or book of Beautiful Theory in which or by which "the mountainous, granite order of creation" can be viewed "in one all-knowing glance" (14–15). Such arguments, as Kushner implicitly acknowledges, unite both Right and Left. The Reagan revolution, Joe tells Louis, represents "the end of a nineteenth-century socialist romanticist conflation of government and society, law and Justice, idea and action." Now, says Joe, there is nothing left but the uncertain prospect of individual "happiness" (*Perestroika* 34). And by the end of the play, Louis is saying more or less the same thing, asserting, "It's all too much to be encompassed by a single theory now" (146). It is also interesting to recall that Kushner's subtitle for the play—*A Gay Fantasia on National Themes*—alludes unmistakably to George Bernard Shaw's *Heartbreak House* (1921), whose subtitle is *A Fantasia in the Russian Manner on English Themes*. Shaw's play is also a sort of elegy for the Work, one that deplores in particular how all the great Victorian reformers from Carlyle to Marx to Shaw himself had proven themselves quite useless to prevent the unspeakable disaster of the First World War.

Then, to summarize very briefly a complex sequence of magical-realistic action, the "Great Work" announced by the Angels turns out to be a Work of ending the Work. The gospel they present to Prior, their chosen prophet, although it is itself embodied in a great Book (46–47), is a call for the end of all "human progress" and "Forward Motion" (50), the cessation of all exercise of imagination, invention, and creativity. Over the course of the play, however, Prior eventually decides to refuse this task. "We can't just stop," he tells the Angels, because "progress, migration, motion is . . . modernity" (132). Nevertheless, Prior speaks once more as a prophet in the final lines of *Perestroika:* only this time he speaks directly to the audience and clearly in the voice of the author as well, at once summing up the play's meditation on AIDS and echoing the final scene of the previous play:

This disease will be the end of many of us, but not nearly all, and the dead will be commemorated and will struggle on with the living, and we are not going away. The world only spins forward. We will be citizens. The time has come.

> You are fabulous creatures, each and every one.
> And I bless you: *More Life.*
> The Great Work Begins. (148)

It is a striking theatrical moment which seems, however, not quite to achieve the thematic clarity of the rest of the play as I have summarized it. In particular, how are we to understand the "Great Work" which here "begins" in the wake of its own announced impossibility? The prophet and the play seem at once to *embrace* the end of the Great Work (the "comprehensive construct" and "Beautiful Theory") and yet *reject* the end of work itself, since progress, invention, creation, and the like are to continue as the very defining characteristics of (post)modernity itself. The world will still be "moving ahead," Louis says in the final scene, since "that's what politics is" (146). But if this motion, this inevitable progress, is itself political, it is also beyond any *particular* politics. Even Roy Cohn, the play's right-wing monster, had previously set his seal of approval on Prior's elegiac final lines by affirming that "Life" is what humanity "is supposed to bless" (82).

In any case, some viewers have found in this final scene a vision, at once classically comic and vitally contemporary, of a new community in its birth throes. Such a community would be the one announced comically, for example, when Prior, who has been taken to the hospital by Hannah Pitt, identifies her to the nurse as "my ex-lover's lover's Mormon mother" (102). In the final scene, argues Ron Scapp, "We find ourselves gathered with the actors on-stage, finally represented, a unified, singularly hopeful crowd of 'fabulous citizens'" (98).[9] But such a conclusion can be drawn only by ignoring much that the play makes unmistakably clear, for the "we" who will be "citizens" evidently refers only to a particular embattled identity (gay Americans), who are promised the full fruits of a specifically *American* citizenship. Indeed, just before these final lines, as a reminder that citizenship is absolutely linked to the state form, Belize and Louis have an argument about another set of extremely embattled identities:

LOUIS: . . . I mean no one supports Palestinian rights more than I do but . . .
BELIZE: Oh yeah right, Louis, like not even the Palestinians are more devoted than . . . (148)

What we are witnessing here, in other words, is an entirely conventional model of progressively inclusive (yet by no means *all-inclusive*) citizenship, a process of identity formation that is itself being depicted as something to be *produced*.[10] Indeed, the play as a whole is entirely grounded in an ethos of production and creativity: in the lines from Emerson cited as the epigraph of the published version, it affirms that "the soul . . . in every act attempts the *production* of a new and fairer whole" (emphasis added). If the comic community realized at the end is perhaps no longer grounded in a traditional affirmation of paid employment, it is also explicitly being understood as itself a Work of the highest order. At stake here is thus precisely the model of citizenship alluded to in the beginning of this chapter, in which the citizen-subject produces his community as his work only to be then (re)claimed by that community as *its* product and Work.

This is also the moment to recall that *Angels in America* was itself canonized as a major Work of theater and literature with a speed, and to an extent, almost unprecedented in American literary history. The play not only won numerous awards (including the 1993 Pulitzer Prize) but was repeatedly declared to be the salvation of serious drama on Broadway, a historic turning point for American theater, and so forth, so that, as Savran observes, a play "deeply preoccupied with teleological process" was itself "positioned as both the culmination of history and as that which rewrites the past" (14). Because the canonization of the play began before the second half of the play had even opened, it is hard not to hear a certain ironic duplicity in its final lines: to hear, that is, the Prophet announcing not the beginning but rather the *end* of "the Great Work" that is *this* play—and that, like all plays, always potentially rebegins at the moment of its own ending. The same ambivalence is articulated in the "Afterword" appended to the published version of *Perestroika,* where Kushner dismisses as a "fiction" the idea "that artistic labor happens in isolation" and yet enthusiastically affirms his own "authorship" of a play that was intended to be "something of ambition and size" (149–51). "We pay high prices for the maintenance of the myth of the Individual," he acknowledges, even as he looks forward to a moment when "the Individual will finally expand to its unstable, insupportably swollen limits, and pop" (151–52). I will end this opening chapter by underlining this hope but questioning the felicity of the metaphor. If the *myth* of individualism, like all myths, indeed has its limits, the figure projected by that myth has none. One must therefore doubt whether the way beyond either an individual or a community understood to be constituted and expressed by its Work could ever be via any process of self-development or self-production.

FREE-MARKET FUTURISM

On the "Postindustrial"

It is perhaps less surprising than it first appears that a contemporary discourse of corporate capitalism, even as it celebrates the historical defeat of Soviet communism and the global ascendancy of a so-called free market, also returns to quasi-Marxist themes of the "liberatory power" of labor (Guattari and Negri 9). Marx himself, of course, always understands capitalism as a progressive and even "revolutionary" social force as well as an exploitative one, a dialectical complexity that his critics regularly forget. Contemporary apologists for capitalism seem to literalize Marx's figure by replacing the rhetoric of thrift, prudence, and conservation (the values that Max Weber once identified as the essential characteristics of the capitalist "spirit") with a rhetoric of speed, diversity, innovation, and global transformation. As Thomas Frank documents with persuasive and sometimes depressing detail, a whole range of contemporary "free-market" discourse seeks to appropriate from the same Marxist tradition whose historical defeat it proclaims and celebrates not only the glamour of the revolutionary but even the utopian appeal of collective struggle (see *One Market under God*). Who would have ever imagined, as Fredric Jameson asks, that "the dreariness of business and private property, the dustiness of entrepreneurship, and the well-nigh Dickensian flavor of titles and appropriation, coupon-clipping, mergers, investment banking, and other such transactions . . . should in our time have proved to be so sexy?" (*Postmodernism* 274).

Certainly thinkers on both the Right and the Left today commonly assume that we are witnessing the advent of a new era of human civilization, an era often named and defined in reference to that which it *follows:* "postmodern," "postcapitalist," "postindustrial," and so forth. It is probably impossible to identify a precise origin of this now-famous latter term. Daniel Bell, who once claimed to have coined it, and who undoubtedly did much to put it into general circulation, observes in the introduction to his *Coming of Post-industrial Society* (1973) that the term was used as long ago as 1918 in the title of an obscure book, Arthur J. Penty's *Old Worlds for New: A Study of the Post-industrial State.* Penty was a follower of William Morris and John Ruskin, and his book advocates "a return to the decentralized, small workshop artisan society, ennobling work, which he called the "'post-industrial state'!" (Bell 37). That this familiar term first conveyed a meaning precisely opposite to the one it commonly has today is perhaps something more than a piece of historical trivia. In fact, this semantic slippage indicates something that emerges in nearly all the writers I am about to consider: how the subject of work evokes a play of symmetrical but opposed impulses toward the past or the future, toward arcadian or utopian modes of social thought, and, accordingly, toward positive or negative critiques of work.

A familiar narrative of the present and near future of capitalism emerges today from a wide range of popular and scholarly writers, a narrative that always begins with one basic claim: something called "information" (ideas, technical know-how, intellectual creativity, new modes of instantaneous communication) has now become not only the most valuable commodity but also the fundamental source of all industrial or productive value. When one invests in a company like Microsoft, it is argued, one does not gain an ownership share in any massive manufacturing power; rather, the value of the company lies in its marketing organization and in its patents for products like software that literally exist in the form of a particular arrangement of information. Thus, information technology saturates both the process and the product of contemporary corporate capitalism. Such technologies necessitate a radical reorganization of material production and the firm itself, even as they also increasingly dominate the marketplace in the form of new commodities for sale (home computers, digital televisions, cell phones, and so forth). And all this, it is further claimed, has revolutionary implications for workers and for work: for this new postindustrial economy is said to create a new kind of employee, who approaches his or her work with an unprecedented degree of interest, involvement, and personal "autonomy."

Alvin Toffler and Peter Drucker

An exemplary version of this argument is that of Alvin Toffler. In a best-selling book from 1980, Toffler announces the advent of a "third wave" of human history, an era understood to follow two others, dominated by agriculture and by industry respectively, and to be dominated, in its turn, by information-processing and "super-symbolic" practices. Among the myriad other social, economic, and political changes that it will bring in its wake, this third wave is thus most clearly defined by its radical transformation of the world of work. "We are moving toward a future economy," he writes, "in which very large numbers never hold full-time paid jobs, or in which 'full-time' is redefined . . . to mean a shorter and shorter workweek or work year" (*Third Wave* 293 – 94). Moreover, under the regime of third-wave production, Toffler argues, "work grows less, not more, repetitive. It becomes less fragmented, with each person doing a somewhat larger, rather than smaller, task. Flextime and self-pacing replace the old need for mass synchronization of behavior. Workers are forced to cope with more frequent changes in their tasks, as well as a blinding succession of personnel transfers, product changes, and reorganizations" (401). Toffler's language here distantly echoes the celebrated descriptions, in the texts of Marx, Engels, and others of their period, of the dehumanizing effects of industrial labor; and Toffler argues, in effect, that information-based capitalism will itself achieve Marx's dream of a nonalienated work. To be sure, he also acknowledges that to give workers greater autonomy is also to make new and bigger demands on their time and energy. Indeed, his ultimate point is that "Third Wave employers increasingly need . . . men and women who accept responsibility" (401). Third-wave workers are said to be improvisational, like jazz musicians, rather than regimented, like classical musicians, and are accordingly "complex, individualistic, proud of the ways in which they differ" (401).

Only occasionally does Toffler acknowledge the inevitable question of whether such an appealing vision can possibly apply to any but a small elite of workers. By the time of *Powershift* (1990), he does concede that many corporations, especially in traditional "white-collar" fields that require massive data-entry operations, are "trying to turn their employees into 'electronic proles'" via technologies of surveillance that allow them to "count keystrokes, monitor breaks, and listen in on employee phone calls" (209). Such methods are, however, merely a kind of exception, a passing regression to the ways of the old industrial era, and Toffler questions whether they will even "pay off," because "truly advanced technologies require truly advanced work methods and organization" (209). In other words, Toffler raises and yet dismisses far too readily the difficult theoretical question inevitably posed by new modes of electronic work which blur the conventional distinction between manual and intellectual labor. His argument, in fact, comes to an impasse at precisely this question, in the face of which he can do no more than reiterate the assumption with which the whole argument begins: that there is an intrinsic and necessary connection between new technology and new work.

And despite such passing glances at the new electronic proletariat, Toffler's overall vision of the future, throughout these two massive books, is profoundly utopian. "It is one of the grand ironies of history," he argues in the later book, "that a new kind of autonomous employee is emerging who, in fact, does now own the means of production. The new means of production, however, are not to be found in the artisan's toolbox, or in the massive machinery of the smokestack age. They are, instead, crackling inside the employee's cranium—where society will find the single most important source of future wealth and power" (*Powershift* 217).

This possibility—that the means of production of the information economy are already in principle "owned" by the workers—is one which curiously unites the contemporary Right and Left in their respective approaches to the question of work. In the face of this intriguing thesis, however, one must ask: why is the skill or know-how in an information worker's cranium not every bit as susceptible to exploitation as the energy or skill in a laborer's hands? Toffler's argument might seem to be built on a kind of Lockean framework stressing the intrinsic or natural connection of labor and property. The worker's skill, competence, and consequent "autonomy" would then be considered products of her work; and in this sense, the worker could be said to "own" this knowledge as a property. But if such an argument were indeed made in terms of some concept of natural law or, as a matter of fact, in any specifically *political* terms, it would seem necessarily as applicable to a shoemaker as to a computer programmer (at least in the democratic society that such arguments otherwise assume will also prevail). The real argument, therefore, seems not to be one of principle but rather to be one of practicality. Toffler and others seem to argue, that is, that the employee's knowledge and skill have in some new way become immanent in him, contained in his head and his hands and taking the shape of heuristic structures that literally *cannot be appropriated.* This knowledge would then be almost a "property" in the sense of an intrinsic quality of its bearer.[1]

Such a possibility, by the way, could be questioned, in real life, with reference to the practice of requiring corporate employees to surrender all claims to legal ownership of their inventions or discoveries and, in speculative fiction, with reference to William Gibson's story "Johnny Mnemonic," which imagines a technology allowing the contents of a person's brain to be bought, sold, or even forcibly removed. Such objections, however literal-minded, do at least clearly indicate the theoretical difficulties at stake. To put it another way, Toffler's argument—seemingly founded in empirical observations about the *material* mode of industrial production—nevertheless falls into a kind of radical idealism: a vision of the future forgetting that even digital work requires physical movements of the eyes and hands and that, as Marx always argues, even the *relations* of production are themselves *materially based.*

The same general arguments, and the same specific claim that the ascendancy of information as value will also require an ascendancy of the worker, are also made by Peter Drucker, who in numerous books over half a century has established himself as perhaps the world's most renowned theorist of business management. Drucker's *Post-capitalist Society* (1993) proclaims at its outset the historical defeat of *"the belief in salvation by society"* (7). And yet, in the postcapitalist world, to cite Drucker's summary at some length:

> The basic economic resource—"the means of production," to use the economist's term—is no longer capital, nor natural resources (the economist's "land"), nor "labor." *It is and will be knowledge.* . . . Value is now created by "productivity" and "innovation," both applications of knowledge to work. The leading social groups of the knowledge society will be "knowledge workers." . . . Practically all these knowledge people will be employed in organizations. Yet, unlike the employees under Capitalism, they will own both the "means of production" and the "tools of production"— the former through their pension funds, which are rapidly emerging in all developed countries as the only real owners; the latter because knowledge workers own their knowledge and can take it with them wherever they go. (8)

Here again, Drucker suggests that capitalism itself will, in its own progress to what he calls a postcapitalist society, give back precisely that which, in Marx's account, it had originally taken away from working people: their ownership and control of the tools and means of production. In Drucker's version, workers own their knowledge both because it is immanent in them ("they can take it with them") and because the workers own shares in the companies that employ them via their pension funds. The latter point at least lends a certain practicality to what is otherwise, as we have seen, an argument that rests somewhat precariously on the unexamined assumption of a self-owning self. At the time of this writing, however, and in the wake of a new disastrous wave of corporate bankruptcies (in which thousands of workers saw their pension funds evaporate), Drucker seems at the very least overly complacent about who the "real owners" of future corporations will be.

Just following this passage, Drucker concedes briefly that there will also be a "*social* challenge" regarding "the dignity of the second class in post-capitalist society, the service workers." These service workers "lack the education necessary to be knowledge workers," and yet they always, in every country, "constitute a majority" (*Post-capitalist Society* 8). Drucker thus goes on to define "a new dichotomy of values" that will divide postcapitalist society. One might assume that such a dichotomy must be between these two classes of worker, especially since the gulf between them has to do with that all-important "knowledge" on which the whole society is founded. In fact, however, Drucker's dichotomy proves to be between two kinds of information worker: "intellectuals" and "managers" (9). Resolving an inevitable conflict between the managers' concern with people and the intellectuals' concern with ideas, says Drucker, "will be a central philosophical and educational challenge for the post-capitalist society" (9). This curious conclusion thus serves to occlude what Drucker otherwise clearly indicates: his projected postcapitalist society will be radically divided between an educated elite of knowledge workers and a majority of uneducated "service" workers. The "dignity" of the latter is marked as a subject of concern, though not as a "central" philosophic or educational issue. And all that would be at stake in this question of dignity anyway would be how service workers are *viewed* socially—and this means, presumably, how they are viewed *by* the other, higher class of knowledge workers, whose own dignity is apparently not in doubt.[2] In every other way, the basic class division described here would be necessary in principle, for it is understood as a kind of epiphenomenon or structural reflection of a mode of production dominated by information. Admittedly, Drucker always emphasizes the importance of active citizenship and rigorous education and envisions knowledge itself as a productive force: something that always involves "increasing the yield from what is known" (192). But Drucker never seriously entertains the possibility that society might *overcome* the basic social divide between the haves and have-nots of the information economy. Knowledge itself is said to be capable of infinite expansion and accumulation, but there will never, apparently, be enough to go around.

Consider, along the same lines, a particular change that Drucker acknowledges in his thinking between his early books and the 1990s. In works such as *The Future of Industrial Man* (1942) and *The New Society* (1949), Drucker envisions the workplace itself as the very site of a future community, to which workers would increasingly look as the absolute source of both social stature and existential meaning. In the 1990s, by contrast, Drucker concedes that the idea of a "plant community" never took root, at least in America. Therefore, knowledge workers "need an additional sphere of social life, of personal relationship, and of contribution outside and beyond the job" (*Post-capitalist Society* 174). It is striking that Drucker limits his point here to information workers, since service workers—whose jobs alone are not even sufficient to guarantee them social "dignity"—would seem to have an even more pressing need to find personal validation somewhere other than the workplace. Drucker also here abandons wholesale what might have seemed an absolutely essential point: that the new centrality of information and knowledge as economic values would make possible—at least for *some*—a mode of labor that was truly self-justifying and self-fulfilling. This possibility is now discounted even for the elite. In postcapitalist society, it is now clear, everyone will still be working for the weekend.

The "Autonomous" Workforce

Other versions of this general narrative about work in the information economy have been repeated with tedious regularity across a wide spectrum of popular writing, including business and professional books of every kind, reviews of these books, and articles in magazines such as *Forbes, Fortune, Business Week,* and younger, hipper rivals such as *Wired* or *Fast Company*.[3] Much of this material constitutes a kind of "conduct literature" for traveling white-collar middle managers, who, waiting in airports and planes, are a more or less captive audience for writers claiming to explain the key to business and personal success. As such, however, there are evident limits to what such writers can possibly think or imagine. Two common themes of contemporary business writing correspond closely to what André Gorz describes as two contradictory strategies with which contemporary capitalism is trying to deal with a newly "autonomous" workforce. The first involves a cutting of the traditional bonds of loyalty and identification between employees and employers in favor of a situation in which each employee "treats himself as capital and valorizes himself as such"; the second involves a "reestablishing [of] pre-capitalist—and indeed, almost feudal relations of vassalage and allegiance" (Gorz *Reclaiming Work* 7).

These strategies exist both in the form of literal employment practices and as discourses that, in interpreting, justifying, or celebrating such practices, sometimes seem to exceed them. The first strategy, always available as an option in some industries, intensified with the "restructurings" and "downsizings" of the 1980s and 1990s and the corresponding rise in temporary and freelance employment arrangements variously called "flextime," "outsourcing," "tele-work," and so forth. All of these have brought forth, especially on the Left, fears of what Ulrich Beck calls the "risk-society"—that is, "the spread of temporary and insecure employment, discontinuity and loose informality into Western societies that have hitherto been the bastions of full employment" (1). Yet a number of business writers attempt to affirm and even celebrate this new regime of insecure employment. Sometimes the argument is made negatively, by assuming, in the classical manner, a *homo oeconomicus* whose behavior stems from a calculus of needs and exertions, and for whom certain forms of economic anxiety have a salutary moral and personal effect. For example, Robert Samuelson, writing in *Newsweek* magazine in 1996, went so far as to argue that a certain level of "job insecurity" is "good for society," because "the anxieties and uncertainties that unsettle people may make them more prudent and productive in ways that strengthen and stabilize the economy" (25). But more often the argument is made positively, by envisioning and extolling what is claimed to be a new social type, variously named the "free agent," the "gold-collar worker," the "intrapreneur," and the like—that is, a fully "autonomous" employee whose knowledge purportedly gives him a kind of sovereignty over the mode of production itself.

The recent term "free agent" has its own particular ideological valence, since it originally referred to a professional athlete not bound by long-term contract to any single team and thus free to offer his services to the highest bidder. Now it begins to refer to the kind of highly skilled "information worker" whose portable knowledge allegedly allows him to move from company to company as what Jeremy Rifkin calls a "techno-nomad."[4] It is also commonly suggested that all enterprise might adapt the model of the Hollywood film, in which, as one writer puts it, "literally hundreds of small firms and individual entities . . . coalesce around a project" (Granthan 120). The term "free agent" thus lends a certain reflected glamour to a situation that was, after all, imposed on contemporary workers, but who are now, by contrast, to be understood as at once the directors and star performers of their own careers. Let me cite at some length the summary of consultants Susan B. Gould, Kerry J. Weiner, and Barbara R. Levin, who at least frankly suggest how a model of free agency is a way of making a virtue of necessity:

As companies radically reconstruct themselves by streamlining their operations, people are living in constant fear of losing their jobs and their quality of life. . . . Wave after wave of restructuring has washed away the promises of lifelong employment that had sustained their confidence in their future. . . . Since the mid 1980s our management consulting firm has been assisting individuals caught in this maelstrom. Our clients . . . have come to recognize a new reality and are beginning to follow a new model, one in which they are in charge of their careers, their lives, and their future. They are becoming Free Agents in the world of business. As Free Agents they define themselves by what they do rather than for whom they do it. They understand and accept that the relationship between themselves and their employers has shifted from "'til death do us part" to "What have you done for me lately?" This realization provides Free Agents with a new psychological freedom. . . . By being dependent on themselves alone, they are able to develop a new kind of security. (xvi)

Several points in this deceptively simple passage require scrutiny. Most obviously, the passage insistently tries to perform a fundamental semantic inversion with which a condition explicitly identified as insecurity is reimagined *as* "a new kind of security," and in which new modes of coercion are somehow said to bring "a new psychological freedom." Such an inversion finally evokes what can only be called a *comic* response. One might be reminded, for example, of George Bernard Shaw's character Andrew Undershaft, who is asked whether social programs that make life easier for people might also be bad for their characters. He replies, "well . . . when you are organizing civilization you have to make up your mind whether trouble and anxiety are good things or not" (Shaw 1:423).

But it is also claimed, more specifically, that free agents are to be defined by how they define themselves, namely, "by what they do rather than for whom they do it." The idea of the free agent thus can be thought about only from within the logical opposition which seems to inform this whole discourse about the new employee: an opposition between work as a means to an end and work as an end in itself. Wage labor would *seem* to be inevitably an instance of the former; and even if one complicates the issue by assuming a strong bond of loyalty and identification to the company, the situation remains one of instrumentality. In other words, there would remain in this context no material distinction between working for the wage and the weekend and working for the company—either way, employees are defining themselves in terms of the organization for which they work. But to be defined by what one *does* (instead of for whom one does it) is at least to glimpse the possibility of work as an autoteleology, something that fulfills itself in its own process. Thus, in this discourse of free agency, the whole deplorable situation of American capitalism at the end of the millennium—the layoffs and restructurings, the rollback of traditional benefits, the transferring of all risk of the business cycle from the employer onto individual employees via various forms of "flextime" or "temporary" employment arrangements—is somehow claimed to have actually *liberated* employees. It is not difficult to see that the logic of such an argument, pursued even one step farther, violates its own premises. The free agent, so to speak, is said to have left behind the realm of necessity and attained what is explicitly called a realm of freedom; yet the freedom of free agents can exist at all only via the crudest kind of instrumentality ("What have you done for me lately?"). The labor of free agents is thus revealed as anything but *self*-fulfilling.

Corporate Culture and Corporate Cant

The concept of free agency can also be turned on its head by suggesting that a strong bond of loyalty and identity between the individual and the company is the very ground of work as an end in itself. This is where corporate capitalism shifts from the first to the second strategy outlined above and attempts to appropriate the autonomous worker by elaborately reconstructing the workplace as a site of transcendental meaning. One of the most striking examples of this project is the idea of "corporate cultures," first given general currency by Terence E. Deal and Allan A. Kennedy in their book of that name from 1982. According to these authors, the most successful business organizations are those whose members share a particular set of values and practices—ranging from their corporate slogans ("Productivity through people!") to various "rituals" and "ceremonies," such as giving commemorative plaques to recognize achievement and as "signs of belonging to the culture" (Deal and Kennedy 21–22). In this account, the assortment of customs, procedures, traditions, and "war stories" that, as the authors acknowledge, exist in more or less every conceivable organization are now to be understood as constituting a full-fledged "culture" in the ethnographic sense. It is only in weak corporate cultures, they suggest, that work remains a mere instrumentality. In strong corporate cultures, by contrast, work truly attains the cherished goal of appearing as an end in itself: "Sometimes [the corporate culture] is fragmented and difficult to read. . . . if you ask employees why they work, they will answer 'because we need the money.' On the other hand, sometimes the culture of an organization is very strong and cohesive; everyone knows the goals of the corporation, and they are working for them" (4).

To be sure, even this brief summary retains the same ambiguity that threatens the promise of free agency: does work performed to fulfill the goals of the corporation really constitute work as an end in itself? In any case, it does not take Deal and Kennedy long to concede that the idea of a corporate culture is really a mere strategy imposed from above and formulated specifically in response to the crisis of work: "In the dispersed, helter-skelter world of the radically decentralized atomized organization . . . the role that culture plays will be even more critical. . . . The winners in the business world of tomorrow will be the heroes who can forge the values and beliefs, the rituals and ceremonies, and a cultural network of storytellers and priests" (Deal and Kennedy 193). Or in other words, "the way to manage [employees] is . . . by the subtle cues of culture" (15) because "a strong culture enables people to feel better about what they do, so they are more likely to work harder" (16).

Even in its own terms, then, corporate culture must be understood as operating via a kind of meta-instrumentality in which managers self-consciously formulate, communicate, and instill in their workers a so-called culture that ensures the workers' loyalty and exertion by making work *appear* to them as though it were an end in itself—a possibility which the very necessity of such a strategy itself reveals to be an illusion. One must also ask: are the managers whom Deal and Kennedy address themselves inside or outside the culture they are enjoined to orchestrate? Can the corporate manager serve, as it were, as at once the shaman *and* the ethnographer? An irreducible uncertainty about this question finally explodes the very concept of culture on which this whole discourse depends even as it perhaps also explains the remarkable staying power of the concept in the discourse of business management. Thus, in his *Corporate Culture Survival Guide* (1999), Edgar Schein suggests at the outset that culture itself is an infinitely adjustable and mobile concept which exists at once in "small teams, families, and workgroups," in "the whole organization," in "a whole industry," and, finally, "in regions and nations." As Schein thus concedes, a corporate culture could in principle only be one culture among many, and every individual is always "a multicultural entity" (13–14). But what are the limits of this concept in either direction? Can a family or small work group really be said to possess a "culture" analogous to the culture of a nation or ethnicity? Or, to reverse the question, could an individual's corporate-cultural identity ever trump his national, religious, or ethnic identity? Although this is not the place to pursue such questions any farther, it is at least worth noting how this vision of a "corporate" culture necessarily implies a radical cultural relativism ("there is no right or wrong culture, no better or worse culture," writes Schein, "except in relation to what the organization is trying to do" [21]) and thus participates in the evacuation of the word and concept of "culture" itself—which in this discourse refers, so to speak, at once to everything and to nothing.[5]

In the 1990s, by contrast, this focus on the rituals and ceremonies of corporate life seemed to expand into and merge with an astonishing new project of corporate self-fashioning, now taking the form of a self-conscious return to the discourses and symbols of religion and spirituality (see Conlin). Deal himself in 1995 coauthored *Leading with Soul: An Uncommon Journey of Spirit,* which argues: "Heart, hope, and faith, rooted in soul and spirit, are necessary for today's managers to become tomorrow's leaders, for today's sterile bureaucracies to become tomorrow's communities of meaning" (Bolman and Deal 12). The profusion of such "spiritual" business books in the 1990s—titles such as *Jesus C.E.O.: Using Ancient Wisdom for Visionary Leadership* (1992); *The Leadership Secrets of Jesus: Practical Lessons for Today* (1997); *Real Wealth: A Spiritual Approach to Money and Work* (1998); *Reclaiming Higher Ground: Creating Organizations That Inspire the Soul* (1998); *Spirit Incorporated: How to Follow Your Spiritual Path from 9–5* (1998); *Building a Business the Buddhist Way* (1999); and many others—is a phenomenon more remarkable as a whole than anything to be found in an individual volume.[6] Most of these books essentially return, with a certain irony which the writers themselves sometimes acknowledge, to what I will call the "moral economy": that is, the paternalistic and prescriptive model of economic behavior descending from Aristotle, the Christian fathers, and medieval philosophy into the homilies, tracts, and conduct literature of the early-modern period and beyond. As Max Weber famously argues, after the Reformation the discourse of moral economy develops two distinctive themes that have long outlived its more specific prohibitions (such as that on usury). The first is the so-called work ethic and its attendant concepts of the "vocation" or "calling": the idea that "hard, continuous bodily or mental labour" should "be considered in itself the end of life, ordained as such by God" (Weber 158). The second is the corresponding doctrine of "justification by success": the belief that wealth can be an earthly reward for a godly life and that, as William Perkins puts it, "any men may accept abundance, when it is the pleasure of God to bestow it upon them" (Perkins 770). These two interrelated themes (which also remain potent ones in political debates over welfare and economic justice) more or less circumscribe the discursive landscape of these spiritual business books, which do not distinguish themselves by either their subtlety or their originality.

Michael Novak's *Business as a Calling: Work and the Examined Life*

(1996), for example, uses a loose assortment of historical anecdotes and personal reflections to argue that business "is not only a morally serious vocation but a morally noble one" and to console business people, who, the author suggests, "get little affirmation for their vocations from the clergy or the general culture" (13, 43). As this astonishing second claim indicates in particular, this is an utterly conventional book that nevertheless constantly claims to oppose some imagined fantasy of a conventional wisdom. For an example of the enthusiastic contemporary return to the doctrine of justification by success, here is Bob Briner, writing in *The Management Methods of Jesus* (1996): "Jesus has the right idea for our individual lives *and* for our businesses. And the good news is that his priorities for our lives are not incompatible with solid, practical, profit-making priorities for our businesses" (111). One might also mention Paul Zane Pilzer's *God Wants You to Be Rich* (1995), a book whose title alone expresses the theme in question with a bluntness and concision unlikely to be surpassed.

These curious texts provoke a certain inevitable comic response; but they also might be said to challenge a familiar narrative of cultural history in which the "political economy" of Adam Smith and his followers gradually supersedes, as a dominant economic system of economic ideology, the simpler system of moral prescriptions and prohibitions in the moral economy. It is still commonly argued that Smith's vision of an infinitely self-adjusting market emancipated economics from the claims of positive religion and thus marks a profound turning point in Western intellectual history (see, e.g., Minowitz). The market allows individual acts of economic self-interest to be harmonized by an "invisible hand" into a larger, collective good; and although this vision continues often to be understood as essentially moral in its intentions and consequences, Smith's distinctive innovation must nevertheless be said to lie in his liberation of economic activity from many of the specific moral prohibitions to which it had traditionally been subjected. In other words, whatever moral effect is ascribed to capitalism even by its most explicit apologists inheres in the system as a whole rather than in the explicit moral intentions or actions of its individual protagonists. The spiritual business book, however, reminds us that this very vision of the market—which "hovers over the earth like the fate of the ancients, and with invisible hand allots fortune and misfortune to men" (Marx and Engels *Collected Works* 5:48)—retains a strong metaphysical component and perhaps indicates that capital, in its irreducible need to control the direct producers of value, is today returning after a protracted historical detour to the directly prescriptive power of moral discourse itself.

In the present context, so pervaded by futurist and technophilic themes, an obvious final example is the work of George Gilder, whose incongruous combination of high-tech "cyber-libertarianism" and Christian theology manages to unite practically all the themes I have considered so far. Gilder rose to prominence with *Wealth and Poverty* (1981), a political polemic defending the essential justice of the market that became the very bible of the resurgent capitalism of the Reagan years and that I will address briefly in chapter 5. His *Microcosm* (1989) is, by contrast, a kind of primer of those new technologies of information and communication that, as everyone today seems to agree, are radically transforming the global economy. The final chapter in *Microcosm,* however, elevates this common idea into a rhapsodic spiritual vision: "Once seen as a physical system tending toward exhaustion and decline, the world economy has clearly emerged as an intellectual system driven by knowledge. . . . The materialist superstition succumbs to an increasing recognition that the means of production in capitalism are not chiefly land, labor, and machines, present in all systems, but emancipated human intelligence" (378). Here again, in perhaps its most extreme form and expressed with a striking rhetorical bravura, is the basic point I have considered throughout: that the new ascendance of "knowledge" in capitalist production will serve as a radically emancipatory force. Gilder goes so far as to claim that the new electronic technologies have literally put an end to materialism itself, both as a philosophic position (which Gilder dismisses, in a piquant rhetorical inversion, as a mere "superstition") and perhaps almost in literal terms: "Giving up the superficial comforts of a human-scale world, mankind moves to mind scale. In the image of his Creator, he exalts the truly human—and godlike—dimension of his greatest gift from his Creator: his creativity. Giving up the material idols and totems . . . he is gaining at last his promised dominion over the world and its creatures" (379).

From this astonishing passage, let me mark for future reference how Gilder envisions human creativity as a typological "gift" from the divine Creator (an ancient trope in which my two central terms obviously intersect) and otherwise observe only how Gilder clearly understands the alleged new economy not merely as a new era of human history, and not merely even as the implicit fulfillment of biblical prophesy, but also, and most of all, as a vehicle or ground of "dominion": that is, of the capitalist Law of Command.

LIBERAL NOSTALGIA

After Work

In this chapter I address a second broad position regarding the contemporary crisis of work, placing here several thinkers who respond to what they vividly acknowledge to be a historical crisis by redoubling their efforts to reaffirm work as a uniquely privileged site of social and personal value. Whereas the futurist position, in any of its versions, at least remains forward looking and begins and ends with an enthusiastic acceptance of the transformation of work, this second position, by contrast, tends to be wistful, nostalgic, and radically uncertain about the current prospects for work in human experience. Although many of the writers I place here associate themselves with what is called today a "liberal" or "progressive" politics, their theoretical strategy is in principle a conservative one. Indeed, in many respects these writers often converge with so-called social conservatives, who, as I will consider in chapter 7, have managed successfully to put an end to "welfare" as a legal entitlement in the United States, doing so precisely in the name of an alleged social obligation of work.

The thinkers of liberal nostalgia begin by trying to make visible, in a salutary way, the human costs of that crisis of work that in other circles is celebrated for its world-transforming potential. For example, William Julius Wilson's *When Work Disappears: The World of the New Urban Poor,* a complex analysis of the roots and costs of urban poverty in the United States, was at the moment of its publication in 1996 (the same year as the so-called welfare reform bill) a valuable intervention into an ongoing policy debate. Even this book's title, however, indicates the extent to which Wilson privileges the determinative force of work among the myriad other factors that, as his analysis vividly demonstrates, contribute to the decline of traditional blue-collar communities.

In broad theoretical terms, Wilson positions his own argument between a "liberal" position which emphasizes "structural factors" such as "the ordering of social positions . . . and networks of social relationships" and a "conservative" position which stresses "the importance of values, attitudes, habits, and styles in explaining the different experiences, behaviors, and outcomes of groups" (xii–xiv). Then he attempts to cut through this familiar dispute over the relative determinative force of social structure or individual agency by seeing the latter as always genetically linked to the former. He argues that a variety of structural factors—the historical inequities of race and class, the challenges of globalization, the pressure put on traditional smokestack industries by the high-tech "information economy," and so forth—eventually produce a set of durable values, attitudes, and behaviors that then become immanent in individuals, so that they *seem* to be the self-sufficient "causes" both of poverty and of themselves.

The indispensability of work in such a schema is therefore self-evident, for it also precisely mediates between structure and agency. Work's availability in urban communities is structurally determined; but work's *significance* (morally, personally, and in terms of a general social psychology) lies in its alleged ability to shape the agential behavior of human beings in fundamentally positive ways. Although Wilson claims to balance agential and structural approaches to the problem of poverty, the centrality of work in his schema forces his argument willy-nilly toward an essentially moral judgment on the urban poor's failures of agency and attitude. As it were, these disadvantaged social subjects are at once the victims of, and themselves responsible for, the disappearance of work from their communities.

This belief in the unique and distinctive role of work in the formation of individual and social identity clearly constitutes one absolute limit of a thought which otherwise rigorously insists that such identity formation is collectively and structurally determined. Thus, Wilson engages in detail with what he calls the "liberal-conservative consensus about welfare reform" (164) in the 1990s, a consensus to which I will return later in another context and which boils down to an insistence that welfare recipients must be forcibly moved from welfare to work. He also observes that such a position could emerge only from the prevailing American belief system that sees poverty itself as an individual moral failure. Nevertheless, in a variety of ways, and even while rightly distancing himself from such essentializing arguments, Wilson himself embraces a privileged role for work in the construction of the social subject. He argues, for example:

As Pierre Bourdieu demonstrated, work is not simply a way to make a living and support one's family. It also constitutes a framework for daily behavior and patterns of interaction because it imposes disciplines and regularities. Thus, in the absence of regular employment, a person lacks not only a place in which to work and the receipt of regular income but also a coherent organization of the present—that is, a system of concrete expectations and goals. Regular employment provides the anchor for the spatial and temporal aspects of daily life. (72)

As envisioned here, work has a double product: it is not "simply a way to make a living" but also the essential ground of a sociopersonal "coherence" that defines at once "society" and the social subject. The opening reference (which is to Darbel and Bourdieu's *Travail et travailleurs en Algerie* [1963], an early and relatively little known text of someone who later emerges as a major social theorist) opens up certain necessary questions, and not merely because Bourdieu is far better known today as a critic of the Work (e.g., in his monumental study *Distinction*) than as the advocate of a sociocultural work ethic, which Wilson takes him for here. Even more broadly, this reference to what Bourdieu himself would later describe as a merely "empirical" study also indicates how Wilson's thought remains constrained by an implicit anthropology of self and Other.[1] The citation could in principle have no value if it were not also assumed in advance that work plays precisely the same role in every conceivable human culture and that it is, indeed, a uniquely privileged site for the construction of a universal human subject. This is the first of many examples that indicate how a certain anthropology remains an unsurpassable horizon for the thought at issue here.

The same understanding of work is even more obviously central to Richard Sennett's *The Corrosion of Character: The Personal Consequences of Work in the New Capitalism* (1998), which, as its title indicates, is a nostalgic lament for a world in which the productive rhythms of daily labor still yielded a sense of meaning for ordinary people. The basic argument of this loosely structured and anecdotal book can be simply summarized. What Sennett calls "short-term" or "flexible" capitalism (i.e., the same situation repeatedly observed by the other writers I mention) "threatens to corrode [people's] character[s], particularly those qualities of character which bind human beings to one another and furnishes [*sic*] each with a sense of sustainable self" (27). The book as a whole describes and deplores how "the conditions of time in the new capitalism," its new reliance on temporary or freelance modes of administering work, threaten "the ability of people to form their characters into sustained narratives" (31). To restate Sennett's point in the terms that govern my argument here is to understand his rather amorphous term "character" as referring to a particular relationship between work and the Work. This "character" is itself an instrumental product, something constructed "through the pursuit of long-term goals, or by the practice of delayed gratification for the sake of a future end" (10). But since mere employment can apparently no longer provide such goals and ends, and thus can no longer offer itself as saturated with meaning, it is envisioned—and only, so to speak, in retrospect—as a site for the construction of a work of self, of a self as a Work.

In Sennett's account, furthermore, the new capitalism threatens only this subjective production, not production itself, which in fact thrives via those same processes of industrial automation that otherwise make possible its corrosive "flexibility." One of Sennett's pieces of anecdotal evidence, for example, is the case of a bakery in Boston where he interviewed workers both twenty-five years ago and again today. Formerly, these workers made bread by hand; they had strong "craft pride," but they "didn't enjoy their work" because "the ovens often burned them, the primitive dough beater pulled human muscles; and it was night work, which meant these men . . . seldom saw their families during the week" (66). Today, workers at the same bakery use computers to tend baking machines. The bakery is now "startlingly cool, whereas workers used frequently to throw up from the heat" (67); and the bread that is produced is "excellent" (69). Sennett readily concedes the terminal ambiguity of this example and repeatedly stipulates that he is not calling for a return to the previous conditions (75, 117). He does want to argue, however, that now workers feel a "detachment and confusion" about their own identities as workers (74): they are no longer able to "organize a life narrative" (117), and their "inner needs" (148) are not being satisfied. In the end, therefore, either for the workers themselves or for Sennett, there are no conclusions, only a vague sense that something has gone missing from the workaday world. To go back is neither possible nor even desirable, but there is no clear plan of future action either. Political change occurs, Sennett asserts in the book's final lines, "on the ground, between persons speaking out of inner needs. . . . What political programs follow from those inner needs, I simply don't know" (148). Given a chance to speak, the laboring self seems to have nothing to say, just as Sennett's own empirical and descriptive argument has, in its own explicit terms, absolutely nowhere to go.

Or perhaps, a little more precisely, this is an argument that can go only one place: it can, so to speak, go "home," to some personal or experiential "outside," beyond work. This is essentially the conclusion of Joanne B. Ciulla's *The Working Life: The Promise and Betrayal of Modern Work* (2000), which has a broader historical focus than Sennett's book but shares his essentially nostalgic point of view. Ciulla critiques Sennett for his assumption "that long-term employment with one firm is the key to character development." By contrast, she suggests that "while work itself is important to form character, there is no reason to believe that changing employers frequently will harm one's character. . . . People can still gain a sense of self-efficacy, discipline, integrity and pride from the work they do and from the fact of employment itself" (232).

In making so fine a distinction, however, Ciulla's own argument simply retreats one step back from Sennett's while retaining all of his key assumptions. Work is said to retain its alleged foundational role in human experience in a manner that wholly transcends its conditions and content, so that, whether inside or outside the regime of capital, and whether or not a person takes pride in what he does or whom he does it for, work remains the sole source of character, discipline, pride, and all the rest of the social and personal virtues.

And yet Ciulla herself proves incapable of remaining entirely faithful even to this straightforward argument. In the book as a whole, Ciulla surveys some of the same recent attempts to invest work with meaning I have briefly mentioned here, observes a "betrayal" of the expectations such efforts raised in American workers, but then finally concludes only that "[o]rganizations do not have a moral obligation to provide meaningful work; however, they do have an obligation to provide work and compensation that leave employees with the energy, autonomy, will, and income to pursue meaning at work and a meaningful life outside of work" (227). It is difficult even to follow what is being proposed here, since Ciulla asserts, on the one hand, that organizations do not have to offer work that is *itself* meaningful but must, on the other hand, offer work that allows employees to "pursue meaning at work." Apparently, workers must somehow find meaning *at* work but not *in* work. Ciulla does make one concrete and specific proposal: employers should be moderate in their demands of time and energy and generous in their compensation. But it is hard to see how anyone could object, from any political position, to so attenuated a conclusion, which—like Wilson's call for a WPA-type federal job program and Sennett's vague hope for some new economic order "which provides human beings . . . deep reasons to care about one another" (148)—leaves entirely unexamined what I have called *the double necessity of work.* Indeed, the thought of each of the writers considered in this chapter invests its whole force in the hope of that double production by which, in work, one both makes a living and makes a (durable, sustainable, coherent, narrativized) Self—a Self that, however, is then defined by its productivity and *constituted in and as a Work.*

Robert L. Heilbroner's World of Work

The essential elements of this liberal nostalgia may be considered in perhaps their purest form in a brief but remarkable text by Robert L. Heilbroner, a distinguished economist long famed for his ability to summarize complex intellectual ideas for a broad audience.[2] This text, which I will discuss in detail, was first delivered as a lecture at the Library of Congress in 1984, published as a pamphlet the following year under the title *The Act of Work,* and then republished with minor changes as "The World of Work," in *Behind the Veil of Economics* (1988), the text I cite here. Heilbroner's subject in this text is something he calls the *idea* of work, which he asserts must be entirely distinguished from all of the more specific aspects of the subject commonly addressed by economists. This project requires Heilbroner to provide a kind of schematic summary of Western economic history from its alleged origins all the way to its multiple imagined futures, a breadth of focus which makes this text exemplary in more than one way. To consider work as a pure idea, Heilbroner claims in opening,

takes us immediately to the territory of the anthropologist—the jungles of Africa and New Guinea, the grasslands and semideserts of the Australian outback, the Kalahari regions of South Africa, the remote islands of the Pacific. In these exotic places we find the bedraggled remainders of what was once presumably the universal form of societal existence—what anthropologist Marshall Sahlins has called "the domestic mode of production." (81)

Heilbroner's vision is thus, in the most literal sense of the term, *archeo-logical,* since the "exotic" ethnographic Other constitutes at once the origin and reference point for his argument.

And Heilbroner goes on to make a surprising assertion: "*there is no work in primitive societies*" (81). The members of such societies, he concedes, engage in bodily and mental exertion of every kind; but the tasks performed to provide material sustenance, such as hunting and gathering, are not distinguished in relative social status from any other activity and "are not carried out under any one's supervision or command" nor "for any extrinsic purpose" (82). Therefore, if one is willing to accept that the primitive societies studied by the anthropologist "are the vanishing remnants of earliest human society—a form of life portrayed in Genesis—it follows that there was indeed no work in Paradise" (82). Heilbroner is here primarily thinking of Marshall Sahlins's famous *Stone Age Economics* (1972), a book that does indeed suggest that a primitive "domestic mode of production" made possible what he audaciously calls an "affluent" society: that is, a society whose members had few possessions but were not poor, and who managed to meet their material needs without working particularly hard. Poverty, Sahlins insists, "is the invention of civilization" (37).

But Heilbroner uses Sahlins's anthropological observations largely to distinguish a category of "work" from a second category that can be defined only negatively, in terms of its lack of certain forms of historical and social elaboration. At the same time, he marks this opposition between two forms of human exertion as not merely historical or archeological but as something still operative in contemporary economic life. "We say that it is a lot of work to take care of a child," he says, "but we do not mean the same as when we say there is a lot of work at the office" (83). Heilbroner's passing example opens up, with painful obviousness, questions about "unpaid" domestic labor and its social status that feminist historians and economists have pursued at length (see, e.g., J. Smith, Wallerstein, and Evers). And even if one holds these necessary questions in abeyance, the proposed distinction would still seem to be a difficult and fragile one. If domestic labor is not "work," then what is it? Correspondingly, how could one precisely delimit the category that Heilbroner considers to be proper work? This category of practice would seem to be almost, but not quite, simply wage labor itself and almost, but not quite, what one calls a "profession." To extend Heilbroner's own hypothetical example, are we to understand that nannies and teachers *are* doing "work" on the job but are *not* doing work when they perform precisely the same tasks for their own children?[3]

At the very least this is evidently one more case of an argument wholly grounded in the assumption of *a work that is not work*. The question is whether such a possibility can ever be extricated from the anthropological (and gendered) thought of the Other to which, in Heilbroner's own discourse, it is so obviously linked. One must also notice how, even as Heilbroner explicitly identifies the "exotic" societies studied by anthropology as an essential limit point for understanding contemporary work, he also marks this anthropological vision as an arcadian myth. His narrative of the history of work is not merely archeological but implicitly theological, for he imagines the present as midway between two moments of historical rupture, between a paradise lost and a paradise regained. As the earliest societies resemble the scriptural paradise, so the historical advent of work is the real event "whose mythic representation is the expulsion from the Garden of Eden. Thereafter, the Bible tells us, mankind lives by the sweat of his brow" (82).

Although it might be objected that Heilbroner evokes the myth of Eden merely for rhetorical effect, this sudden conjunction of economics and anthropology on the ground of an archeo- or teleological history is no coincidence, given that both disciplines begin by assuming a particular human subject whose perhaps unknowable presence can nevertheless be reconstructed from its observed practices. To be sure, Heilbroner claims specifically that these primitive societies where Sahlins's domestic mode of production prevails, and where work therefore does not exist, must be seen as *preceding* the birth of *homo oeconomicus*—that "new hero of work" who emerges only much later in classical political economy (89). In other words, Heilbroner tries to sidestep that fundamental conceptual error with which (as Marx suggests and Althusser summarizes) the classical political economists make "the conditions of capitalist production the eternal conditions of all production, without seeing that these categories were historically determined, and hence historical and transitory" (Althusser and Balibar 92). Indeed, the book in which Heilbroner's essay appears claims in its title to take us "behind the veil of economics" and begins with a ringing denunciation of the discipline not entirely unlike Althusser's. Economics itself, Heilbroner claims, too often merely obscures the fact "[t]hat the price system is also a system of power; that the work of analysis is inescapably colored by ideology and initiated by unstable 'visions'; that the object over which the veil is spread is not a collection of individuals but a specific social order to which we give the name capitalism" (7–8).

But despite these ringing assertions of an apparent materialistic historicism, he continues implicitly to ground his discipline in an anthropological determination of man—by indirectly positioning the status of that discipline as a historical stand-in for anthropology. Economics, in other words, picks up the narrative of humanity right where the latter lets it go, at the birth of work in its proper sense. For a further example, in his *Twenty-first Century Capitalism,* Heilbroner once again mentions Sahlins and asserts this time that there is no "economics" in primitive cultures, "whereas economics seems to pervade life in [contemporary] Western countries" (24). Anthropology is thus at once the predecessor *and* an unsurpassable horizon for economics as a discipline and for the economic facts or phenomena which that discipline addresses.

In "The World of Work," Heilbroner proceeds to describe humanity's "leap from primitive freedom and equality to subordination and inequality," and the consequent construction of a world in which work would henceforth always involve some form of exploitation (*Behind the Veil* 68). Work in this new historical form of "submissive striving" (100) is, he insists, necessary for the achievements of civilization (87). "Without work, in the exploitative sense . . . there would be no pyramids, Great Walls, temple complexes, cathedrals, irrigation systems, or road systems—nor the high culture that arose within and from these material underpinnings" (87). In other words, the opposition between primitive, or domestic, labor and proper work has now been displaced in favor of the opposition between work and the Work: on the one side, a submissive, exploited, and wholly instrumental labor that always functions merely as a means to an end; and on the other side, the "achievements" of civilization and high culture, which presumably transcend the exploitative conditions of their creation.

Heilbroner also largely follows Marx in identifying capitalism as at once the ultimate historical form of such exploitation and an economic system that ultimately makes possible a transcendence of itself. What Heilbroner has in mind with this transcendence, however, is something rather different from what Marx had in mind. Heilbroner suggests that capitalism is the first mode of production "in which the upper class 'works' in ways that would have been regarded with disdain by the upper classes of previous social orders" (94). Marx, of course, always suggested that the capitalist *as such* does no work; if an individual capitalist personally manages his business, he is simply to that extent also a worker.[4] But Heilbroner observes persuasively that the historical mode of "general industriousness," the defining characteristic of the historical regime of capital, has now in fact subsumed all social subjects. And in all acts of capitalist work, "there remains a core of submission," a "surrender of the autonomy of the body and mind to a pace and to movement designed by another" (97).

Following this somewhat disheartening narrative of paradise lost, Heilbroner finally allows himself briefly to imagine a world beyond this submission to the rhythms and structures of production, a time when humanity might return "to the blissful state of primitive society"—in other words, "a world without work" (100). He begins with what he calls a "necessary qualification": "The vision of a world without work is not to be interpreted as a world without effort, perhaps exhausting effort, or a world without personal achievement . . . indolence is not at all the quality we seek in a world without work. What is at stake is not a society without striving and effort but a society without submissive striving, without subordinative effort" (100). Heilbroner here momentarily entertains the possibility of a world without *work* (in the proper sense he has been at pains to define throughout), but in which remain both "effort" and "achievement," and in which any pure negation of work ("indolence") is to be strongly rejected. This passage thus occludes a crucial question that it also allows to remain in plain sight. Heilbroner refuses to entertain the possibility of mere idleness, and he insists on a perpetually repeated progress from "effort" to "achievement." But such a progress, as the etymology of the latter term indicates, would necessarily always be a movement *upward,* a coming to a *head* (*à chief venir*). Is not to affirm such a progress necessarily to reinscribe the same hierarchies of "submissive striving" which Heilbroner is otherwise laboring to reject?

Such a question will prove to be moot, however, for Heilbroner is soon going to demolish this evanescent vision of paradise regained in a crescendo of successive qualifications and negations. First he briefly imagines, only to reject, two specific scenarios for this world without work. The first is technological, "a world in which submissive effort will become unnecessary because machines will take over all tasks," leaving humanity "free to consume their output, much as the hunters and gatherers consume the output of nature" (100–101). Notice that this ultrafuturist fantasy of a fully robotic mode of production is explicitly associated with the vanished arcadian world of Sahlins's "first affluent society." This imagined future, Heilbroner also claims (echoing very briefly the whole debate about "the problem of leisure" that attends the earliest recognitions of work's historical crisis), is "already near enough to raise disturbing questions with respect to the possibilities for employment" (101). In fact, this automated world is one that Heilbroner himself can scarcely bear to contemplate:

A *fully* robotized world would indeed be one in which there would be *no need* for men and women to submit to the relationship of subordination, because machines would perform their tasks, yielding up *all* their returns. What sort of world would such a regime of machinery be? The prospect is disconcerting and unnerving. I will venture *only one* speculation with regard to it. Surely the emplacement of such a robotic mode would render the present social order as obsolete as the emplacement of centralized power rendered obsolete the domestic mode. It would be the end of capitalism, the beginning of *we know not what.* (101; emphasis added)

As the italicized words indicate, the analytic voice here strongly reveals its own limitations relative to the extremity of the vision it reluctantly considers. What, precisely, is so disconcerting about these generous and efficacious machines? Heilbroner here marks a significant point where this liberal vision diverges radically from both free-market futurism and most varieties of classical or contemporary Marxism, all of which embrace in principle the socially ameliorative potential of technology. Heilbroner, by contrast, rejects almost without explanation what he oddly calls a "regime of machinery," even as he acknowledges that such a regime perfectly solves the very problem (of submissive striving) that he has identified as fundamental.

But there is still one more possibility Heilbroner wants to consider. Here I again add italics to indicate how multiply qualified is this second possible future:

> The second vista is more attractive. It asks us to imagine whether our existing system would not *gradually* expand its prestige and power-oriented jobs until *virtually all* work was conducted under the aegis of ambition, not duress, so that subordination and submission would simply disappear.
>
> I have no doubt that *a great many* constraints that now encumber work—especially its sapping division of labor and its hierarchical disposition of jobs—can be *lessened*. (101–2)

As against the sinister or benevolent extremity of the technological future, this is a vision of incremental improvement in which the end of *all* duress, or of *all* hierarchy, cannot even be imagined. Heilbroner acknowledges as much in the next lines, which, with an astonishing rhetorical violence, shut down the utopian hopes that have resounded through the entire essay, insisting that

> work—and I now stress to the utmost its inner core of submission to social direction—is essential to maintain civilization as we know it. A world without work is a fantasy, and a dangerous fantasy at that. (102)

Here, then, is what we are left with: work is intrinsically and inescapably submissive, and yet a world without work is a dangerous fantasy. It is thus only *after* the full force of Heilbroner's rhetoric had associated these imagined futures with the arcadian past that he finds it possible to say that there is no going back; and in the wake of such utopian hopes, which were apparently raised only so as to be dashed, he offers nothing more than the vague possibility of gradual progress (the very idea, by the way, that one would have thought had already been disposed of by the anthropological vision of primitive affluence which had served as the essay's starting point). Thus, at the end of this curiously self-destroying text, only one possible conclusion remains. Freedom *"within* work" is at most a tenuous improbability; and freedom *"from* work" cannot—and *must not*—even be imagined (103, emphasis added).

MARXISM AND POST-MARXISM

Toward a Liberation of Work

At the point where these various free-market and liberal visions of work reach their common impasse, Marxism necessarily interposes itself again, not least because it represents the earliest sustained attempt to grasp work as a historical crisis. Indeed, Marxism both begins and ends, so to speak, with a radical critique of labor under the regime of capital, a critique that, however, continues to be haunted by a certain tension between work and the Work. This tension sets its mark on a variety of contemporary Marxist thinkers, who join to constitute a third broad approach to work's contemporary crisis. I have in mind, on the one hand, writers such as Stanley Aronowitz and William Di-Fazio in the United States and André Gorz and Ulrich Beck in Europe, all of whom argue in broadly similar terms for the necessity of moving past a "work-based society," and, on the other hand, the circle of Italian and American theorists of so-called autonomist Marxism, especially Harry Cleaver, Félix Guattari, Michael Hardt, and Antonio Negri (the last two are coauthors of the monumental study *Empire*). All these writers perhaps have at one level more in common with the free-market futurists than with contemporary liberals or progressives. Like the futurists, these writers too grasp the crisis of work not as a problem to be lamented but as an opportunity to be seized; and they envision humanity standing at "the threshold between suffering and the moment when history's potential will realize itself" (Guattari and Negri 34). They also, of course, depart from the apostles of the market in recognizing the ethos of "general industriousness" as a historical product of capitalism that has finally outlived its usefulness. It is, however, their common inability to follow this insight all the way to its limit that will be my particular interest in the analyses that follow.

At the same time, these two groups of writers can be distinguished in terms of their different theoretical approaches to the future of work. To put it in schematic terms: both groups advocate the abolition of something called "work," but they differ in their understandings of precisely what this means and how it is coming to pass. Whereas the first group commonly argues that technology makes possible a reduction of industrial or instrumental labor in favor of "autonomous activity," the second group commonly argues that industrial labor itself, in its own technological evolution, is producing a newly autonomous social subject. In other words, one group seeks autonomy *outside* capitalist labor; the other seeks autonomy *inside* it. The goal of the first group (here I cite Ulrich Beck as he cites Gorz) "is no longer to regain full employment in the classical sense" but rather "'to capture, alongside and beyond the apparatus logic, greater spaces of autonomy . . . that permit a fairly unrestricted blossoming of individual existence'" (Beck 15, citing Gorz *Farewell* 11–12). The goal of the second group, by contrast (here citing Félix Guattari and Antonio Negri), is a "liberation of work" that "can now be accomplished by workers in the most advanced sectors of science and technology" (Guattari and Negri 15). This brief summary does not, of course, do full justice to either side, but the opposition between these two positions will, in any case, prove to be an extremely slippery one. In all these writers—as indeed throughout this entire debate—the very idea of work continues to serve as a kind of floating signifier whose meaning changes at different points.

The first group of Marxist writers begins exactly where so many others do: by announcing a profound historical rupture in the theory and practice of work. Gorz, for example, has argued repeatedly over the course of his long career that "there can no longer be full-time waged work for all, and waged work cannot remain the centre of gravity or even the central activity in our lives. *Any politics which denies this, whatever its ideological pretensions, is a fraud. . . .* The right to work, the right to a job and the right to an income have been confused for a long time. They cannot be confused any longer" (*Paths to Paradise* 34).

Beck, similarly, begins his *Brave New World of Work* (2000) by describing what he calls the "Brazilianization of the west": the spread to the industrialized nations of the conditions that prevail in the semi-industrialized countries of the south, where "those who depend upon a wage or salary in full-time work represent only a minority of the economically active population" (1). And Beck too denounces the absurdity with which societies no longer able to provide full-time, secure paid work for all retain their ideological commitment to work as "the only valid measure for the evaluation of human beings and their activities" (10).

Finally, Aronowitz and DiFazio have for some years been making a similar case, arguing strongly against the continuing prevalence of "the dogma of work" in a world where full employment is no longer possible or necessary. In *The Jobless Future* (1994), these authors demolish the conventional arguments of free-market futurism by documenting in convincing detail that new informational technologies have in no way improved the lives of most workers. Rather, they conclude, "for the immense majority, computerization of the workplace has resulted in further subordination, displacement, or irrelevance" (33). Both here and in their later "Post-work Manifesto" (1998; coauthored with Dawn Esposito and Margaret Yard), these authors join Gorz and Beck in arguing for an immediate reduction in the workweek combined with a guaranteed income, in order to produce "a world beyond compulsory labor . . . where human freedom is the measure of social life" (Aronowitz et al. 75).

In the most fundamental sense, all of these authors strive to bring an end to what Beck calls "the value imperialism of work" and to embrace, instead, "a multi-activity society in which housework, family work, club work and voluntary work are prized alongside paid work and returned to the centre of public and academic attention" (Beck 15).

André Gorz: Reclaiming Work

The importance and urgency of these arguments must be acknowledged in the strongest possible terms. Nevertheless, I suggest that all these varied critiques of work continue to ground themselves, at least implicitly, in an anthropological determination of Man and allow themselves to be governed by the problematic of a *subject* in its alleged potential for creativity and self-development. The exemplary case here is Gorz, who across numerous polemical books forcefully and eloquently critiques the prevailing (social) ethos of work, only to insist on an (individual) ethos of the Work. Gorz's thought always seeks at once to move beyond work and to reclaim it in some higher or different sense, a theoretical trajectory indicated by the titles of his books, which begin by saying *Farewell to the Working Class* (1982), proceed through

Paths to Paradise (1985) and finally arrive at *Reclaiming Work* (1999). In the earliest of these books, Gorz divides the field of work into two modes, which he calls *heteronomous* and *autonomous*. The first refers to "an activity carried out: for someone else; in return for a wage; according to forms and for a purpose not chosen by the worker"—in other words, work as an instrumentality, a means to an end. The second refers to "self-determined activity, which is its own end"—in other words, work as an autoteleology, an end in itself (*Farewell* 2). Gorz's thought as a whole absolutely depends on this opposition, and he always, of course, privileges autonomous and self-determining labor. In doing so, I suggest, he also repeatedly allows to return through the back door the unwelcome guests he has so resolutely thrown out through the entrance.

Indeed, for Gorz, it is not sufficient to lessen or even abolish heteronomous work; rather, he insists that "the abolition of work will only be emancipatory if it also allows the development of autonomous activity" (*Farewell* 2). In other words, Gorz envisions autonomous work not merely as a possibility to be somehow freed and facilitated but, rather, as itself an obligation, a necessary component of the project of liberation. He writes in *Paths to Paradise:* "Reduction of work time has nothing to do with emancipation if it merely leads to more time being spent on material and non-material consumption. It can be an emancipatory project only if combined with contraction of economic and market activity and expansion of activities performed for their own sake—for love, pleasure or satisfaction" (53).

For Gorz, therefore, liberation itself is a *positive* and *constructive* project involving the making-present of an individual self presence and thus "the creation . . . of self" (*Reclaiming Work* 4). The extent to which such arguments recall Marx's 1844 manuscripts, with their celebrated denunciation of the "alienation" of labor under capitalism, is also obvious. Yet by his own account, Gorz goes considerably farther than the early Marx by insisting on a realm of "individual existence" which "can never be entirely socialized," because "it involves areas of experience which, being essentially secret, intimate, unmediated and incapable of mediation, can never be had in common" (*Farewell* 90). Gorz thus envisions autonomous work as the definitive characteristic and product of a singular being who, precisely *in* his singularity, is impervious to community. His vision is also radically conditioned by a largely unexamined historico-anthropological narrative. In "pre-capitalist societies," he writes, "work was given its rhythm by festivals and celebrations, with their songs and dances; the tools themselves were beautifully decorated"; and in these antediluvian societies where men whistled as they worked, all labor was "a way of *being in the present*" (*Paths to Paradise* 49). For Gorz, work is something that once was, and might again return to be, a bringing of singular being to full self-presence in the world; and thus (autonomous) work remains the absolutely privileged site for a Work of self.

These assumptions are so deep-rooted in Gorz's thought that his arguments seem to become steadily more problematic across the course of his career. The introduction of his most recent book, a text whose severe internal tensions I will illuminate in some detail, begins with a ringing exhortation: "We must dare to prepare ourselves for the Exodus from 'work-based society'" (*Reclaiming Work* 1). Gorz then proceeds to restate and rename his opposition of autonomous and heteronomous work. When one speaks of the end of work, he argues, one does not mean

the end of what everyone has become accustomed to call "work." It is not work in the anthropological or philosophical sense of the term. It is not the labour of the parturient woman, nor the work of the sculptor or poet. It is not work as the "autonomous activity of transforming matter," nor as the "practico-sensory activity" by which the subject exteriorizes him/herself by producing an object which bears his/her imprint. It is, unambiguously, the specific "work" peculiar to industrial capitalism: the work we are referring to when we say "she doesn't work" of a woman who devotes her time to bringing up her own children, but "she works" of one who gives even some small part of her time to bringing up other people's children in a playgroup or a nursery school. (*Reclaiming Work* 2)

Here, Gorz distinguishes the work which today might be reaching its end, the work peculiar to industrial capitalism, from a work which, by contrast, must not be allowed to end. The latter, which he now bluntly calls "real work" (*Reclaiming Work* 3), comprises at least three different things: (1) work in an anthropological sense: that is, presumably, Sahlins's "domestic mode of production," those alleged archaic practices with which humanity once labored so as to make itself present in the world; (2) work in a "philosophical" sense: a kind of Hegelian and idealist concept of work as the *poiesis* or expression of a fully self-present subject; and (3) the unpaid, gendered, reproductive, and (in a different sense) "domestic" labor that clearly accompanies industrial capitalism but is apparently not, at least for Gorz, "peculiar" to it.

One observes, first of all, the obvious parallel to the examples and argument of Robert Heilbroner that were discussed in the previous chapter. Gorz's arguments raise similar questions in a somewhat more intense form, since he, unlike Heilbroner, allows himself to be directly prescriptive. But how, then, can the mode of work which we must "rescue and sustain" (*Re-*

claiming Work 3) even as industrial labor fades away be understood at once as a primitive labor (which, as Heilbroner suggests, is actually characterized by its *absence* of sociocultural elaboration) *and* as artistic and poetic "creation" (the Work as a sociocultural *presence*)? Or, to ask essentially the same question in a completely different way, can domestic labor really be seen as somehow self-fulfilling and authentic simply because of what it *lacks*—that is, because it brings neither a wage nor the social status associated with full-time paid employment?

Gorz immediately goes on to denounce "the fraudsters who, in the name of the philosophical or anthropological definition of work, justify the value of a form of 'work' which is the very negation of that definition" (*Reclaiming Work* 2). He is presumably thinking of contemporary ideologues who (in the context, for example, of debates over welfare) often deploy some quasi-anthropological notion of "human nature" to demand that society continue to enforce full-time labor for all whether or not it is materially necessary. No wonder Gorz is anxious to distinguish himself from such arguments, given that he too is inclined to speak of autonomous, "real" work as something to be mandated, both for the individual and for society. Indeed, Gorz's critique of a fraudulent work ethic (in which I would readily join) here again proves itself inseparable from a reaffirmation of the autonomous Work:

Efforts to deny "the end of work" in the name of the necessity and permanence of work in the anthropological or philosophical sense demonstrate the opposite of what they were attempting to prove: it is precisely in the sense of self-realization, in the sense of "*poiesis,*" of the creation of a work as *oeuvre,* that work is disappearing fastest into the virtualized realities of the intangible economy. . . . One cannot demonstrate that "the work-based society" must exist in perpetuity by invoking its anthropologically necessary character. In fact, the opposite is the case; we have to exit from "work" and the "work-based society" in order to recover a taste for, and the possibility of, "true" work. (*Reclaiming Work* 2–3)

This passage continues to mix positive and negative critiques in a most problematic way. Gorz suggests that to defend the moral or ethical necessity of work on the ground of some anthropological or philosophical concept of the subject is to "demonstrate the opposite." It is not mere labor but "true work" that is threatened by the general industriousness, and the new technologies, of "work-based society." One will wonder in passing how the work-based society can threaten true work at the same time that the former is itself threatened by new technology and our increasing inability to provide jobs for all who seek them. But one must then ask, far more broadly: can true work be defended as an anthropological and philosophical necessity as mere labor cannot? If so, then the argument makes itself instantly vulnerable to those capitalist apologists who, as we saw in chapter 2, tirelessly reconstruct the capitalist workplace as a place of spiritual and existential self-realization. If not, then on what grounds can Gorz insist on the necessity of true work in the first place? And in any case, Gorz is here defending *poiesis* against a nonexistent threat. It is quite absurd to suggest that the same technologies that are threatening or transforming industrial work are also threatening the Work; any of a myriad possible examples (electronic music, video art, digital research tools, and the like) make abundantly clear that technology has in fact fostered cultural production of every kind. Gorz's final assertion ("we have to exit from 'work' . . . in order to recover . . . 'true' work") is thus quite untenable, because "artistic, sporting, or philosophical activities" (*Reclaiming Work* 5) clearly thrive in contemporary work-based society, as defenders of "the market" are only too eager to remind us.

Finally, Gorz's argument becomes, if possible, even more problematic as he returns to his implicit analogy between artistic and domestic labor. He asks, "Why do we say a woman 'works' when she takes care of children in a nursery school and 'does not work' when she stays at home to take care of her own children?" (*Reclaiming Work* 3). It is not, he argues, simply because the nursery school teacher is paid and the mother is not. Rather,

the essential point is that work performs a socially identified and normalized function in the production and reproduction of the social whole. . . . In other words, it has to be a "job," a "profession": that is to say, the deployment of institutionally certified skills according to approved procedures. None of these conditions is fulfilled by the housewife-and-mother: her work is not part of the process of social labour; it is not subject to approved procedures, institutionally monitored for their conformity to professional standards (or susceptible of such monitoring); it is not subject to public criteria in terms of hours and efficiency. In short, it is not in the public sphere, does not meet socially codified, socially defined needs. This is something it shares with the work of slaves or personal servants who wait upon the personal desires of their masters, not to mention the work of artistic or theoretical creation. (3–4)

The myriad difficulties of this passage begin with the manifest inaccuracy of his allegation that domestic and reproductive labor is somehow free from public or professional scrutiny—as any welfare mother, for example, could readily attest. (For that matter, is it even true that "artistic or theoretical creation" is completely free from institutional "monitoring" of various kinds?) As Gorz describes it, furthermore, "work" in the common sense of the word (i.e., the work whose impending abolition is announced and celebrated) seems to subsist, much as it does for Heilbroner, in a curious limbo between mere wage labor and "the profession," neither quite one nor the other. The last lines of the passage then silently associate "true work" with what the classical political economists call "unproductive" labor. The very paradigm of such unproductive labor is what Adam Smith identifies as "a menial servant" (260), because a servant's wages represent a pure consumption of value, as opposed to the factory worker, who produces value in excess of what he is paid. And unlike Marx himself, who, as I argued in chapter 1, empties this distinction of its moral or ethical content, Gorz seems simply to overturn Smith's opposition so as to privilege the "unproductive" work of the mother or the artist. To do so, it seems to me, is not only to fail to escape the imprisoning categories that haunt the historical idea of work but, in effect, to reinvest them with a new discursive and theoretical power.

Indeed, whereas Marx meditates on the unexpected analogy of the servant and the artist in order to grasp the peculiarity of capitalist production, Gorz brackets these incongruous categories for quite a different reason: in order to argue, here again, that true work is an activity whose aim "is the creation of meaning, or self" (*Reclaiming Work* 4). This creation, he always claims, "is not socializable or codifiable" but "is, in its essence, a transgression and recreation of norms and codes; it is solitude and rebellion and contestation of 'work'" (4). It is only here, for Gorz, that the mother, the servant, and the artist converge. In other words, true work is the activity of a singular being *in* her absolute self-presence and separation from all that is common or social. Rejecting this as strongly as possible, I nevertheless mark for future reference something that still manages to emerge from this welter of overlapping and problematic categories: the idea, not merely of a work that is not work, but, rather, of a work that exists only as a kind of forever-to-be-repeated transgression and exposure of its own limits, and whose purely *negative* power one does perhaps sometimes glimpse in art or in philosophy, in music or in motherhood.

Michael Hardt, Antonio Negri, and Autonomist Marxism

The second and final group of writers to be considered under the heading of "post-Marxism" comprise a distinct school of thought that is now commonly referred to, following the coinage of Harry Cleaver, as "autonomist" Marxism. At the time of this writing, this school has emerged into new prominence following the publication in 2000 of Michael Hardt and Antonio Negri's *Empire:* a monumental attempt to produce what has been called a "communist manifesto" for the twenty-first century, and a book that has already received perhaps more than its share of both extravagant praise and bitter criticism. Useful summaries of the history and development of autonomist Marxism are already available in Hardt's introduction to the anthology *Radical Thought in Italy* (edited by Paolo Virno and Michael Hardt, 1996), in Nick Dyer-Witheford's *Cyber-Marx* (1999), and in the preface to the second edition of Cleaver's *Reading Capital Politically* (2000), and I do not propose to retell this story in full. Rather, I will consider autonomist Marxism as a kind of limit case for the kind of arguments I have considered throughout this chapter, for this is yet another mode of thought that, like so many others discussed here, presents itself as a response to a historical crisis of work. Autonomist Marxism, however, responds to this perceived crisis not merely by reaffirming the creative potential of the laboring subject but also by wholly grounding itself in an ontology of production. This thought begins, in other words, by assuming what Hardt and Negri call "the fundamental productivity of being" (Hardt and Negri 387), proceeds to celebrate a "subject of labor" understood as essentially "productive, creative, and inventive" (Ryan 195), and defines communism as "activity in which people can develop themselves as they produce" (Guattari and Negri 13). Although the autonomist Marxists frequently speak of the "refusal" of work and of an "exodus" from work-based society, they are also as clear as possible that "this refusal of work should not be confused with a denial of one's own creative and productive powers" (Virno and Hardt 262).

As such formulations make clear, at the heart of autonomist Marxism is an intimate union or imbrication of positive and negative critiques of work, a double movement of rejection and reaffirmation. Cleaver explains the genesis of the field in precisely such terms. He first distinguishes two broad traditions of Marxist thought: one a "structural" and merely theoretical approach associated in particular with Althusser, which allegedly neglects class struggle; the other an approach stressing, by contrast, the historical agency of the working class, their "real struggles and revolutionary trials" (Cleaver *Reading Capital Politically* 49). Earlier examples of the latter approach, he suggests, "clung to the very orthodox belief that the object of revolution was the liberation of work from the domination of capital, and hence from alienation and exploita-

tion" (17). Later, autonomist Marxism itself would emerge as a theoretical response to two socioeconomic trends:

First, the continuing spread of Taylorist and Fordist deskilling produced such an
alienation of young workers from work that, by the 1960s, the desire to take over work
and make it less alienating was being more and more replaced by its simple refusal. . . . Second, the refusal of work on the job was increasingly accompanied by a
refusal of the unwaged work of reproducing labor power in life outside the formal job.
Moreover, the refusal of both kinds of work was accompanied by new kinds of nonwork activity. (17)

As examples of nonwork activity, Cleaver cites, among other things, "the
women's movement, the student movement, [and] the environmental movement." As a result of all such projects of identity formation, Cleaver suggests,
the research agenda of Marxist theory shifted "to the study of what Toni Negri
has called working class self-valorization, i.e. the autonomous elaboration of
new ways of being, of new social relationships alternative to those of capitalism" (18). To summarize, Cleaver claims three sequential forms of revolutionary struggle: (1) a liberation of work, (2) a refusal of work, and (3) new kinds of
nonwork activity. Let me underline in particular that the final, *positive* phase
of liberation—which succeeds two negative ones and in itself replaces or
transforms work in its traditional (capitalist) sense—once again takes the
shape of a work which is not work, whose precise model and instance, moreover, is the construction of particular communities or group identities.

So far, however, this is not unlike how Stanley Aronowitz and his associates, for example, envision a "new world of post-work" in which people can
develop their "individual and social potential" (Aronowitz et al. 69); or how
André Gorz and Ulrich Beck seek to open "new spaces in which a variety of
activities—family work and public-civil labour—are able to develop" (Beck
15). But autonomism goes on to envision an even more profound historical
rupture, which occurs *within* the realm of work, even though it is constituted
by what is paradoxically still described as a *refusal* of work. A variety of overlapping technical terms, some recast from Marx's own text, join to describe
and designate this rupture. The contemporary mode of production is characterized, it is argued, by a universal shift from conventional industrial and manual work to "immaterial labor"; this shift, in turn, raises the level of "general
intellect" and "mass intellectuality" in society as a whole; and these developments then join to produce a new "self-valorization" of the laboring subject

and a new "autonomy" of workers and work. This summary is of course a schematic one, and some formulations, for example, envision general intellect as conditioned by the self-valorization of labor instead of vice versa; but autonomist Marxism as a whole always centers on some such identification of a fundamental historical rupture or crisis *within* the realm of work, which in turn makes possible a new liberation *of* work.

Let us consider these crucial terms in a little more detail. "Immaterial labor" refers, according to Maurizio Lazzarato, to "the labor that produces the informational and cultural content" of commodities. This must be taken, however, in two different senses: it refers, first, to "workers' labor processes in big companies in the industrial and tertiary sectors," which increasingly involve "cybernetics and computer control," and, second, to "the kinds of activities involved in defining and fixing cultural and artistic standards, fashions, tastes, consumer norms, and, more strategically, public opinion" (132). Hardt and Negri identify, by contrast, three types of immaterial labor that are akin to, but not precisely the same as, Lazzarato's categories: first, "industrial production that has been informationalized"; second, "analytical and symbolic tasks"; and third, "the production and manipulation of affect," that is, a labor which "requires (virtual or actual) human contact" (293).

For all their internal variations, these definitions all seem to risk a similar methodological confusion of producer and product, for the term "immaterial" seems to denote more precisely a property or quality of the postindustrial *commodity* than it does of postindustrial *labor*. One may well assume that software, for example, is indeed a purely and absolutely immaterial commodity, something that literally exists only in the form of a particular pattern of information. Yet it is difficult to imagine any conceivable process for the production and distribution of software that would not involve material labors, even if only the bodily movements of eyes or fingers fixed on screens or keyboards. Hardt and Negri's final category, which is literally a "labor in the bodily mode," and which refers in particular to what they frankly acknowledge to be common forms of "women's work," raises similar questions in a different way. Such labor, they acknowledge, is "entirely immersed in the corporeal," and therefore it is only its product that is affective or immaterial. I note in passing how once again a work of *caring*—the often gendered work of the nurse, the nanny, or the mother—emerges as one of the alleged paradigms of a work that is not work, in this case joined somewhat incongruously to the new "super-symbolic" labor characteristic of postmodern industrial production.

Although one might thus suspect that the term "immaterial labor" does little more than gesture toward a new blurring of conventional oppositions between mental and manual work, Hardt and Negri's ultimate point is the historical rupture delineated by their remaining terms. They point to a rise in what is called "general intellect" and "mass intellectuality," two terms that refer to the general level of collective social knowledge. These terms are absolutely linked to the idea of immaterial labor: it is argued that as conventional industrial production becomes increasingly reliant on "information technologies and cybernetic machines," so "general intellect has become . . . the primary force of social production," and that these same "technico-scientific knowledges and practices are spreading to invest all spheres of life to a greater extent" (Virno and Hardt 261–62). The epochal significance of such developments is designated, in its turn, by the remaining two terms. It is argued that the universal saturation of society by technical knowledge and cultural activity has now made possible, for the first time in history, a "self-valorization" and consequent "autonomy" on the part of workers whom capitalism previously had merely alienated and exploited in the manner famously described by Marx. In brief, the profound structural changes in the texture of industrial production indicated by these overlapping terms has produced a whole spectrum of new forms of resistance and liberation: "activities, resistances, wills and desires that refuse the hegemonic order, propose lines of flight, and forge alternative constitutive itineraries" (Hardt and Negri 48).

Here again, the general similarity of such observations and arguments to those of free-market futurism will perhaps be obvious. In a footnote, Hardt and Negri concede briefly that Peter Drucker also envisions a new contemporary ascendancy of immaterial labor, and they cite the same passage I quoted in chapter 2, where Drucker claims that "knowledge workers own their knowledge." Yet in response, they argue only that "Drucker does not understand that knowledge is not given but produced and that its production involves new kinds of means of production and labor" (462–63). One needs no theoretical sympathy with Drucker to stipulate that this critique is quite inadequate, since the very crux of Drucker's argument is that technology and knowledge have radically transformed both production and labor. I will venture to suggest, by contrast, that the key difference between futurism and autonomist Marxism lies in what we earlier observed to be Drucker's abandonment of any possibility of community through work, for Hardt and Negri further argue, most broadly of all, that all these technological developments have themselves produced

a more radical and profound commonality than has ever been experienced in the history of capitalism. The fact is that we participate in a productive world made up of communication and social networks, interactive services, and common languages. . . . Producing increasingly means constructing cooperation and communicative commonalities. . . . it is the community that produces and that, while producing, is reproduced and redefined. (302)

As the technologies essential to all production become in principle collective, so, it is argued, they literally produce community. Note again that, as in the Cleaver passage discussed earlier, such production of community is here understood as precisely analogous to, and in every way imbricated with, material production itself. Community and communism are themselves being grasped here as Works—indeed, as the very instances of the Work which succeeds and transforms work. Marx himself argues at length for the socially transformative power of the large-scale "cooperation" that capitalist production necessarily entails; and autonomist Marxism in one sense simply puts a renewed emphasis on this point. But self-valorization and autonomy are also, in strict theoretical terms, absolutely definitive of autonomist Marxism as a school, for they designate precisely that working-class agency and struggle that the "structuralist" Marxism of Althusser was allegedly incapable of grasping. Thus, autonomist Marxism, in the most basic sense, always celebrates the worker, in Dyer-Witheford's words, as "the *active* subject of production" and affirms, by extension, that the technological revolutions of contemporary industry have compelled capital "to set in play agents and subjects whose capacities outrun its control" (Dyer-Witheford 65, 237).

The extraordinary interest of these arguments (and a certain quality of utopian audacity which is central to them) must be clearly acknowledged. Nevertheless, these characteristic themes of autonomist Marxism raise a variety of theoretical questions, particularly with regard to the basic argument they share with all the other writers surveyed in this chapter: that is, the fundamental vision of a contemporary rupture or crisis of work. Hardt and Negri's basic concept of "Empire," a new postnational model of global sovereignty, would seem to be entirely predicated on some such rupture. "In our times," they argue, "*modernization has come to an end,*" and the defining characteristics of the postmodern economy are its "highly mobile" and "flexible" jobs which emphasize "knowledge, information, affect, and communication" (285). Hardt and Negri grasp these changes in the literal facts of employment as the source both of Empire and of "the Multitude" who resist it. "Empire takes form," they argue, "when language and communication, or really when immaterial labor and cooperation, become the dominant productive force," for at this point, "capital tends to be constituted and represented . . . in the brains, bodies, and cooperation of productive subjects" (385). Here again, this seems more or less identical to Alvin Toffler's assertion, cited earlier, that the "means of production" of a postindustrial economy are neither tools nor machinery but "are, instead, crackling inside the employee's cranium" (*Powershift* 217). The only real difference is that Hardt and Negri further envision such developments as changing, or at least intensifying, the socioeconomic *form* of exploitation itself. From now on, exploitation will always specifically be "the expropriation of cooperation," and therefore "resistances to command continually emerge within Empire" (385).

What is centrally at issue here, as such formulations would surely seem to suggest, is a crisis and an "event" (Hardt and Negri 386), a specific moment (*our* moment) when "the increasingly intense relationship of mutual implication of all social forces that capitalism has pursued throughout its development has *now* been fully realized" (24–25; emphasis added), and when, accordingly, there has been a new birth of resistance in the laboring subject. Is, then, liberation truly announcing itself here and now, as it has never done before? Is its advent present, *in* the present? In one sense the autonomist answer would have to be yes, in that the evolution of industrial production and the full capitalist subsumption of social relations are precisely what liberate liberation, so to speak.

In fact, however, Hardt and Negri seem frequently to hedge their bets on this all-important point. "The decline and fall of Empire," they further suggest, "is defined *not as a diachronic movement but as a synchronic reality*" (385; emphasis added). Such an assertion seems difficult to reconcile with their general argument about the revolutionary potential of "immaterial labor" and the new rise in the level of "general intellect." How can such developments possibly be grasped except as intimately conditioned by a range of social and technological processes that unfold diachronically?

Even more broadly, one must stipulate that the diachronic and the synchronic, terms drawn from Saussurean linguistics, cannot in any rigorous sense be taken, as they seem to be here, as referring to discrete *alternatives* or to two discrete forms of empirical "reality"; nor can one be ontologically privileged as more "real" than the other. These terms denote two different modes of analyzing the same phenomenon and join to form the irreducible opposition that Derrida famously terms *différance*. This is a specific instance of a broader theoretical problem also manifest in Hardt and Negri's larger claim that the resistance to Empire takes shape as "pure immanence," pure synchronicity or becoming, and is characterized by "a refusal of any transcendence" (91–92). This refusal of transcendence, they always stipulate, "should in no way be confused with a negation of the *vis viva,* the creative life force" (92). Is it not obvious, however, that this so-called life force is itself a transcendent Idea? How can a process of resistance that, in its very essence, involves not only industrial organization of a sophisticated kind but also, of course, intellectual discourse itself be characterized as pure immanence? Thus, Hardt and Negri seem at once to *indicate* by their own argument, and yet absolutely refuse to acknowledge, that signification itself always involves a *relation* between immanence and transcendence, between the ontic and the ontological, between becoming and Being. As Jean-Luc Nancy argues, in the context of a very different approach to communism and community that I discuss later, to consider immanence as a kind of radical innocence or purity finally itself amounts to a merely *mythic* attempt to transcend the limits of being. A more rigorous model would then understand liberation itself as involving, not some impossible refusal of transcendent ideas in general—which would mean, after all, a refusal of thought itself—but a process by which singular beings, and their communities, are understood as "stripped of immanence *as well as* transcendence" (Nancy *Inoperative Community* 77; emphasis added).[1]

Correspondingly, to return to the passage, one now sees that, for Hardt and Negri, resistance is both historical and actual, both remembered and anticipated, both recognized as a (transcendent) Idea and merely glimpsed as a possibility:

Crisis runs through *every moment* of the development and recomposition of the totality. . . . With the real subsumption of society under capital, social antagonisms can erupt as conflict *in every moment.* . . . Crisis and decline are not a hidden foundation nor an ominous *future* but *a clear and obvious actuality, an always expected event, a latency that is always present.* . . . nothing manages to illuminate *our destiny ahead.* Nonetheless, we have acquired a *new* point of reference . . . which consists in the fact that Empire is defined by crisis, that its decline has *always already begun,* and that consequently every line of antagonism *leads toward the event* and singularity. (385– 86; emphasis added)

Whereas other formulations seem to indicate a contemporary crisis of work that creates new possibilities of resistance, it now appears that rupture and crisis, and hence the all-important potential of liberation, saturate *all* history and *every* moment. Once this possible interpretation is recognized, a whole variety of other arguments and observations from autonomist writings can be recalled to support it: from Hardt and Negri's celebration of Saint Francis's "opposition to nascent capitalism" and their corresponding claim, in the final lines of the book, that *"once again* in postmodernity, we find ourselves in Francis's situation" (413; emphasis added), all the way to Cleaver's enlistment, as allies in the autonomist project, of "a new generation of historians . . . studying crime and social struggle and the formation of the British proletariat" (Cleaver *Reading Capital Politically* 16).

But if liberation itself is made possible only by the revolutionary transformation of the productive forces in the postmodern era, then must not these historic instances of resistance to capitalism be seen, in effect, as *tragedies*— that is, heroic but doomed struggles for a liberation that could not possibly have been attained at that time? And if so, then when Hardt and Negri, for example, look back in time in order to "take inspiration from Saint Augustine's vision" (207), do they not start to resemble the kind of mythic-romantic scholars who, as Raymond Williams once suggested, merely discover in the struggles of the past a sort of consolation prize for the despairs and defeats of the present (Williams *The Country and the City* 36)? These unexpected moments of historical inspiration also seem to contradict *Empire*'s more persuasive critique, elsewhere, of any "primordialism that fixes and romanticizes social relations and identities" (44–45) and its corresponding insistence that "[w]e cannot move back to any previous social form" (206).

These already difficult questions also return us one more time to the horizon of that arcadian anthropology that so often becomes visible in the thought at issue here. One of the theoretical sources identified by Hardt and Negri and other autonomist Marxists as primary influences on their shared project is the work of Gilles Deleuze and Félix Guattari, especially their *A Thousand Plateaus.* In this celebrated and difficult text, the central figure of the "plateau" is itself a product of an anthropology of the Other. Originally used by Gregory Bateson to describe what he claimed was a quality shared by certain sexual or aggressive practices in Balinese culture, the term is used more generally by Deleuze and Guattari to denote "continuous regions of intensity constituted in such a way that they do not allow themselves to be interrupted by an external termination, any more than they allow themselves to build toward a climax" (158). A "plateau" in this theoretical sense would seem to correspond to the *second* possible interpretation summarized above: that is, the idea of a homogeneous pattern of history uninterrupted by rupture or, rather, saturated with it. This is also the apparent point of Deleuze and Guattari's celebrated image of the "rhizome," which is intended to reject the dominant Western image of "the root-foundation" (18) in favor of an "acentered, nonhierarchical, nonsignifying system," an "antigenealogy" that "connects any point to any other point" (21).

Yet Deleuze and Guattari simultaneously suggest, more than once, a vision of history that at least flirts with archeo- or teleological themes, associated here again with the question of work and employing the same anthropological sources that have emerged in previous writers. They write, for example, of "primitive societies" that "do not, strictly speaking, work," because work in the proper sense requires "a capture of activity by the State apparatus, and a semiotization of activity by writing" (400–401). Elsewhere, they cite "certain outstanding ethnologists" who clarify that "primitive societies are not societies of shortage or subsistence due to an absence of work, but on the contrary are societies of free action and smooth space that have no use for a work-factor" (491). Such references, which of course refer us, once again, to Marshall Sahlins's analysis of "the first affluent society," necessarily imply some form of subsequent socioeconomic rupture—which Deleuze and Guattari variously associate, at different moments of their text, with the development of writing and the division of labor, or with the "capture" of human activity by the state apparatus and by capital itself.

Deleuze and Guattari also then speak of another corresponding moment of rupture, this one in either the present or the imminent future, when a "threshold" shall be crossed so that "there is no longer a need for a State, for distinct juridical and political domination, in order to ensure appropriation" (453). This is precisely the moment that Hardt and Negri also describe: the moment of the global genesis of both Empire and the Multitude, the moment, as we have seen, of maximum exploitation and maximum liberatory potential. Both pairs of writers, then, seem at least to *allow,* if not quite deliberately to *employ,* an implicit narrative of history with a three-part structure: from "smooth space" to "striated space" and back again; from the imposition of work to its final refusal and abolition; from paradise lost to paradise re-found(ed).

A final series of theoretical questions surrounds the last two of the terms identified above as definitive of autonomist Marxism: autonomy and self-valorization. The first of these, obviously enough, attempts to name something that is absolutely central to this whole school of thought and yet that also raises particularly vexing methodological and theoretical questions, for how is a notion of autonomy, of separateness, of absolute singularity, to be reconciled with the all-important imperatives of community and the collective? One can hardly forget in this context that a so-called autonomy of the worker is equally privileged in the discourse of free-market futurism, where the term refers to the historical apotheosis of the atomistic individuality always demanded by the regime of capital. As the various contemporary guides to "free agency" and so forth attest, the autonomy of the capitalist worker goes hand in hand with a process of exclusion based on relative levels of autonomous self-development.

André Gorz, for example, cites an illuminating interview with the head of training at a German automobile manufacturer, who boasts of the "cultural revolution" by which his company has been "transferring entrepreneurial skills to the shopfloor" and thus producing "a large enterprise made up of independent small entrepreneurs." As Gorz observes, however, this process "presupposes that the workers have the capacity to analyze, predict, communicate and express themselves, capacities which the 'mass intellectuality' theorists regard as belonging to the 'general intellect.'" Asked what happens to workers who do not manage to succeed with these complex new responsibilities, the manager replies: "They are pushed to the fringes of the labour market" (*Reclaiming Work* 44).

Even a quick look at the vast contemporary literature of business management of recent decades will provide abundant further evidence for the same conclusions. To briefly cite just one additional example, British management guru Charles Handy celebrates the new "flexible" corporation, in which employees no longer have secure lifetime or even full-time employment, and then concludes that those who are displaced by "down-sizings," "restructurings," and the like are simply those who lack the "urge or energy" to succeed (Handy 100).

The all-important question therefore remains whether autonomist Marxism can retain its vision of *homo faber,* its general ethos and ontology of production and self-production, while escaping the exclusionary practices these processes seem to necessitate. Clearly aware of such potential objections, autonomist writings attempt a variety of carefully formulated definitions of this crucial term. Guattari and Negri, for example, attempt to forestall one possible objection to this notion of autonomy: that it leads away from classical Marxism toward a kind of anarchism. By contrast, they stipulate that "there is nothing anarchic about [autonomist Marxism], since it essentially has to do with a qualitative autonomy, capable of apprehending the social complexity of movements, and of grasping it as a process of subjective convergence" (79). They suggest, in other words, that in the moment of ultimate liberation, "each autonomy, each minoritarian movement will coalesce" (80).

But if each group is in itself "autonomous" or *self-governing,* then the process of transition between such particular instances of self-governance and any necessary broader form of communal organization ("coalescence") would seem necessarily to involve a struggle over relative priorities, which would finally amount simply to what is often today called identity politics. In other words, to deploy the concept of autonomy in this double or multiple fashion is to raise a series of questions which these confident formulations simply elide. For example, at the point of coalescence, would autonomy itself cease to be a "minoritarian" phenomenon, and hence a form of resistance? With the coalescence of separate autonomies, does autonomy itself cease to exist? Or does such coalescence produce, by contrast, a kind of meta-autonomy?

It is also important to note that, in *Empire,* autonomy is not merely being understood as a condition or a quality but rather as itself a form of productive activity, something constituted by and manifest in the active construction of "new figures of subjectivity" (Hardt and Negri 29) and new social "movements." Thus, autonomy is at once all forms of (noncapitalist) work and in itself a Work of the highest order, for this term refers, more than anything else, to the positive self-development of personal or group identities, "the continuous constituent project to create and re-create ourselves and our world" (92). On the one hand, "by working, the multitude produces itself as singularity" (395); and, on the other hand, "the multitude promotes through its labor the biopolitical singularizations of groups and sets of humanity" (395). As such rather confusing formulations indicate, Hardt and Negri deploy the concepts of singularity and autonomy in a manner that finally explodes their meaning by ascribing them at once to individuals, to groups, and to a larger collectivity (the Multitude). One must at least wonder whether such a strategy again contradicts their own insistence that "Empire cannot be resisted by any project aimed at a limited, local *autonomy*" (206; emphasis added).

In any case, it quite clear, at least, that autonomy and self-valorization finally refer to more or less the same thing: singular beings *make themselves* and in so doing *make themselves autonomous.* At the most fundamental level of this thought, *to be is to produce.* Thus, the last set of questions one must raise about this thought will surround "self-valorization," a term that Negri takes originally from Marx's own text but applies in a different way. For Marx, the term refers to the ultimate goal of capitalist production: the creation of surplus value. Because workers can produce more value in a full workday than would be required for the reproduction of their own labor power, the capital invested can produce a surplus value above and beyond the net price of the raw materials, means of production, and wages expended in the production process. When this happens, accordingly to Marx, the capital has *valorized* itself. This term thus refers to capital's "constant drive to go beyond its quantitative limit" and to the absolute structural necessity by which capital "*preserves* itself . . .

only by *constantly multiplying itself* " (Marx *Grundrisse* 270). For Negri and autonomist Marxism, by contrast, valorization refers to the *subjective* value produced, beyond this material value, as a secondary (and wholly unintentional) surplus of the postindustrial capitalist order. Indeed, like immaterial labor, self-valorization seems to refer at once to the worker and to the worker's product, except that here the process of value creation goes backward, so to speak, from the work back to the worker, from material to subjective production.

Now, Cleaver himself acknowledges that "this term has its problems" (*Reading Capital Politically* 18) because "the self-valorization of the working class is *not* homologous with that of capital" (Cleaver, interview). But this terminological coincidence is anything but coincidental. In the chapter "Co-operation" in *Capital*, Marx begins by reiterating that "the driving motive and determining purpose of capitalist production is the self-valorization of capital to the greatest possible extent, i.e. the greatest possible production of surplus value, hence the greatest possible exploitation of labour-power by the capitalist." This means that capital must always strive to increase the number of workers under its control; but "as the number of the co-operating workers increases, so too does their resistance to the domination of capital, and necessarily, the pressure put on by capital to overcome this resistance" (*Capital* 449). This brief passage can be taken as a virtual map of the whole field of autonomist Marxism, which, as we have seen throughout, invests its full force in the identification of a moment of historic rupture or fulfillment in which what Marx describes only abstractly has finally presented itself in person. But this means that the two meanings of "self-valorization" (surplus value and subjective self-production) are homologous after all; for they are, in every possible sense, genetically and structurally linked. The new subject in which autonomist Marxism invests its utopian hopes is coterminous with and determined by capitalist production, even if only via its refusal of the latter. Liberation itself consists in the shift from mere industrial production to subjective production.

The inescapable connection of the terms further begins to show itself as a problem when one recalls that the one absolutely definitive and inescapable characteristic of self-valorization in the capitalist sense is that it has no certain limit or terminus. Although the cycle of exchange C-M-C (exchanging commodities for money, which is used to buy other commodities) "is limited to procuring the articles necessary to existence and useful either to a household or the state," the economic cycle of M-C-M' (buying in order to sell) strives only to make money, and therefore "there are no bounds to its aims." The movement of capital's self-valorization "is therefore limitless" (*Capital* 253). But then, what about subjective self-valorization? Is it, too, limitless? For autonomist Marxism, the answer must in some sense be yes, since as we have seen, this thought always celebrates the historical and experiential progress from the self of work to the Self as a Work. And although I have repeatedly suggested affinities, on the empirical level, between the autonomists and the free-market futurists, in this the autonomists finally seem to provide merely a more positive and forward-looking version of what I have called liberal nostalgia. In other words, autonomist Marxism affirms and celebrates a Subject defined by its productivity and *constituted in and as a Work.* For autonomist Marxism, *all* work, in any conceivable sense of this word, is "oriented toward that end— in other words, as self-valorization and self-production of singularities" (Guattari and Negri 41). And yet, once again to phrase the necessary questions as simply as possible: If the productive Subject is in every sense a product of capital, then is it not a capitalist Subject? Or at the very least, once we have decided that the self-development of Subjects remains the central project of history, then why should such a Subject ever reject the conditions of its own development?

I am arguing, in other words, that autonomist Marxism, for all of its extraordinary utopian audacity and theoretical innovation, still reaches an impasse at what I have called, following Nancy, the aporia of Marxism itself: a dilemma clearly indicated, in this case, by the inescapable convergence of capitalist *valorization* and subjective *self-valorization.* As Negri himself argues, the Law of Value is *always* inseparable from the Law of Command: "there is no value without exploitation" (Negri 83). But this also means that every effort to subdivide the field of human exertion in order to affirm some "autonomous activity" beyond mere wage labor, some work that is "liberated from work" (Negri 160), still leaves us with an ethos of *homo faber,* a fundamental injunction to produce. Although Hardt and Negri claim they are employing what Negri elsewhere calls "a new paradigm," a "new—postdeconstructive—ontology," intended specifically to respond to a "change in the paradigm of productive labor" (Negri 12), in the end their schema merely once again privileges work, in the most traditional of ways, as the very site of personal and social value—and, thus, too, although this is surely not their intention, the very site of hierarchy and exclusion. The fact remains, however, that *all* working—the work of group identity and personal self-fashioning no less than industrial wage labor itself, however "immaterial" its texture—remains always in principle a *working for,* which is entirely other than a *being-with.*

This is why, to anticipate briefly the thought to be considered in part 3 of this book, any future communism worthy of this name "cannot arise from the domain of work," because community itself "is not the work of singular beings, nor can it claim them as its works"; rather, "community is simply their being—their being suspended upon its limit" (Nancy *Inoperative Community* 31). Among other things, Nancy's vision of community cuts through the confusing autonomist formulations about singularity and autonomy: for in this model we recognize that all being is at once absolutely singular and absolutely connected, and that being itself is not a process of production nor a form of immanent identity but simply an exposure, a *being-in-common*.

It is not yet time to pursue these alternative formulations any further, so I will conclude part 1, instead, by summarizing my critique in aphoristic form, with reference to perhaps the most infamous assertion ever made about the ends of work. This is a formula that, to cite Nancy one last time, began its life as a "sanctimonious bourgeois ideologeme" and ended up "inscribed in frightful derision above the gate of Auschwitz" (*Sense of the World* 98):

> *Arbeit macht frei.*
> (Work liberates; work makes us free.)

Guattari and Negri at one point claim this phrase should be considered the motto of postmodern capitalism, which, they argue, has "succeeded in appropriating the discourse of communism—an analysis of labor and its liberatory power" (9). I can readily see their point, one that indeed recalls, one last time, the troubling similarities between free-market futurism and autonomist Marxism itself. But I must also suggest that all the modes of thought mentioned here, including the latter, seem in the end merely to slightly revise a formula that has already, one would think, been emptied of its promise as perhaps no other before or since. In other words, although no longer quite willing to affirm that

> Work makes us *free*

the thought at issue here, both on the Left and on the Right, continues stubbornly to affirm that

> Work makes *us.*

And that, as I have been trying to suggest, is something worse than insufficient.

PART TWO | THE WORK OF THE GIFT

FROM RESTRICTED TO GENERAL
ECONOMY—AND BACK AGAIN?

Of Sinking

Any reading of James Cameron's film *Titanic* will probably have to interpret the doomed ship in much the way Fredric Jameson interprets the shark in his reading of Steven Spielberg's *Jaws:* that is, less as a symbol of something in particular than as a site for the process of symbolization itself. If the huge ocean liner inevitably signifies the Ship of State (an allegorical microcosm of class and gender conflict, which the film represents in its central melodrama), it also seems to signify the process of (its own) representation. Both the film and the ship are in every sense *titanic.* The film, a kind of parable of the Work, joins the many previous representations of its story in interpreting the famous shipwreck as a cautionary tale of technological and social hubris. In its own day, the *Titanic* was already being celebrated as "the largest moving work of man in all history"; and in the aftermath of its disastrous encounter with the iceberg in 1912, most commentators joined Joseph Conrad in blaming the wreck on its owners' excessive concern for "size, speed and profits" (quoted in Lubin 12; see also Howells 112–13). The film obviously evokes the same ethos of heroic production and the same moral critique. Cameron misses no opportunity to emphasize the sheer magnitude of the doomed liner, his camera lingering on images of its huge screws turning beneath the water, its flaming boilers fed by men with blackened faces, and its enormous staterooms with their carved wood paneling and private promenade decks. The film also depicts Bruce Ismay, the White Star Line's managing director, encouraging the captain to keep the ship at maximum speed because he wants *Titanic* to break the transatlantic speed record. Later, informed of the collision by the ship's designer, Thomas Andrews, Ismay exclaims: "But this ship can't sink!" Andrews responds, "She is made of iron, sir. I assure you, she can. And she *will*" (Cameron 48, 93).

The same narrative conventions seem also to enfold the drama of the film's literal creation, whose details have been recounted in numerous articles and a best-selling book (see, e.g., Marsh; Shapiro). As *Titanic* was in production, and as its budget swelled to something like twice its original figure (Shapiro 293), many commentators began to anticipate a financial disaster for the film that, had it occurred, would have mirrored the disaster within its narrative. To some observers (arguing against the general tide of critical praise), even the finished film seemed, like the ship, to be no more than the catastrophic wreck of a grandiose idea. Movie critic Kenneth Turan, reviewing the film in the *Los Angeles Times,* suggests: "Just as the hubris of headstrong shipbuilders who insisted that the *Titanic* was unsinkable led to an unparalleled maritime disaster, so Cameron's overweening pride has come unnecessarily close to capsizing this project."

Nevertheless, it seems doubtful that the film's phenomenal commercial success can be fully accounted for by either its moral critique of the Work or the various much-publicized off-screen conflicts that attended its production. In fact, there is another, contrary way to understand the film's appeal, which I will use to introduce a theoretical terminology that will be at issue throughout this chapter, and that will allow me to add to the question of the Work its counterpart or antithesis, the question of the gift. I refer to the theoretical opposition—emerging first in Marcel Mauss's famous *The Gift* and developed and transformed in the work of George Bataille and his interpreters—between what Mauss called the commodity and the gift or what Bataille called, much more broadly, "restricted" and "general" economies. To summarize very briefly a theoretical terrain that I will consider in a variety of ways in the rest of this book, a "restricted" economy assumes that the central economic issue is *scarcity.* Such an economy therefore involves productive investments of time, energy, or money made in the expectation of profit, or "return." Bataille's restricted economy is also precisely the economy of work and the Work. One sows in order to reap; one labors in order to make a living; one writes or speaks or thinks in the anticipation of communication, comprehension, and the circular return of all these to the writing, speaking, or thinking subject. A "general" economy, by contrast, assumes that the central economic issue is *surplus.* Such an economy therefore involves consumption, sacrifice, and reckless expenditures, in the expectation of loss without return or reserve. And if, in some obvious sense, the general economy is at least associated with an economy of the gift, it also seeks to name a certain transgression of the limits of economic reason itself.

With such terms in mind, one can conclude that *Titanic* as a story of hubris must be understood, like the tradition of Judeo-Christian ethics from which it stems, as inscribed within a "restricted" economy. It would be a story, in other words, of reaping what you have sown, of a moral and material investment and its proportionate "return." But the popular appeal of Cameron's film might also be thought to stem from what Bataille calls the "principle of loss": the idea that human subjects are finally motivated not by rational economic calculation (the "economism" always assumed in classical theory) but rather by the impulse to sacrifice and squander. Such an interpretation returns to the same cinematic details but sees them in a different light. *Titanic* now becomes the story of a city-sized ship with solid oak stairways and crystal chandeliers, equipped, as the aged Rose puts it, with china that had never been used and sheets that had never been slept in, that goes to the bottom with two-thirds of its passengers only days after its first launch. The film would then be, so to speak, an extended version of the narrative offered by one of the salvagers to the aged Rose in the framing story, in which every detail of *Titanic*'s destruction is re-created and relished in a kind of ecstasy: how the iceberg punches holes in it "like Morse code," how its massive stern, weighing "maybe 20 or 30 thousand *tons*," rears vertically in the air until the whole enormous ship finally splits and sinks. "Cool, huh?" says the salvager (Cameron 14–15). This representation of loss in the narrative would, here again, rejoin the drama of the film's creation, in which Cameron spent some two hundred million dollars (the most money to date ever spent on a film) and even relinquished his own salary and profits to build a nearly full-sized version of the doomed ship with its every detail, even those unused plates, obsessively re-created—and then destroyed it, in order to represent its destruction.[1]

Reading the film this way also invites consideration of the enigmatic scene at the end, when the aged Rose takes the priceless gem, the Heart of the Ocean, the object on which the inner and outer plots have both centered, and casts it into the sea. We are asked, apparently, to regard the gem as a gift, a sacrifice, for Jack Dawson, the beautiful boy who perished to save Rose from the icy waves. Yet in this incident, the film seems pointedly both to invite and to reject economistic questions, such as: wouldn't the young Rose, after her rescue and inadvertent acquisition of the gem, have used it to support her genteel but penniless mother, whose economic terror is vividly expressed in one

scene of the central melodrama? Or wouldn't the gem at least have freed Rose
from the necessity of prudent marriage and financed the long and adventur-
ous life that the audience glimpses in her photographs and mementos? Or
even if she had managed somehow to keep the gem so long, wouldn't the aged
Rose want to bequeath it to the granddaughter who takes care of her in the
framing story? Hurrying us beyond such implicit questions, the film seems instead to indulge us with what Bataille calls our "*interest* in considerable
losses" (*Visions* 117). Indeed, when read this way, *Titanic* invites us to recall
how frequent in all popular cinema are these spectacles of ecstatic destruction
and loss: cars exploding in fireballs, rooms shattered by bullets, great buildings toppling under the onslaught of bombs, aliens, or mythical beasts. So
common are such images that, in the aftermath of the 2001 terrorist attacks on
the World Trade Center buildings in New York, a few critical voices dared to
remind us that in fact we have been imagining such attacks on our public
buildings for decades.

As one might put it, then, the narrative of Cameron's *Titanic* turns on the
idea of the gift as much as it does on the idea of the Work, and yet it seems to
exceed and transform the conventional associations of both. The film's plot
concerns a jewel intended to purchase a young woman and bind her to a love-
less marriage; and it goes on to depict, not merely her escape from this familiar
domestic tragedy, but also how the jewel itself escapes from the economic calculus altogether to become a figure of irrational expenditure, of loss without
return. And yet, of course, this interpretive reversal must then be reversed one
more time. The story of destruction is framed by a story of salvage: Jack Dawson, who asserts, "Life's a gift and I don't intend on wasting it,"[2] heedlessly
sacrifices himself—but only so as to save Rose "in about every way a person
can be saved" (Cameron 57, 149). And Cameron himself comes through the
threats of bankruptcy and scandal to achieve a phenomenal personal and
commercial success (see Shapiro 311).

To put all this another way, *Titanic* indicates not just the continuing appeal of the idea of a "general" economy but also a certain vulnerability of that
vision. Bataille's theoretical project was always intended, at least in part, as a
critique of historical capitalism, which must be seen as the very paradigm of a
restricted economy based on calculation, investment, and return. In my example, however, it remains easy to see that *Titanic*'s unforgettable vision of
sacrifice and expenditure is still circumscribed by a restricted economy of the
most literal kind and that the film's material expense, like its representation of
loss, is still first and last a capitalist investment, which has grossed, at last
count, over a billion and a half dollars worldwide. Indeed, in the aftermath of

the film's extraordinary commercial success, it was for a time possible to buy commercial reproductions of the Heart of the Ocean itself, either with or without genuine precious stones: a fact that provides perhaps an even more piquant image of what might be called, to mangle Bataille's formula, loss *with* return.

Rethinking the Gift

My opening example also suggests why the title of this chapter echoes but alters the title of Jacques Derrida's influential reading of Bataille: "From Restricted to General Economy." As Derrida's original title suggests, Bataille's thought always strives to move *from* economic restriction *to* an economy in which the universal movement of energy might be considered in its "general" aspect. But what will continue to be at issue here, on the contrary, is a kind of displacement—not merely theoretical and symbolic but also, as we will see, practical and political—in which economic restriction (investment with return; the economy of work) seems always to reemerge amid the attempt to consider a general economy of giving and loss. In this persistent displacement, we first glimpse clearly what I suggested at the outset is a fatal discursive conjunction of work and the gift.

It is quite clear, first of all, that a broad resurgence of intellectual interest in the question of the gift occurs in roughly the same years in which many writers begin to identify a historical crisis of work. A continuing contemporary debate on the gift more or less begins with Mauss's famous *The Gift*, the continuing influence of which not only in anthropology itself but also across a wide range of other disciplines can hardly be overestimated. In this celebrated text, Mauss marshals an array of ethnographic and linguistic evidence to argue that archaic human economies around the world were organized, not around the production and conservation of scarce resources (like capitalist societies), but, instead, around mutual gift giving and ritualistic expenditure—such as the famous potlatch. Mauss then contrasts this archaic gift economy to what Derrida paraphrases as "those two economisms . . . capitalist mercantilism *and* Marxist communism" (Derrida *Given Time* 44) and finally asserts that a new economy "is at present laboriously in gestation," in which the ancient values and practices will reemerge (Mauss 78). Bataille's work on expenditure and general economics emerges in large part from his study of Mauss and similarly begins with an anthropological history that envisions how the "great and free forms of unproductive social expenditure" that prevailed in archaic cultures were gradually superseded by the restricted economic values of thrift, prudence, and economic calculation (*Visions* 123–24).

A continuing fascination with the gift can also be noted across a range of other disciplines in the last decades of the twentieth-century and beyond. Within anthropology itself, Mauss's book itself has been critiqued and reinterpreted in well-known texts by Claude Lévi-Strauss, Raymond Firth, Marshall Sahlins, Chris Gregory, and many others. One can also cite, among many other possible examples, Pierre Bourdieu's *The Logic of Practice* (1980), an influential attempt to move beyond the structuralist analysis of culture by generalizing insights emerging from a study of precapitalist gift economies; Lewis Hyde's *The Gift* (1983), a widely cited book that theorizes the aesthetic as a kind of gift-giving practice; Natalie Zemon Davis's *The Gift in Sixteenth-Century France* (2000), which joins the work of other historians and literary scholars in its fascination with aristocratic gift exchange in early-modern Europe;[3] and several important texts by Jacques Derrida, especially *Given Time* (1992), which have established the gift as one of the fundamental themes of contemporary thought.[4]

It is also clear that, just as the gift itself seems to present itself as the Other of work, so an ideal of generous giving now presents itself, at least to some thinkers, as an ethical and political alternative to Marxist socialism, particularly in the aftermath of the fall of socialist governments around the world and the worldwide triumph of the market. As James Carrier puts it: "With the apparent fall from favor of the Marxian framework, the Maussian may be the alternative that is more attractive to those who continue to be interested in economic forms and understandings and who continue to search for a powerful critique of economic life and thought in the West and elsewhere" (viii). Or as Alan D. Schrift argues, even more specifically, "the appeal of the gift as a topic of consideration and research may reflect a renewed concern for the establishment of more politically acceptable relations between citizens in response to recent neoconservative attacks on . . . social welfare" ("Introduction" 19). Thus, the idea of the gift presents itself today in a whole series of radically different ways: as a hypothetical building block of human culture; as a historico-anthropological Other of "the market" and capitalism; as a marker or expression of some realm of self-presence and aesthetic Work wholly separate from the utilitarian calculus; and as the rubric for a possible politics, at once post-Marxist and postliberal, founded in what Schrift calls an "ethic of generosity."

Indeed, even at the simplest level, the idea of the gift in any of its versions is something that seems impossible to consider except in opposition to something else. The act of giving opposes the act of selling; an economy founded in gift exchange distinguishes itself from both communism and the market. The same is true, as I have suggested, with the idea of work, which in some allegedly proper sense is always being distinguished, on the one hand, from primitive exertions not yet incorporated into the burdens and divisions of the workaday world and, on the other hand, from the Work as autoteleology and labor of love. In either case, such distinctions are themselves inseparable from an opposition of *act* and *object*. "Work" refers both to corporeal or mental labor in its own process and to the product of this labor, either in itself or in terms of the social identity it indicates and manifests (one's "work" as one's vocation or profession). A gift is similarly both an act and an object. In this case, each of these two senses reciprocally defines the other and remains inseparable from it. Literally anything might conceivably be a gift, but nothing is a gift in its own essence: an object becomes a gift only within the act of giving. In this case, therefore, both the act and the object of the gift must be distinguished from its opposite. Giving must be distinguished from buying or selling; and the gift must be distinguished from the commodity or the wage, from any form of remuneration or compensation. A certain symmetry thus emerges in the relation of these two terms. The Other of the gift (something given in return for something else or as a reward for something performed) presents itself as work; the Other of work (the self-fulfilling Work as it hypothetically exists outside every calculus of profit or return) presents itself as a kind of gift.

As we have also already seen, however, the conceptual divisions with which the domain of work is always being divided are ambiguous and unstable at best. Is it work in the proper sense to clean one's own house or care for one's own children? Was there really no work, properly considered, in primitive human culture? In the case of the gift, however, the allegedly proper sense of the word seems, more ruinously still, to exist only in imminent threat of violation from its opposite. Can a gift truly be given freely, with no thought of reciprocation, which would necessarily reinscribe the gift in an economy of exchange—and thus reveal the gift to be itself a form of work? Such questions, as I will shortly suggest in more detail, always haunt the ethnographic observations of the gift economies that alleged precede (or coexist with) the economy of market exchange. Even more broadly, as Derrida demonstrates rigorously in *Given Time,* a gift in the strict sense requires far more than an absence of reciprocation. Rather, "the gift not only must not be repaid but not be kept in memory, retained as symbol of a sacrifice, as symbolic in general. . . . From the moment the gift would appear as gift, as such, as what it is, in its phenomenon, its sense and its essence, it would be engaged in a symbolic, sacrificial, or economic structure that would annul the gift" (23). Therefore, the gift is the "very figure of the impossible" (7), and therefore Mauss, in *The Gift,* is really writing of "economy, exchange, contract," that is, "of everything but the gift" (24).

Such insights make possible another schematic summary of my two central terms. As the (negative) attempt to think the end of working encounters the paradox of *a work that is not work,* so the (positive) attempt to think the possibility of giving encounters the paradox of *a gift that is not a gift.* These two formulations are linked to one another, this time, with reverse symmetry. Working presents itself urgently and immediately as a means to an end (of sustenance and survival) and only in some secondary sense, after necessity has run its course, opens to the utopian possibility of the Work as a self-fulfilling freedom. This is precisely the trajectory and historical vision of the classical Marxist project. The gift, conversely, presents itself right from the start as something absolutely defined by its own self-sufficiency, something that cannot be solicited or appropriated, and that thus can only exist (if indeed it does exist at all) as an absolute end in itself. And yet, across a tangled web of discourse and history, the gift seems, on the contrary, to be always ruinously contaminated with obligation, revalued and reinscribed in economies of every kind. Therefore, the utopian vision of *the Work as gift* is inseparable from the belittling instance of *the gift as work.*

Even this, however, is not the last stage of the discursive structure I am trying to describe. In the continuing conversation which Mauss's text inaugurates, and in which Derrida and others have drawn Bataille's thought to its limits and beyond, the gift finally confronts a different Other. Now the gift does not simply reveal itself as always-already a form of work or as no more than a guise or mask of some market economy that thus allows itself to be taken as "natural" and inevitable. Rather, both the Work and the gift reemerge, in their very likeness or inextricable connection, as heralds, at least, of a wholly different set of relations: a "placing in common of that which is no longer of the order of subjectivities" (Derrida and Ferraris 24), an "allegory of a thought . . . which sustains itself beyond the loss of the subject" and "keeps on thinking when its subject has been spent" (Hollier 71). This would be a working and a giving that are, in either case, always and only a *sharing.* And in this sense, as I will be able to suggest only gradually, the theoretical and practical promise of the gift reveals itself not as some transcendence of Marxism but as its very fulfillment, and not as some return of an ancient ethic of generosity but as the recognition or uncovering of a community where, as Marx always imagined, mere generosity would be quite irrelevant.

General Economics in Retrospect and Prospect

All this will of course require further consideration. For the moment, I consider in more detail the situation indicated in my opening example: a kind of recuperation or displacement that haunts the attempt to represent a "general" economy of loss without return. It might be argued that this motion of recuperation is inscribed in the very idea of the gift and therefore, too, that the anthropological and philosophical speculations that elaborate and rethink the idea of giving are always constrained at once to *address* and themselves *reiterate* it. Bataille's general economics, for example, begins by responding to a certain invisible recuperative strategy that it uncovers at the heart of Hegelian philosophy and to which it interposes its own "barely perceptible displacement," which finally "makes the entire old shell crack" (Derrida "From Restricted to General Economy" 260).

Let me briefly follow the initial stages of this threefold reading of Hegel via Bataille via Derrida, a reading that lends a further urgency to the suspicions raised by my initial example. In Hegel's celebrated dialectic of the master and the slave, the master's victory stems from his willingness to risk his life absolutely, to put at stake his entire existence. By contrast, "the servant is the man who does not put his life at stake, the man who wants to conserve his life, wants to be conserved" (Derrida "From Restricted to General Economy" 254). For Bataille, this encounter is the center of Hegel's thought, where it serves as "an obligatory stage in the history of self-consciousness" (254). Precisely as such, however, the master who *risks* his life does not in fact *lose* his life. On the contrary, in this encounter the master must, in principle, remain alive, in order to enjoy the fruits of his victory. In a sense (to adapt a sardonic figure Derrida uses elsewhere), one might even say that the master has simply played his cards well (Derrida *Gift of Death* 97), for the very structure of his encounter with the slave ensures that no one will have called his bluff. The life that is exposed to risk must be preserved, because "[t]o rush headlong into death pure and simple is . . . to risk the absolute loss [of] . . . the effect and profit of meaning which were the very *stakes* one hoped to *win.*" By contrast, Hegel argues that "the negation characteristic of consciousness" is one "which cancels in such a way that it preserves and maintains what is sublated" (Derrida *Gift of Death* 255, citing Hegel 234).

But at this point there is, as Derrida puts it, a "burst of laughter from Bataille" (*Gift of Death* 255): for the master's victory, and the crucial theoretical operation of *Aufhebung* (sublation) that it represents and constitutes (and that takes the shape of a kind of productive synthesis of death and life, risk and conservation), are a kind of ruse. It is laughable because the risk of absolute loss—the master's crucial willingness to expend all without reserve and put his life absolutely in the balance—has all along really been an *investment.* Hegel's operation of self-consciousness thus "*amortizes* absolute expenditure and . . . gives meaning to death" (257). For Bataille, therefore, "philosophy is *work* itself," but this work of philosophy in some sense merely simulates or refuses that all-important gift of being which the master had *seemed* to be willing to give. To put it schematically, and once again in the terms at issue here: at the heart of the Work of philosophy is the gift; but that gift is, so to speak, always-already in service of the Work.

Thus, played out in the "form and torment" of Bataille's writing is an exposure of that which remains unseen and unsaid in philosophy itself, which willfully blinds itself "to the baselessness of the nonmeaning from which the basis of meaning is drawn" (Derrida *Gift of Death* 257). This project—or non-project—is the impossible itself. Bataille laughs at philosophy (253) and yet also strives somehow to convey or represent this laughter, to think and write "a negativity that never takes place, that never *presents* itself" (256), a negativity so radical that "it can no longer be determined as negativity in a process or a system" (259). Bataille uses the name *sovereignty* to indicate this confrontation with absolute loss and sacrifice, a confrontation that finally displaces the merely spurious risk that inaugurates Hegelian self-consciousness.

One might, for further example, apply something like Bataille's reading of Hegel to Freud's famous account of the primal opposition of *eros* and *thanatos,* the life instinct and the death instinct—terms that already join with the Hegelian dialectic to inform Bataille's own opposition of restricted and general economies.[5] In *Beyond the Pleasure Principle* (1920), Freud seeks to explain how the mind, which is ultimately governed by the desire to maximize pleasure, can nonetheless sometimes embrace unpleasure, a project he describes as "introducing an 'economic' point of view into our work" (18:7). His explanation will, of course, involve far more than the now familiar idea of "deferred gratification" that he mentions in passing. Understanding unpleasure as positive and pleasure as negative, Freud argues that whenever there exists in the mind a certain energy or "excitation" that is not yet "bound," then unpleasure will correspond "to an *increase* in the quantity of excitation and pleasure to a *diminution*" (18:8). The pleasure principle is thus an economic principle: its dominance of psychic activity takes the form of an attempt "to keep the quantity of excitation . . . as low as possible" (18:9).

Later, moving into a realm he frankly identifies as "speculation," Freud imagines that the earliest forms of life on earth faced an environment of radical surplus, a world charged with far more potential energy than life-forms could possibly master, and that indeed would destroy the organisms with excessive stimulation were they not protected by some kind of shield (18:27). The negative pleasure principle thus first manifests itself, with profound paradox, in an instinct toward dissolution, a desire on the part of an organism to return to its earlier and simpler state of death. At the same time, Freud acknowledges, the organism must have a "puzzling determination . . . to maintain its own existence in the face of every obstacle"; it "wishes to die" but "only in its own fashion" (18:39). Being itself, with respect to its instinct toward death, is sovereign; the instinct of survival, by contrast, is servile, reactive, at the mercy of chance.

Thus, Freud's analysis, like Bataille's, portrays life as contingent upon a precise *relation* between two contradictory economic impulses, which in Freud's schema are in fact doubly related. The death instinct is *conservative* in that it seeks to restore an earlier state of things; and yet such restoration takes the form of an annihilation or abandonment to absolute loss. The life instinct is progressive or creative and yet also, precisely as such, is essentially concerned with conservation and preservation—a preservation that, moreover, it achieves only via circuitous strategies by which the organism simply makes "ever more complicated *détours* before reaching its aim of death" (18:39).

One might thus suggest that at the heart of Freud's schema is a kind of ruse not unlike Hegel's, in which the subject at its origin wholly embraces death and yet manages to remain alive. Such an insight then might be extended far more broadly to what Andrew Ross describes as a familiar strain of contemporary theory in which "the limited and mundane libidinal economy of *plaisir* is contrasted with the higher, transgressive experience of *jouissance*," an opposition, first invoked by Roland Barthes, that was "itself based on the Freudian distinction between the 'economic' pleasure principle and the destructively 'spendthrift' death drive" (Ross 184). The reading of Freud briefly outlined here would then suggest, by contrast, that *jouissance* (that "general" economy of limitless transgression and expenditure without reserve) is actually governed by the merely "restricted" economy of *plaisir* and, by the same token, reveal the latter as no more than a sort of fancy-dress version of classical utility itself.

And yet, to turn such arguments back toward Bataille, one might finally suspect that general economics has also been, as it were, hoist with its own petard, subject to a kind of displacement or appropriation not unlike those described in Hegel and Freud. In a remarkable essay, Jean-Joseph Goux suggests precisely this possibility. Goux juxtaposes the work of Bataille to that of

George Gilder, whose peculiar combination of technological determinism and metaphysical bravura I briefly considered in chapter 2. Specifically, Goux compares Bataille's three-volume work of political economy, *The Accursed Share*, to Gilder's *Wealth and Poverty*, a book often cited approvingly by Ronald Reagan and now commonly seen as the very bible of the resurgent market capitalism of the 1980s and beyond. This incongruous juxtaposition reveals a striking and unexpected convergence of thought. Gilder strives to provide what he calls a "transcendental justification" for capitalism by envisioning it as a kind of general economy grounded in selfless giving and extravagant expenditure. Citing Mauss's anthropological theory of the gift, Gilder argues that "the unending offerings of entrepreneurs, investing jobs, accumulating inventories—all long before any return is received, all without any assurance that the enterprise will not fail—constitute a pattern of giving that dwarfs in extent and in essential generosity any primitive rite of exchange." Indeed, Gilder manages to conclude that "giving is the vital impulse and moral center of capitalism" (*Wealth and Poverty* 30).[6] Such astonishing assertions seem to indicate a broad historical displacement in what Goux calls the *mise-en-scène* of capitalism. Beginning in the late twentieth century, capitalism no longer presents itself as the quintessential restricted economy, and it claims guiding virtues quite unlike the frugality, prudence, and calculation that Max Weber once famously defined as its essential "spirit." Thus, entrepreneurial investment can now be envisioned as a process of reckless expenditure and ecstatic dissemination; and it is Marxist socialism which now seems to suggest dreary, old-fashioned bourgeois calculation (bread lines and five-year plans).

Such observations also displace the anthropological history that informs Bataille's theory of general economics. Bataille's early essays on "expenditure," written while he was a member of the short-lived College of Sociology in Paris before the war, suggest that all human cultures prior to the birth of capitalism were organized around various forms of "unproductive expenditure" such as "luxury, mourning, war, cults, the construction of sumptuary monuments, games, spectacles, arts, perverse sexual activity." Such practices, according to Bataille, "have no end beyond themselves," and in them "the accent is placed on a *loss* that must be as great as possible in order for that activity to take on its true meaning" (*Visions* 118). Accordingly, he argues, such practices satisfied "not the need to acquire" but rather "the need to destroy and lose" (121). Then, at some epochal moment, these "great and free forms of unproductive social expenditure . . . disappeared" (124). This fundamental moment of historical rupture in the past will finally rejoin a corresponding rupture in the future. Like Mauss, Bataille always also affirms a "basic movement" that is merely obscured "under present conditions," by which all wealth will finally be returned to its original function, that is, "to gift-giving, to squandering without reciprocation" (*Accursed Share* 1:38).[7]

From a certain point of view, however, the displacement in capitalism's ideological self-presentation exemplified by Gilder might almost seem to embody precisely this predicted movement of wealth and power back to an ethic of generosity. At the very least, as Goux persuasively suggests, "advanced capitalism" has already, in its own movement, begun "to exceed the principle of restricted economy and utility that presided at its beginning" (199). Goux thus confronts us with a dismaying possibility: that the future historical rupture anticipated by both Mauss and Bataille has already been achieved, but only within the very domain that the thought of the gift was intended to oppose, and therefore, the theory of general economics was simply too little and too late. Continuing to view capitalism, through the lens of Weber, as no more than a restricted economy of thrift and utility, Bataille perhaps never grasped the paradoxical power with which postindustrial capitalism would so transform its ideological self-presentation, and do so, moreover, via a strategy not unlike Bataille's own: by reference to an "unchanging, anthropological base, most clearly revealed by primitive societies," and in which "the gift alone creates the glory and the grandeur" (Goux 204).

At any rate, one must join Goux in pronouncing Gilder's "sustained praise of the irrationality of capitalism" as "thoroughly remarkable" (202), even as one also joins him in renouncing any sympathy for Gilder's politics. The latter, in fact, are not even consistent, since in the main lines of his book Gilder abandons his vision of generosity and expenditure and returns to the kind of moralistic economism that I will consider in chapter 7, arguing, in the all-too-familiar way, that "welfare erodes work and family" (*Wealth and Poverty* 127). But whatever Gilder's limitations, it would indeed seem that any social critic who ignores him risks "overlooking once more capitalism's resources and metamorphoses" (Goux 203) and, by extension perhaps, overstating the value of mere generosity as a tool of social transformation.

In chapter 6 I consider further how Bataille's thought seems to be always-already implicated with the ideas it claims to question; and in part 3 I will join Derrida and others in trying to wrench his model entirely free from its historico-anthropological frame. I close the present discussion, however, by raising a tentative question about the basic conception of historical rupture on which even Goux's critique seems, at least in part, to depend. In Goux's essay, two slightly different historical schemas are opposed to Bataille's implicit narrative of paradise lost and regained. Goux suggests, first, that Bataille's thought emerges precisely "at a turning point in the history of capitalism, in the 1920s and 1930s" (200), and became obsolete only in the postmodern moment, "after the upheavals of the 1960s" (211). Yet Goux also suggests, using brief references to the nineteenth-century economists Jean-Baptiste Say and Auguste Walras, that the transformation of capitalism's ideological self-image needs to be traced farther back. Both "Say's Law" (the doctrine that supply creates its own demand) and the theories of "marginal utility" developed by Walras and others (which shift the theoretical focus of economics from production to consumption) already mark what Goux calls a "radical break with all normativity . . . of the useful" (210).

As Marx himself points out (and as I considered briefly in chapter 1), the classical political economists never quite give up an implicit moral economy in which "productivity" refers solely to the creation of tangible value and in which, accordingly, products of excessive luxury are viewed with suspicion. By contrast, the redefinition of market value in terms of marginal utility (the final increment of consumer desire) allows an economics capacious enough to enfold even what Bataille claims are "unproductive expenditures"—everything from luxury goods to avant-garde art or literature. Viewed from the aspect of marginal utility, in the words of William S. Jevons, another pioneering marginalist, "the problem of Economy" is not the production of value but, rather, the quest "to satisfy our wants to the utmost with the least effort . . ., in other words, to maximize comfort and pleasure" (44). Thorstein Veblen, writing at the turn of the century, disputed some aspects of the marginalist theory of consumer behavior but went it one better on this score by identifying what he famously called "conspicuous consumption" as the primal and fundamental economic impulse. For the most part, as Jevon's formula indicates, the marginalists continue to emphasize a restricted economy in their assumption of a utilitarian and "hedonistic" calculus balancing needs and prices in both individual and aggregate consumer behavior. According to Veblen, however, even though the consumer tries "to obtain goods of the required serviceability at as advantageous a bargain as may be," he will also "reject as under grade such goods as do not contain a large element of conspicuous waste" (158).

Such observations constrain us to push back the alleged moment of rupture in the history of capitalist discourse. It might, however, be better still to consider another possibility: that both Bataille and the mode of modern or postmodern capitalist apologetics with which his thought inadvertently converges are but two of many possible instances of an interrelation or mutual saturation of the restricted and general economies, the Work and the gift. We would then be dealing with a discursive or logical structure of interrelation that, although by no means timeless or ahistorical, would have to be analyzed outside any particular (past or future) moment of *positive* rupture.

It is also finally possible to state clearly something that has perhaps been implicit throughout: these questions of work and gift necessarily involve what might be called the question of *culture,* taking the latter term in either its anthropological or its humanistic sense. I have suggested that what remains unthought within the growing debate on work is the double necessity in which work presents itself at once as a *negative* overcoming of irreducible material need and as a *positive* self-production whose absolute token and instance is culture as Matthew Arnold famously describes it: that is, the progressive development of "all sides of our humanity" and "all parts of our society" (8). But this double necessity of work, as we have also seen, commonly evokes in its turn the anthropological definition of culture as the ensemble of meanings and practices shared by any conceivable human group. Under this horizon, the ideas of work and the gift directly parallel one another, and the hypothesis of an archaic society before the invention of work goes hand in hand with the hypothesis of an archaic gift economy. This evolutionary vision of work and gift as basic building blocks of culture also rejoins the question of individual self-development insofar as "high" culture (the Work) is alleged to be at once its absolute vehicle and exemplary case.

In the three chapters that follow I try to untangle this complex discursive structure in which the ideas of work and the gift entwine with the idea of culture in both of its senses. First, I return to the kind of explicit anthropological questions that emerged only peripherally in part 1, pursuing the Work and the gift to their hypothetical point of origin in the archaic "gift economy"—finding there, however, merely one more instance of their ambiguous unity. Next, I consider the question of the gift as it conditions a contemporary debate about poverty, charity, and welfare, a debate that has seemingly left us, at the time of this writing, farther than ever from any meaningful prospect of mutual provision. Finally, I consider contemporary debates about literary and cultural value and suggest how such debates remain conditioned by ancient figures and habits of thought regarding self-development and the spiritual "gift."

ANTHROPOLOGIES OF THE GIFT

Marcel Mauss: The Gift Economy and Its Other

One obvious yet disconcerting conclusion emerges unmistakably from the thought of the gift: such thought always both *requires* and *throws into question* the idea of some fundamental (past or present) moment of economic rupture. The gift economy is first and foremost a thought of the Other, something that would appear to be knowable at all only in its difference from a profit or market economy. Yet this opposition between gift and commodity, between moral and political economy, seems always to collapse into identity. Indeed, the very idea of an economy founded in gifts made and reciprocated instead of commodities bought and sold seems to present itself at once in two incompatible ways. Such an economy sometimes appears as a distinct historico-anthropological alternative: that is, a characteristic of "primitive" cultures past and present that, in the Western world, was at some identifiable historical moment superseded by the market. Sometimes, on the contrary, this gift economy appears as merely one form of exchange among many or as one pole of a timeless spectrum of economic practice: something that continues to coexist with the market as it has always done. Mauss acknowledges this double temporal structure in the first few pages of *The Gift*. He claims to be offering "conclusions of a somewhat archeological kind concerning the nature of human transaction in societies around us, or that have immediately preceded our own" (4), societies in which "exchanges and contracts take the form of presents" (3). But he also promises to "note that this morality and organization still function in our own societies, in unchanging fashion and, so to speak, hidden, below the surface" (4).

In Mauss's book as a whole, this doubleness opens up three possible readings of his argument, each characterized by a different implicit relationship between the book's moral and political conclusions and the conditions of knowledge under which those conclusions are understood to be produced. In a first reading, one might describe Mauss's project as an arcadianism in service of a utopianism. Long ago and far away, Mauss claims, there was a radically different economy; and once we recognize such an economy in the past, we can realize it again in the future. At this level, the utopian vision would seem contingent upon the accuracy of the ethnographic observations, since only the knowledge that a radically different economy once really existed makes it possible to conclude that both capitalism and its social subject, *homo oeconomicus,* are neither natural nor inevitable. Such a reading could, then, be critiqued by questioning the accuracy of Mauss's observations (as some anthropologists have tried to do) or, more broadly, as Vincent Pecora does, by dismissing Mauss's whole project as mere arcadian "nostalgia" which is "recuperated from ethnographic materials" but actually "arises in reaction to what Max Weber calls the disenchanted rationality of modernity" (Pecora 13).

A second possible reading of Mauss's book involves a curious displacement of its original premises and, especially, of this apparent empirical project. Precisely because the thrust of Mauss's book is toward what he calls its "moral conclusions," the argument seems, in Mauss's own account of its genesis and development, to exhaust and transcend the factual observations with which it begins. Although Western society has "recently made man an 'economic animal,'" Mauss also stipulates that "we are not yet all creatures of this genus. . . . happily we are still somewhat removed from this constant, icy, utilitarian calculation" (76). By the book's final page, Mauss goes so far as to assert: "It is useless to seek goodness and happiness in distant places. It is there already, in peace that has been imposed, in well-organized work, alternately in common and separately, in wealth amassed and redistributed, in the mutual respect and reciprocating generosity that is taught by education" (83). The goodness and happiness that Mauss had *seemed,* throughout this text, to be seeking in distant places has never passed away and is still among us. This may be read, perhaps, as simply a supplementary discovery to which the earlier evidence inexorably leads, with a kind of conventional narrative logic— like the classical comedy in which the girl next door proves really to be the hero's long-lost daughter after all. Nevertheless, if practices of generous giving are still so clearly discernible—and if, as he states confidently at the end, "there is no other morality, nor any other form of economy, nor any other social practices than these" (83)—then do we really need to look for such practices among the Tlingit Indians or the Maori or in ancient Hindu literature? Pushed to its limit, this reading of the book seems to neutralize its arcadian nostalgia and displace the operation of knowledge with which the whole project began.

Finally, Mauss's text is susceptible to a third reading, which highlights a basic ambiguity in the idea of a gift economy. Throughout, even as Mauss always insists that archaic cultures organized their economic life around systems of "gifts made and reciprocated," he also concedes, in a variety of ways, that "if one so wishes, one may term these transfers acts of exchange or even of trade and sale" (37). In other words, members of archaic cultures exchanged so-called gifts in the rational expectation of receiving ever-larger gifts later, making the gift economy merely a kind of rudimentary capitalism under a different name. Mauss's commentators have debated at length this curious uncertainty, which also, as Christopher Bracken documents, "haunts the official inquiry into the truth about 'Potlatches' in northwest Canada" (Bracken 32). As Bracken shows, even within the texts of a single observer, "the Euro-Canadian understanding of the 'Potlatch' revolves from exchange to the gift and back to exchange again" (58).

In Mauss's text, a similar uncertainty allows one to take the argument as precisely opposite to that which I summarized above. If in one sense Mauss discovers a radically different economy in distant places and the past, only to rediscover it, still alive and well, in the contemporary world, in another sense he can be taken as arguing that banking and borrowing, trade and exchange—in a word, capitalism—have always existed, merely masked by different names and forms. It is not so much that there were *once* economies of generosity and gift giving that were superseded by economies of exchange and profit but rather, as Mary Douglas concludes in her introduction to Mauss (echoing though reversing the apparent thrust of Mauss's own elegiac summary), that there are *no* free or "pure" gifts, and there have *never* been any "other social practices" than those we already know (vii–viii).

Such a conclusion, carried to its limit, would neutralize at once the arcadianism and the utopian cultural critique of Mauss's text. Within this reading, *homo oeconomicus* remains the assumed agent of social practices that were, Mauss claims, "noble," "replete with etiquette," and engaged in by people who "were less sad, less serious, less miserly, and less personal that we are" (81) but that also, after all, were always part of a process of investment and return. Moreover, if the utopian reading could perhaps be rethought as having the salutary by-product of reducing the discourse's reliance on empirical (historical or anthropological) "facts," this third reading recuperates the crucial value of such knowledge. In fact, the project of knowing and interpreting archaic cultures here seems to provide further proof of the inevitability of market exchange, and even of capitalism itself.

In the "moral conclusions" that conclude the volume, however, Mauss summarizes what I have called the first reading of his book, arguing quite explicitly that there was *once* an economy of generosity, which is *now* in process of revival.

First of all, we return, as return we must, to habits of "aristocratic extravagance." As is happening in English-speaking countries and so many other contemporary societies, whether made up of savages or the highly civilized, the rich must come back to considering themselves—freely and also by obligation—as the financial guardians of their fellow citizens. . . . There must be more good faith, more sensitivity, more generosity in contracts dealing with the hiring of services, the letting of houses, the sale of vital foodstuffs. (68–69)

And yet, Mauss further stipulates, "The individual must work. He should be forced to rely upon himself rather than upon others" (69). This vision of a salutary combination of freedom and obligation, of paternalistic care and individual self-reliance, remains a potent one in contemporary discourses about charity and welfare (as I discuss in chapter 7). The fact remains, however, that Mauss's two sets of prescriptions are by no means symmetrical: people can be forced to work, but they cannot be forced to be generous. Neither Mauss's demand for the rich to "consider themselves" the guardians of their fellow citizens nor his demand for greater "good faith" in business could ever be defined or enforced in some juridical manner; indeed, as Mauss's own description makes all too clear, such obligations could exist at all only subjectively—only as a kind of *manner,* a way of seeing and interpreting practices such as contracts, leases, and commercial exchange, which will not, apparently, be *materially* different from what they are now. Mauss considered himself a socialist, but the specifics of his description here seem virtually indistinguishable from, for example, a frankly procapitalist text such as Andrew Carnegie's famous "Gospel of Wealth" (1900), an essay that similarly extols the moral and social value of accumulation. The wealth accumulated by rich men, Carnegie argues, finally points toward an "ideal State, in which the surplus wealth of the few will become, in the best sense, the property of the many, because administered for the common good" (23). This paternalistic, top-down brand of so-

cialism, and not, say, some literal revival of the potlatch, is clearly what Mauss
too has in mind.[1]

Knowledge and/of the Gift

The thought of the gift, either in Mauss's writings or in various later applications or adaptations of his work, always proceeds via this double temporal
structure, moving back and forth from interpretations of the past (themselves
formulated via empirical observations of existing "primitive" cultures) to critiques of contemporary Western culture and its possible futures. The beginning and ending points of this trajectory, the gift economy and the market
economy, are conceived as absolutely different (after all, their historico-
anthropological difference is the very thing that motivates this thought in the
first place) and yet always allowed to collapse into an identity that appears
both as a historical destination and as something retrospectively revealed as
having been always-already the case. This alternation allows the second conclusion (the "hidden" identity of giving and exchange) to coexist with the first
without quite neutralizing or canceling it. Yet in effect such cancellation inevitably also takes place, in that the relationship between gift and market economy is not really a symmetrical one. To attribute some qualities of gift giving to
commerce is merely to provide an ideological mask for the latter; to interpret
gift giving as no more than a process of exchange is to annul the gift.

I also observe in passing that, even when one entertains the possibility of
some fundamental historical shift from the gift economy to the market, from
the general to the restricted economy, one finds no consensus on its moment
or period. For Mauss, it was "the Semitic, Greek and Roman civilizations"
that, "after a veritable, great, and admirable revolution, went beyond . . . this
economy of the gift" (54). Bataille locates the end of "unproductive expenditure" as a dominant model of social organization somewhat later: in the rise of
an ascetic Christianity, the decline of the feudal nobility, or (following the Weber thesis), at the time of the Reformation and the birth of capitalism. Subsequent historians are also in no precise agreement about where some crucial
turning point of Western economic history might be located. Marc Bloch
identifies AD 1020 as a dividing line between two different ages of feudalism, a
moment of transition that another historian summarizes as a transition from
gift economy to profit economy (Bloch 60–61; Little 3–18). Other historians
envision a moment of historical shift between gift and market that coincides

somehow with the moment of transition from medieval to Renaissance as traditionally conceived; and, not surprisingly, such a shift is then intimately related, even if not simply identical to, the birth of capitalism itself. For example, Jean-Christophe Agnew, in an influential study of the historical development of the market, both as literal practice and as idea, describes the medieval marketplace as a fluid combination of gift and commodity exchange in which the latter only gradually comes to predominate.[2] Natalie Zevon Davis joins many other historians in describing the sixteenth century as one with "special consequences for gift practices" (Davis 22): a period in which gift and market exchange coexisted and in which their relation was at once closer and more sharply divided than it is today. In this period, there was a particular "sensitivity to the relation between gift and sale" and to "the border between them"; and it was always possible to move "back and forth between the gift mode and the sale mode, while always remembering the distinction between them" (44). Since then, "gift-systems have contracted and expanded"; yet today, she suggests, "the dream returns of a world restored, replenished, even expanded in generosity" (132). Here again, the gift economy manages to remain in focus at once as an ever-vanishing horizon and as a kind of ever-present harbinger of its own imminent return.

Once one recognizes this paradoxical structure as a defining characteristic of this thought, even George Gilder's identification of postmodern capitalism as a reborn gift economy reveals itself as in no way exceptional. I have already briefly referred to Pecora's *Households of the Soul*, in which he suggests that the thought of Mauss and Bataille, among others, remains in thrall to a kind of anthropological or "enchanted" economics, a nostalgia for precapitalist social relations whose details are, in any case, merely read back into ethnographic materials in reaction to modernist rationality. To place Pecora's persuasive critique alongside the writings of postmodern apologists for capitalism is to be struck, however, by how the latter celebrate the alleged anthropological underpinnings of the market in a manner that at once further confirms Pecora's thesis and yet in some sense evades its force. In other words, contemporary ideologues of the market no longer find it necessary to announce, as Mauss or Davis or many others do, some imminent historical "return" of the archaic economy; instead, the gift and the commodity, moral economy and political economy, are seen as always-already saturating one another, and the social virtues of "good faith" and "generosity" are claimed to be always-already immanent in commercial exchange.

One might recall here the various instances cited in chapter 2 of writers who insist, as Michael Novak does, that "business" is "a morally noble" profession (Novak 13), and who otherwise engage in what Francis Fukuyama celebrates as a general "spiritualization of economic life" (Fukuyama 355). Fukuyama himself—already well known for his argument, in *The End of History and the Last Man* (1992), that liberal democracy and capitalism have become the only conceivable political and economist systems—argues in a later book, *Trust* (1995):

The liberal democracy that emerges at the end of history is . . . not entirely "modern." If the institutions of democracy and capitalism are to work properly, they must coexist with certain premodern cultural habits that ensure their proper functioning. Law, contract and economic rationality provide a necessary but not sufficient basis for both the stability and prosperity of postindustrial societies; they must as well be leavened with reciprocity, moral obligation, duty toward community, and trust, which are based in habit rather than rational calculation. (11)

Fukuyama's argument here is doubly dependent on an anthropological economics: he assumes, on the one hand, a "raw selfishness of human nature" that "all cultures seek to constrain" and yet, on the other hand, argues throughout that "certain kinds of traditional moral and social virtues," even those practiced "in an arational way," in fact function to "advance utility maximization . . . in a narrowly materialistic sense" (34, 37–38).[3]

At one level this is perhaps no more than another instance where one must join Goux in remarking on the specious but ideologically effective "praise of the irrationality of capitalism" (Goux 202) that pervades contemporary economic discourse. But this is also the place to recall how Gilder proceeds from an assertion of capitalism as a "general" or gift economy to an even more extravagant celebration of a new information economy, an economy that is "driven by knowledge" (*Microcosm* 378). This alleged historical ascendancy of knowledge, information, and communication as key factors of material production is, as I have observed in part 1, the insight that unites a variety of contemporary economic thinkers from free-market futurists to the Marxist theorists of "autonomy." Taken together, the two stages of Gilder's work indicate a certain ambiguity in his approach to the question of knowledge that obliquely echoes the temporal ambiguity inscribed in the thought of the gift. For Gilder, the very essence of capitalism, and the conceptual point where it converges with (and surpasses) the archaic gift economy, lies in the absolute necessity with which entrepreneurs invest their time and money "long before any return is received, all without any assurance that the enterprise will not fail." It is precisely in this, Gilder suggests, that capitalism becomes "a pattern of giving that dwarfs . . . any primitive rite of exchange" (*Wealth and Poverty* 30). In other words, the greatness of capitalism, according to its apologists, is that it tolerates or even requires an *absence* of rational knowledge. And yet, just as certainly, capitalism in its moment of historical fruition must also embrace knowledge at once as the supreme commodity and as a uniquely privileged factor of industrial production.

For capitalism, then, at least in Gilder's remarkable anthropological re-visioning of it, knowledge must be both present and absent. The same thing is true of the gift economy, not so much in its alleged practical existence in past or present primitive cultures but, rather, considered *as* a hypothesis or in-stance of thought. For Mauss himself, the specific interpretation of archaic practices offered in *The Gift* would seem to depend, as I have suggested, on a set of particular empirical observations. In this case, the situation is compli-cated by the fact that Mauss did no fieldwork of his own, although his conclu-sions could, of course, still be questioned even if he had. A sequence of prior observation and subsequent reinterpretation is characteristic of this thought: Marshall Sahlins, for example, begins his own reinterpretation of Mauss by conceding that his version is "unjustified . . . by any special study of the Maori or of the philosophers . . . invoked along the way" (149). But even in Mauss's own text, the specific thesis in its broadest form—that an economy of gift exchange united a whole range of otherwise disparate archaic cultures—is itself finally subordinate to a disciplinary imperative: a commitment to the production of anthropological knowledge in general. For example, when Mauss mentions the potlatch again at the very end of the book, this time he emphasizes what he calls its "aesthetic aspect," something which heretofore he has "deliberately omitted from this study" (79). For the original partici-pants of this "total" event, he suggests, the potlatch organized society juridi-cally, religiously, and economically and was also "a cause of aesthetic emo-tion." This passage, describing and celebrating the possibility of such an intricately unified event, leads Mauss to his concluding celebration of anthro-pology as "the study of total social facts" (80). That is, he affirms the possibil-ity of *knowing* an object even as he defines that object in terms of a kind of general-economic abundance or dynamism: "numbers of men, forces in mo-tion, who are in movement in their environment and their feelings" (80). The complex totality of the object suggests the totalizing possibilities of the an-thropological discourse that re-creates it.

Pierre Bourdieu: From Gift Economy to Cultural Capital

Thus, the hypothesis of a gift economy depends on the empirical production of anthropological knowledge; yet the reverse is also true, in that the gift economy is the privileged example of the hidden cultural truth that a totalizing discourse such as anthropology can bring to light. This interrelation of knowledge and its object also conditions Pierre Bourdieu's critique of structuralism in *The Logic of Practice*. Here, Bourdieu addresses the all-important link (or gap) between culture as experienced by its participants and culture as known by the ethnographic observer and holds up the gift economy as a privileged instance of this very issue. The "detemporalizing" logic of scientific analysis, Bourdieu argues, is ill suited to interpret practices such as gift exchange that unfold over time as a succession of distinct but related acts: "'Cycles of reciprocity,' mechanical interlockings of obligatory practices, exist only for the absolute gaze of the omniscient, omnipresent spectator who, thanks to his *knowledge* of the social mechanics, is able to be present at the different stages of the 'cycle'" (*Logic* 98; emphasis added).

Within an economy in which apparent gifts are expected to be reciprocated, there must at least be an interval between the gift and its reciprocation, an interval which thus serves as "an instrument of denial which allows a subjective truth and a quite opposite objective truth to coexist" (*Logic* 107). By contrast, the anthropologist puts two and two together; and the resulting knowledge allows him to reconstruct a cycle of exchange that must remain hidden from its participants. Gift exchange, Bourdieu concludes, "is one of the social games that cannot be played unless the players refuse to acknowledge the objective truth of the game" (105). Therefore, the anthropologist must murder to dissect, so to speak, being compelled to seek the very knowledge that the culture's participants renounce and that, being brought to light, dissolves the charmed circle of the gift by revealing it to have been always-already a circuit of exchange.

On the other hand, Bourdieu also argues that the gift economy as lived by its participants is inconsistent in its own terms, for it often "proceeds otherwise than as laid down by the 'mechanical laws' of the 'cycle of reciprocity.'" It always remains possible, for example, that "the gift may remain unreciprocated, when one obliges an ungrateful person," or "it may be rejected as an insult, inasmuch as it asserts or demands the possibility of reciprocity" (*Logic* 98). These more or less self-evident facts, Bourdieu suggests, are sufficient in themselves "to change the whole experience of practice and, by the same token, its logic" (99) and thus also to destabilize the totalizing pretensions of anthropological knowledge.

Notwithstanding this conclusion, Bourdieu himself still claims to *indicate* (if not quite describe in its full detail) the "logic" that governs social practice and, as it were, to recognize a cultural dynamic that is lived in the form of misrecognition. It thus appears, in other words, that just as the gift presents itself at once as the absolute Other of economic rationality and as its very truth, so knowledge is at once the opponent of the gift and the only vehicle by which the gift economy can be known in its muddled, inconsistent, but still distinctive practical texture. The point of misrecognition, of absent knowledge, is also the very point at which a market economy can be wrested (as we have seen George Gilder do) into some paradoxical resemblance of the gift economy. It is claimed that the capitalist entrepreneur invests exactly as the gift giver gives: by renouncing all possibility of knowing in advance the future returns of the value he puts in play.

Thus, the two discursive fields, gift and market, whose apparent irreducible difference is the very thing that sets the anthropological project in motion, prove once again to mutually saturate one another. On the one hand, anthropology can do nothing but annul the gift and endlessly re-reveal it as a misrecognized form of the market; on the other hand, the anthropological knowledge thus produced makes it possible for the market to claim for itself the ethical values (generosity and trust) that apparently define the gift.

Since this mutual saturation of gift and market is precisely the result that Bourdieu's exhaustive attempt to define the "logic" of cultural practice is intended to avoid, it is thus hard to escape the impression that Bourdieu's analysis tries, and yet fails, to have it both ways. Bourdieu always insists—as he does, for example, in a essay from 1996 revisiting the question of the gift—that one must never make the error of "seeing the two agents involved in the gift as calculators who assign themselves the subjective project of doing what they are objectively doing" ("Marginalia" 234). Yet he also argues, above all, that even practices that "give every appearance of disinterestedness because they escape the logic of 'economic' interest (in the narrow sense) and are oriented towards non-material stakes that are not easily quantified, as in 'pre-capitalist' societies or in the cultural sphere of capitalist societies . . . , never cease to comply with an economic logic" (*Logic* 122).

Thus, the project of defending the logic of gift giving in precapitalist cultures, a logic apparently founded in a kind of general economy of disinterested abundance, finally leads Bourdieu to reaffirm the primacy of an even more fundamental economism: a restricted economy of investment and return that is, so to speak, invisibly present even in its own absence and that is perfectly complete in its incompletion. Bourdieu at once reproaches anthropological knowledge for an "objectivism" that *fails* to hold together "what holds to-gether in the object, namely the double reality of intrinsically equivocal, am-biguous practices" (*Logic* 118), and yet himself enjoins the "drawing up [of] a comprehensive balance-sheet of symbolic profits," which makes it "possible to grasp the economic rationality of conduct which economism dismisses as absurd" (120). Two things, however, remain clear. First, as the examples of contemporary capitalist discourse attest, the "economic/non-economic di-chotomy" that Bourdieu asks us to abandon is in fact always-already being abandoned by that very "economism" that Bourdieu denounces. Second, what remains very much at stake in Bourdieu's own project is a "science ca-pable of treating all practices" (122): that is, an intellectual work that, some-where above and beyond the uncertainty written into its object (the experi-ence of the gift), will itself be rewarded with a knowledge that thus remains, in the fundamental sense, anthropo-*logical*.

One notices, finally, how Bourdieu, in the passage cited above, makes a passing analogy between "pre-capitalist societies" and "the cultural sphere." This analogy reminds us that Bourdieu uses the term "cultural capital" to re-fer to two quite different things whose possible interrelation is, here again, mediated by the aspirations of anthropology itself. Cultural capital refers, first and foremost, to the misrecognized form of accumulation or debt that occurs within a gift economy and is the product of a "symbolic alchemy" that "en-ables the gift or counter-gift to be seen as inaugural acts of generosity, without a past or a future, that is, without calculation" (*Logic* 112). But it also refers to what Bourdieu elsewhere calls the "'creative' power, the ineffable *mana* or charisma," possessed by the artist, the writer, the professor, and so forth— which is similarly a product of "a vast operation of *social alchemy* jointly con-ducted . . . by all the agents involved in the field of [artistic and cultural] pro-duction" (*Field of Cultural Production* 81).

The idea of symbolic or cultural capital in this latter sense is now well es-tablished within the lexicon of contemporary cultural studies (see, e.g., Guil-lory). Yet, as I will suggest in chapter 8, the vision of art and literature as a kind of cultural "gift" that wholly transcends the utilitarian calculus remains equally widespread, despite the exhaustive demystification to which such a vision has been subjected by many writers—notably including Bourdieu him-self, especially in his magisterial *Distinction*. In this text, a comprehensive "critique of the judgment of taste," Bourdieu demolishes the idea of art for art's sake, of the aesthetic as a self-fulfilling end in itself, and systematically reveals the institutions of art and culture as no more than vehicles for the production, transmission, and enforcement of class difference.

It appears, however, that Bourdieu constantly tries—and fails—to preserve for the idea of the gift just such a status of absolute autoteleology. In his 1996 essay, Bourdieu attacks Derrida's contention in *Given Time* that an absolutely free or pure gift is strictly impossible. But Bourdieu's attempted critique merely further confirms Derrida's point. Bourdieu claims that a gift is genuinely "a generous act" within a social universe in which such acts of disinterested generosity are recognized as such ("Marginalia" 233). In other words, as Bourdieu frankly and repeatedly argues, the generous gift within a gift *economy* tends "toward the *conservation* and *increase* of symbolic capital," and such economies as a whole are "organized with a view to the *accumulation* of symbolic capital (a capital of recognition, honor, nobility, etc.)" ("Marginalia" 233–34; emphasis added). However radical its apparent rejection of calculation and self-interest, the gift economy is by no means a general economy of abundance and excess but rather, in both its lived texture and its essence, a restricted economy of accumulation and conservation, of investments and returns that are no less certain for being somehow intangible or misrecognized. Correspondingly, in the end Bourdieu can only argue prescriptively for the social creation of "institutions" that allow (or force) people to "have an interest in disinterestedness and generosity" ("Marginalia" 240). At least as concerns the question of the gift, therefore, Bourdieu's reflexive sociology ends up more or less at the same place where Mauss and others do: anticipating a return of "good faith" and "generosity" or even of a certain "aristocratic extravagance."[4] This, as Pecora suggests, is also precisely the place where the thought of the gift as utopian cultural critique so often collapses back into mere arcadian nostalgia.

Georges Bataille: Beyond Anthropology

As I have already in part suggested, Bataille's general economics is itself apparently grounded in a kind of anthropological history and thus obviously susceptible to the same critique. Indeed, Bataille's theoretical opposition often seems inseparable from a conventional historical narrative in which an archaic general economy (manifest in, e.g., the human sacrifices of the Aztecs and the potlatch of Northwest American Indians) was gradually superseded by the quintessential restricted economy of bourgeois capitalism. But at the frontiers of his thought, and especially in the interpretations of subsequent theorists, it becomes clear that the restricted and general economies do not finally refer to discrete historical alternatives, or even to two poles of a spectrum of reciprocity; rather, they exist only in the form of an absolutely irreducible ontological *relation*. Correspondingly, as Denis Hollier and others suggest, "the major interest of Bataille's theory of expenditure" finally reveals itself as being not "of an economic or anthropological order but, rather, of an epistemological one" (Hollier 138). Bataille's theoretical opposition must finally be applied both to the material economy (i.e., "economics" itself as conventionally understood) and to a certain economy of knowledge. He argues that the "global movement of energy" is always characterized by an unusable surplus; and thus, the fundamental problem of material existence is really not scarcity and survival but, rather, how to expend the excess heat and light that flows unceasingly to the earth from a sun that "gives without ever receiving" (*Accursed Share* 1:28). This literal surplus of energy in the terrestrial biosphere cannot be fully expended and so "can only be lost without the slightest aim, consequently without any meaning" (for this quotation from Bataille, see Derrida "From Restricted to General Economy" 270). By extension, Bataille suggests that epistemology must come to terms with the terminal absence of meaning beyond all traditional operations of knowledge and thus, too, beyond the aiming or knowing Subject.

The general economy thus becomes the rubric and theoretical framework for an economy of knowledge radically different from classical Western empiricism. Derrida, in particular, has read Bataille as suggesting that all classical philosophic systems must be considered restricted *theoretical* economies. Such systems, as Arkady Plotnitsky summarizes, "configure their objects and the relationships between those objects as always meaningful and claim that the systems that they present avoid the unproductive expenditure of energy, containing within their bounds multiplicity and indeterminacy" (4). In other words, classical systems of theory construe the world as finally limited or "restricted" enough to be graspable by thought; and they assume that intellectual "work" will be rewarded with the wages of knowledge. Such systems thus might be understood as forms of epistemological capitalism, in which knowledge, like any other resource, is produced, accumulated, conserved, and expanded. By contrast, using an ingenious French pun that opposes "thought" (*la pensée*) to "expenditure" (*la dépense*), Bataille calls for a "general" theoretical economy, which has subsequently emerged in the tradition of thought today commonly referred to as *deconstruction:* in which there is always a surplus of signification, and in which meaning itself remains open, unstable, infinitely disseminated, and ultimately uncontainable. Derrida has acknowledged, for example, that his influential early texts are all "situated *explicitly* in relation to Bataille" (*Positions* 105–6 n. 35), and that in them he pursues "a 'general economy,' a kind of *general strategy of deconstruction*" (*Positions* 41).

At one level, then, Bataille's argument has the same shape as my first reading of Mauss: that is, an arcadianism in the service of a utopianism, which is thus wholly contingent upon a traditional empirical knowledge of the past, or what Bataille frankly calls "historical data."[5] But at another level, the idea of unproductive expenditure refers to a kind of excess or surplus of meaning forever ungraspable by philosophic "work" or reason. Bataille's recurrent image for this unthinkable truth, in both its material and its theoretical senses, is the sun, which is both (1) the paradigmatic philosophic symbol (from Plato onward) of enlightenment and (2) a literal heavenly body that is the "source of life's exuberant development" (*Accursed Share* 1:28), pouring into space far more heat and light than could ever be utilized. In other words, the material excess of terrestrial existence indicates the space of "senseless loss" at the heart of all meaning and productive work. Bataille's sovereignty, naming the stance that confronts this absolute loss, thus remains contingent on, even as it thus exposes the limits of, a traditional operation of knowledge: an empirical and at least quasi-scientific vision of the sun's "solar conflagrations" and the terrestrial biosphere. Materially, the "prodigality" of the heavens produces a "pressure of life" that constrains all living beings to "squander" their excess energy; theoretically, it destabilizes the "anthropocentrism" that, in what Bataille calls the "error of the stationary earth," contaminates "all that we recognize as truth" ("Celestial Bodies" 76). Such anthropocentrism arises, paradoxically, *in response to* the same unthinkable excess that it then denies and occludes by postulating an object (the universe) that is "restricted," graspable by thought.

Even more broadly, however, one must also understand a crucial link between the two levels of Bataille's argument itself, which I will describe in the terms that Jean-Luc Nancy derives, in part, from his reading of Bataille. Bataille's general economy, both materially and theoretically, can be grasped by the finite, singular beings who populate the earth only in terms of what Nancy calls their being-in-common. "The universe spends," Bataille asserts in an early essay, "while remaining wholly free of the shadow cast by the possibility of exhausting its prodigality," but this is not the case "for those fragile existences which multiply in cruel combat on Earth's surface" ("Celestial Bodies" 76). In *The Accursed Share*, similarly, Bataille stipulates that, although the "global movement of energy" is always defined by an unusable surplus, this does not alter the "indigence inherent in separate beings (which are constantly short of resources, which are nothing but eternally *needy* individuals)" (1:23). The general economy of our being-in-common always stands in relation to the restricted economy inherent in singular, finite, material (mortal) beings.

Despite this conclusion, which Bataille often acknowledges to be necessary, he elsewhere allows his thought to return to the level of *individual* experience, allowing his thought to remain, as Nancy puts it, "governed by the theme of the sovereignty of a *subject*" (Nancy *Inoperative Community* 23). "Just as the herbivore relative to the plant, and the carnivore relative to the herbivore, is a luxury," Bataille writes, "so man is the most suited of all living beings to consume intensely, sumptuously, the excess energy offered up by the pressure of life to conflagrations befitting the solar origins of its movement" (*Accursed Share* 1:37). Some subjective excess, some desire to consume in a manner that has nothing to do with subsistence or survival (what Bataille calls "servile utility") but that is, rather, ostentatious and "sumptuous" (rather like what Mauss calls "noble"), corresponds to the material excesses of terrestrial existence. Bataille declares himself to be concerned with what he calls "the apparently lost sovereignty to which the beggar can sometimes be as close as the great nobleman, and from which, as a rule, the bourgeois is voluntarily the most far removed" (*Accursed Share* 3:197–98). This familiar-sounding impulse to affront the middle class frequently serves as the theoretical counterpart of a fascination with (material and individual) consumption as the very locus of expenditure and loss, within a discourse that thus sometimes descends, as it were, from epistemology to psychology. The same antibourgeois sentiments often similarly seem in service, here again, of a merely paternalist and arcadian vision of aristocratic extravagance and paternalistic generosity.

Perhaps even more seriously, however, such arcadianism finally seems to disjoin the theoretical and material aspects of general economy, whose unity is otherwise crucial to the theory as a whole. As I have already observed, Bataille suggests that a particular social class, the bourgeoisie, led humanity away from the "great and free forms of unproductive social expenditure" (Mauss's archaic general economies) and toward "the principle of balanced accounts" (the restricted economism of capitalist production). But on the level of epistemology, Bataille follows his solar metaphor to suggest that humanity *always* averts its eyes from the blinding truth of *dépense*. "With respect to all great and violent expenditures," Bataille suggests, "we are concerned to admire them from afar. The sun corresponds most conveniently to that prudent concern. It is all *radiance,* gigantic loss of heat and of light, *flame, explosion;* but remote from men, who can enjoy in safety and quiet the fruits of this great cataclysm" (Bataille "Van Gogh" 59).

If, at one level of the argument, the defining moment of history was the ascendancy of a bourgeoisie characterized by an aversion to expenditure in literal, material terms, so, at another level, humanity as a whole retains an epistemological aversion to *dépense* (the unthinkable truth, the sun, at which we cannot bear to look). This truth is, at least in part, the truth of the literal surpluses of the body, whose repression in the name of "civilization" also characterizes bourgeois culture. (Indeed, as in the passage cited just above, Bataille's critique of the bourgeoisie is grounded in the assumption of a "human nature" into which humanity always sinks back, despite its attempts to evade and lose this nature.) Thus, "mankind as a whole resembles those parvenus who are ashamed of their humble origin" (*Accursed Share* 2:62). Even the great classical philosophic systems such as Hegel's, characterized by what Mark Taylor calls their 'comprehensive aspirations," always encounter some "unavoidable limit" that forces them to exclude and occlude some unthinkable excess of which the literal excrements of the body are a vivid material example (Taylor 32). Bataille's project aspires to be a critique of the (epistemological *and* material) repressions on which philosophy and bourgeois culture are alike founded.

This project, however, always seems riven by an internal tension: on the one hand, it is a historical account which describes, and attempts to undo, the ascendancy of bourgeois economism; on the other, it is an epistemological theory conceding that every labor of thought or writing is economistic because all thinkers and writers, as Derrida argues, "never give anything without calculating, consciously or unconsciously, its reappropriation, its exchange, or its circular return" (*Given Time* 101). Each side of this argument seems to threaten the other, a conceptual vulnerability that might then be said to produce the more obvious failures of Bataille's text, the places where his theoretical bravura gives way to oddly disappointing practical applications. The most obvious example, as Goux and other commentators have already observed, is the way in which Bataille suggests that the Marshall Plan following World War II represents an example of expenditure without return. As Allan Stoeckl summarizes, Bataille suggests that with the Marshall Plan Americans "were seeking no immediate gain, no conventional profit," but were, rather, "spending like the Tlingit chiefs of the American Northwest, without, in principle at least, any thought for the future, any plans for later construction or return" (Stockl 249). In thus suggesting that American postwar capitalism exemplifies a kind of "gift" economy, Bataille concludes precisely where Gilder and other recent capitalist apologists begin.

Correspondingly, Bataille suggests, in an argument spread out over volumes 1 and 3 of *The Accursed Share,* that Marxist socialism as realized in Soviet Russia was the very paradigm of a restricted economy. For example, here are a few excerpts from a long passage in which Bataille provides a sort of schematic mininarrative of Western economic history after the Renaissance. "What is called 'accumulation,'" he argues first, "signifies that a number of wealthy individuals declined to engage in the unproductive expenditures of an ostentatious life-style and employed their available funds for the purchase of means of production" (*Accursed Share* 1:153). Notice how Bataille seems here to accept a central ethical assumption of capitalism that Marx always derided: namely, that capitalist entrepreneurs in some sense deserve to appropriate the surplus value of material production because their investment in such value represents their own "abstention" from consumption. This is no mere oversight: Bataille is *constrained* to accept this assumption by his own description of the birth of capitalism as a move from "unproductive social expenditure" (emphasizing consumption) toward expenditure in the name of reserve and return (emphasizing production).

Bataille then suggests that "the success of workers' claims," through collective bargaining and the like, "augments the cost of production and reduces not only the share reserved for the luxury of the bosses but that reserved for accumulation. . . . If the worker had worked more and earned less, a larger and larger quantity of capitalist profit could have been used for the development of the productive forces" (1:154). Here, Bataille largely follows Marx in assuming a battle between labor and capital over the appropriation of surplus value. But then Bataille seems to suggest that Soviet Russia, confronted by the challenge of modernization, went in precisely the wrong economic direction. Soviet communism "put an end to nonproductive spending" in order to "reserve the resources for equipping the country" (1:155), "closed itself firmly to the principle of nonproductive expenditure," and demanded "the maximum productivity from each individual" (1:158–59). In one sense, as I briefly suggested in chapter 1, Bataille's critique here anticipates other salutary Marxist critiques of a Soviet socialism that ruinously embraces a capitalist ethos of general industriousness. But Bataille perhaps goes even farther along these lines, for he at least risks suggesting that *any* fully realized socialism would be, in principle, more economistic than capitalism. Socialism creates a world in which "passion, be it happy or sad, is only a brief episode" because "all of one's waking hours are dedicated to the fever of work" (1:160). In other passages throughout *The Accursed Share* in which Bataille discovers examples of general economy in transgressive eroticism, in the artistic genius, in "luxury products . . . and amusements" (2:187), he sometimes seems to repeat Mauss's trajectory and neutralize both his arcadian and his utopian visions with an implicit celebration of the capitalist world—where passion and luxury survive at least as remnants of the archaic societies of expenditure.

In other words, Bataille's thought often seems to dwindle into the mere affirmation of an ethic of generosity or even something that sounds suspiciously like praise of consumer culture. The general and restricted economies here relate as an essentially moral opposition between the economistic commodity and the generous gift. Or perhaps, more precisely, one might also see the relation between the two economies as a self-canceling tension: a traditional restricted empiricism (philosophic "work") finally reasserts itself as originary and fundamental within what is then revealed as a merely nominal vision of general excess, much as *homo oeconomicus* seems to reassert himself within anthropological attempts to reimagine archaic practices of gift giving. The restricted economy would then be a kind of dead weight sinking the very labor of thought into a "nature" or a "reality" seen therefore as inescapable; and the general economy, correspondingly, a mere mirage or veil for its antinomy.

In part 3 of this book, by contrast, I will follow other writers who take Bataille's thought to its frontiers and beyond, in order to discover there a rather different relationship of restricted and general economies, of the Work and the gift. Before moving on, however, let me state clearly a conclusion that has been only implicit so far. Whatever traces of arcadian nostalgia or ethnographic sentimentality remain in Bataille's text, his theoretical model, pursued to its limit, necessarily breaks with anthropology, for anthropology always confronts a pattern of behavior by discrete agents (a "culture") with a generalizing discourse that abstracts that culture's underlying patterns and hence its truth. From such a perspective, the so-called gift economy can be revealed as merely a system of economic exchange or celebrated as a fundamentally different economic system. Either way, whether grasped as radical Otherness or reclaimed in its alleged continuity with the anthropological observer's own assumptions, the set of practices in question can be known and identified as a gift economy only *in* its distinctive particularity. By contrast, for Bataille, the economy of surplus and loss is understood as *general* because it denotes the economic condition of the universe grasped in its greatest possible generality; and the economy of scarcity is understood as *restricted*, similarly, because it constitutes the economic condition of singular beings, who are "eternally needy." In other words, anthropology (and even empiricism itself) can grasp the gift economy only by positing it as restricted, particular, individual. For Bataille, conversely, the general economy in a material sense cannot in principle be understood as manifest by some particular instance of culture or history, but only from the "general" point of view: as the community (or the "economy") of an "all" that remains forever *open*—an "all" so radically conceived that this word would no longer even be an appropriate term to calculate it.

CHARITY AND WELFARE: THE GIFT AS WORK

The End of Welfare

In the 1990s, even as theorists and scholars in a variety of fields were contemplating the end of work, politicians and policymakers in America were, by contrast, reaffirming work's absolute moral and social necessity via a process of so-called welfare reform. For some years, it had been repeatedly argued by conservative commentators that the constellation of New Deal social programs today known loosely as "welfare" promote a so-called dependence on the part of the poor and thus hurt the very people they were designed to help. In 1992, as is well known, Bill Clinton campaigned for president stressing themes of personal responsibility and promising to "end welfare as we know it." That same year Lawrence M. Mead defined a "new politics of poverty" whose "leading question" should be, he suggested, "how to . . . minimize dependency by people who many feel could support themselves" (Mead *New Politics* 3). Two years later, Nancy Fraser and Linda Gordon acknowledged regretfully that "'welfare reform' today means reducing 'dependency' by getting claimants off the rolls" (Fraser and Gordon 618). And two years after that, President Clinton's election promise was finally fulfilled with the passage and signing of the Personal Responsibility and Work Opportunity Reconciliation Act of 1996, which ended the idea of a federal "entitlement" to welfare, established strict work requirements in return for benefits, and set limits on the amount of time an individual family could receive cash relief.

Many other writers have described in detail the debate leading up to this "reform" (or repeal) of welfare in 1996 and explored the racist and misogynist fantasies that inhabit its margins: the threatening specter of the so-called welfare queen and the obsessive claims, in the face of every kind of contrary evidence, that welfare merely subsidizes crime and illegitimacy in inner-city ghettos. Here, I simply observe how both the intention and the material effect of the 1996 bill is, more than anything else, to compel welfare recipients to work. The bill provides poor people with an "opportunity" to work by forcing them to work, either directly (in so-called workfare programs) or indirectly (by removing a safety net of support).

Of course, even long before the latest round of debate, an assumed connection between welfare and work was written deeply into the history of American social policy. As has frequently been observed, nearly all American welfare programs since the New Deal—including unemployment insurance, workmen's compensation insurance, and, of course, Social Security—were exclusively intended to assist workers (see, e.g., Hansan and Morris 1). The notable exception is Aid for Families with Dependent Children (AFDC), the program that most people mean when they refer to "welfare," and whose historic rollback was primarily addressed in the 1996 bill. Now, even "a parent or caretaker receiving assistance" is required "to engage in work" (Personal Responsibility and Work Opportunity Reconciliation Act, HR 3734, sec. 402)—a provision which seems, by the way, to contradict the bill's manifest concern with specifically *parental* forms of responsibility. The plain fact that, as William Julius Wilson summarizes (and as, e.g., a study released by the General Accounting Office of the federal government in 1987 concludes), there is "no conclusive evidence to support the prevailing common beliefs that welfare discourages individuals from working, breaks up two-parent families or affects the childbearing rates of unmarried women, even young unmarried women" (Wilson 163), indicates clearly that something else is *at work* in this obsessive concern for setting the poor to labor.

I suggest that the welfare reform bill is another site where the unmistakable connection of the ideas of *working* and *giving* reveals itself with painful clarity. Senator Barbara A. Mikulski, speaking on the floor of the U.S. Senate on August 1, 1996, asserted: "We all acknowledge that our current welfare system does not *work*. It has failed to move people from welfare to *work*" (emphasis added). The awkward repetition conveys precisely how the rhetoric of welfare typically evokes or expresses what I have called a double refusal of the gift in the name of work. The project of "reforming" welfare is about being cruel to be kind, about helping people by giving them *less*.

The sheer speciousness of this alleged affirmation of responsibility and work was acutely in evidence as the nation approached the five-year lifetime limit for recipients of welfare required under the 1996 bill. The *New York Times* of December 17, 2001, for example, recounts the stories of "Daisy Torres, a 34-year old mother of three who was raised on welfare," and "James Howard, 42, a 10th grade dropout who did odd jobs off the books to supplement his family's public assistance grant in years past." Both of these people had been cleaning subways for months on New York's workfare program without a wage or benefits but simply in return for their regular welfare checks and a promise that diligence would eventually result in a permanent job. Both had excellent performance evaluations and near perfect attendance. And both "got a double dose of bad news last month. Because of the deepening recession, the [transit] authority had imposed a hiring freeze. And, under federal law, the city's Human Resources Administration informed them, their welfare benefits were at an end" (Bernstein).

To place such examples side by side with the blithe pronouncements, by President Clinton and many others, that "welfare reform works"[1] is to confront a policy so contradictory in its underlying logic and so cruel in its practical effects that the words of necessary critique almost wither before one can articulate them. Nevertheless, and for what it may be worth, I join many other writers in observing the fundamental contradiction of this obsessive concern with forcing people to labor in a society where the dream of a workerless world is already announcing itself. Why, as Fraser and Gordon ask, do we continue to demonize a so-called economic dependency in a world so obviously characterized by "ever higher relations of interdependence, based on an ever increasing division of labor, from the global to the neighborhood level" (630)? Why is work the one thing whose social, economic, and political necessity remains above all question, so that, in the words of Viviane Forrester, "no one ever officially questions its deep-rootedness, its obviousness, still less its necessity" (1)?

Welfare and Work

The national debate leading up to the 1996 bill was widely influenced by the writings of an interrelated group of conservative social scientists and historians, including the above-cited Lawrence M. Mead and also writers such as Martin Anderson, George Gilder, Charles Murray, Gertrude Himmelfarb, and Marvin Olasky. Even the briefest consideration of the argument these writers share reveals how it turns absolutely on two interrelated obligations (to work and to give) and on an implicit anthropological history which envisions a self-present human subject forever leaving its traces in discourse and events. All these writers assume that poverty is essentially an individual moral failure rather than the consequence of structural inequities in the economic fabric of society. (Indeed, welfare policy is also a site where the celebrated theoretical debate about the relative determinative force of "structure" and "agency" emerges most clearly into the public sphere.)[2] Poverty occurs, according to these writers, when individuals fail to support themselves and their dependents by their own labors. Some people, they acknowledge, are literally unable to work because they are too young or too old or because they are physically or mentally disabled. In this case, they are "deserving" of support and the community at large is obligated to give it. But more often people are simply unwilling to work because of some intrinsic moral weakness such as drug addiction or because they are just plain lazy. In this case, it is argued, to relieve their poverty merely rewards and encourages their moral failure; and our obligation to withhold support from these "undeserving" social subjects is perhaps even greater than our original obligation to give.[3]

Even on the surface, this latest round of "welfare reform" obviously relies on the same assumed connection between work and personal self-development considered in the previous section. Thus, President Clinton claims, in a speech on August 4, 1999, that companies who hire welfare recipients are helping "to develop the human capacity of our people" (Harris). It is this unexamined faith in work as the one irreplaceable mode of human self-fashioning that has made possible what William Julius Wilson describes as a "liberal-conservative consensus on welfare reform" and what Judith Shklar calls the "astonishing" agreement among "critics and defenders of welfare," both of whom "want to make good citizens of the 'underclass' by getting them a job" (Wilson 164; Shklar 96). What is wrong with organized welfare, according to its critics on both the Left and the Right, is that it fosters dependency instead of independence. But what this really means is that welfare breaks two assumed cycles of exchange: between work and its rewards and between the gift and its obligations. "The fatal weakness of federal programs," argues Mead, "is that they award their benefits essentially as entitlements, expecting next to nothing from the beneficiaries in return" (*Beyond Entitlement* 2). And what should be expected in return, of course, is *work,* something which, Mead suggests, "must be treated as a public obligation, akin to paying taxes or obeying the law" (82). As this argument suggests, the point where personal and moral obligations become public obligations is also precisely the point where the assumed narrative of individual self-development rejoins a historical or cultural narrative of collective social progress, and where, in other words, the project of forcing individuals to work is believed to be the very Work of society as a whole.

Other writers arrive at the same conclusion indirectly, arguing that government welfare simply interferes with the "natural" process of impersonal economic coercion by allowing people to survive without working for it. In his introduction to Marvin Olasky's *The Tragedy of American Compassion* (a book itself arguing, as its title suggests, that the whole history of American organized welfare has been counterproductive), Charles Murray asserts baldly that "the problems of the underclass are not caused by poverty" (Murray xiii). This brief text then proceeds via a sequence of equally blunt assertions, each of which, however, implicitly contradicts the previous one. First Murray asserts that there simply is not enough socially available funding to end poverty but then nevertheless goes on to consider a hypothetical possibility. Even "if we *could* put everyone above the poverty line with a check," he asks, "*should* we?" (xiii). Even to pose this second question reveals the spuriousness of the first one, since if providing comprehensive welfare was literally impossible, there would be no point in assessing its potential social effects. As one might put it, the very existence of Murray's discussion implicitly acknowledges that the funding of welfare *in any amount* is always in principle available, since the source of such welfare lies in a collective wealth that has no predetermined limit, and whose level is decided by political choices, not by brute necessity.

Murray's point will of course prove to be that, even if we could do so, we should not use welfare to end poverty. Murray provides two different reasons for this conclusion that are mutually incompatible. Assuming, on the one hand, that work in its social existence is bound up in a calculus of needs and exertions, Murray claims that, if a guaranteed minimum income was available, "Families that once managed to stay above the poverty line through their own labor," would begin "to take it a little easier" (xiii). Therefore, any kind of guaranteed income "will produce significant reductions in work effort" (xiv). This is what can be called the *negative* critique of welfare: the all-too-familiar idea that people require the goad of subsistence in order to keep them working hard enough. But Murray then goes on to suggest an entirely different *positive* critique, claiming that to give welfare to the urban poor is absolutely useless because "[m]ore money is not going to make competent mothers of incompetent ones, nor conscientious mothers of irresponsible ones. More money is not going to bring fathers back to the children they have sired and then abandoned. . . . A guaranteed income is not going to reduce drug abuse or alcoholism" (xiv). These familiar claims are obviously open to question on their surface, but for the moment what interests me instead is the theoretical slippage that they (almost) conceal.

Murray always assumes what I have called the double necessity of work. All social subjects must labor both to overcome scarcity and because work is a uniquely privileged sign of social and personal responsibility. Thus, Murray argues, in the familiar way, that we must never allow welfare to completely relieve poverty since people will not work unless forced to do so by material necessity. Yet he then goes on to claim that no level of material well-being will ever induce the incompetent mother, the deadbeat dad, or the drug addict to mend their ways. At one and the same time, Murray imagines humanity in quasi-utilitarian terms, as governed by the carrot and stick of the economic calculus, and also as somehow impervious to that calculus, governed and defined by an essential moral strength or weakness. To be sure, this slippage occurs precisely along the line of the shift from public to domestic modes of work and behavior; and in this Murray's argument anticipates the welfare bill of 1996, which similarly mandates both paid employment *and* parental responsibility. This observation does not, however, in any sense redeem the contradiction at the very core of the argument since—as the legislation produced under the influence of arguments like Murray's further attests—mothers and fathers, no matter how competent, responsible, and loving, will, if they have no other means to support themselves and their children, still be required to succeed in paid employment in order to qualify as a full-fledged moral subject and citizen.[4]

It is hardly surprising, however, that such contradictions should so haunt contemporary polemics against welfare since the logic at work in such arguments is always deeply paradoxical. What Martin Anderson calls the "common-sense view" that "if someone has the option of working or not working to obtain the same or virtually the same amount of income, all other things being equal, he will choose not to work" (88) is an argument that can only be made in the first place by forgetting what is otherwise also being assumed: namely, that work is also supposed to be the very site of personal self-fulfillment. It is because such a point needs to be forgotten that ideologues like Murray find themselves compelled to shift so confusingly from negative to positive critiques of welfare: claiming first that society must preserve the goad of material necessity in order to keep people on their toes and then also claiming that some people simply won't work because of an essential irresponsibility. But even the negative critique of welfare is, in its own terms, similarly founded on an invisible contradiction. In this case one argues *both* for the absolute importance of the daily battle against necessity *and* that such necessity must never be entirely overcome through guaranteed welfare. But this mean that subsistence itself must always be both present and absent, for only the threat of its absence produces its presence. Or, to phrase this fatal argument in its most absolutely paradoxical form: *in order to overcome scarcity we must never overcome scarcity.*[5]

The contemporary conservative approach to poverty, and the underlying connection of work and the gift that it instantiates, can be effectively summed up in a single sentence from Josephine Shaw Lowell, one of the leaders of the so-called scientific charity movement in the nineteenth century and a writer often cited approvingly by these contemporary writers. "No man," writes Lowell, "can receive as a *gift* what he should earn by his own *labor* without a moral deterioration" (66; emphasis added). As Lowell herself already conceded about her own book, published in 1884, "There is not, perhaps, an original thought or suggestion in it" (preface, unpaginated). In the same way, contemporary conservatives often present this argument as at once something new and innovative (a revolutionary reform of long-standing American policy) and as a kind of perennial wisdom long known by "the practitioners of effective compassion" (Olasky *Renewing* 159). In fact, it is quite obvious that contemporary welfare policy remains almost wholly determined by an ideological approach to poverty that can be traced at least as far back as the early-modern period.

To observe this continuity, however, is to reopen the vexed question, raised most famously by Max Weber and repeatedly debated by subsequent writers, of an economic and cultural rupture that takes place at the dawn of modernity, and in which both the mode of production and a range of social and religious attitudes and practices were fundamentally transformed. Such a rupture, at least as commonly described, involves in particular the ideas and practices of working and giving. On the one hand, it has often been argued that a medieval ideal of "indiscriminate charity as a spiritual good" is replaced by "a concept of charity as a duty to be carried out circumspectly, distinguishing carefully between deserving and undeserving poor" (Woodbridge 276). On the other hand, as Weber in particular suggests, a medieval vision of work as no more than a means to the end of "daily bread" was transformed into a so-called work ethic, an idealization of work as a god-given vocation or "calling," a uniquely privileged site of spiritual achievement.

Such a moment of past historical rupture would also be the analogue and antecedent of the contemporary rupture whose possibility I previously entertained via Jean-Joseph Goux's reading of George Gilder (chapter 5). It was precisely that capitalist "spirit" of thrift and industry, whose genesis Weber locates at the founding moment of modernity, from which a postmodern or postindustrial capitalism would be seen to depart. The earlier moment could then also be seen as the birth or ascendancy both of capitalism itself and of Bataille's restricted economy: that is, the economic logic of scarcity and productive self-interest that finally supersedes the archaic or medieval systems of gift exchange and puts an end to those "great and free forms of unproductive social expenditure" with which earlier cultures indulged their taste for loss and sacrifice (Bataille *Visions* 124). Correspondingly, the contemporary moment would also be seen, as the ideological bravura of Gilder and others attests, as the reappropriation by capitalism (that quintessential restricted economy) of the spirit of the gift and the never-quite-extinguished promise of the general economy.

When considering this hypothetical contemporary shift in the mise-en-scène of capitalism, however, we found it necessary to move its moment progressively farther back—far enough, in fact, to sunder its connection with any conceivable model of postmodernity. In the same way, one cannot consider the hypothetical past moment of historical rupture without encountering a range of scholarship that questions or at least complicates its defining characteristics. Even if one focuses on the unmistakable difference between medieval notions of holy poverty and the denunciations of the "sturdy beggar" that are so frequent in later homiletic texts, one finds no definitive moment of change nor even a coherent linear progress from one extreme to the other. As Bronislaw Geremek observes, "the writing of St. John Chrysostom and the imperial legislation of Justinian [fourth to sixth centuries] scrupulously distinguish between those among the poor who are capable of work and those who are not," and "Merovingian society [sixth to eighth centuries] was hostile and contemptuous in its attitude toward the poor," so that "it was not until the eleventh and twelfth centuries . . . that poverty began to be recognized as a spiritual value" (16–17). Correspondingly, as Michel Mollat concludes, "the idea of the pauper as an image of the suffering Christ remained alive" through a wide range of humanist and reformation discourse in the sixteenth and even the seventeenth centuries (299).

Indeed, whatever changes in attitudes and practice can be discerned over the course of these centuries, at least one fundamental vision of charity and poverty survives virtually unchanged from early Christianity to the present moment. In the fourth century, Saint John Chrysostom argues that "God appointed almsgiving not only for the needy to be nourished, but also for the providers to receive benefit" (Chrysostom 141–42); in the seventeenth century, popular sermonist Isaac Barrow argues that God allows economic inequality so that "some mens industry and patience might be exercised by their poverty" and "other men by their wealth should have ability of practising justice and charity" (Barrow 95–96); and in the late twentieth century, Marvin Olasky (advisor to President George W. Bush and coiner of the term "compassionate conservatism") denounces government welfare and praises private charity because of its alleged "emphasis on affiliation, bonding and . . . *suffering with*" the poor (*Tragedy* 148). Charity, apparently the very domain of generosity, the very site of the gift, is thus affirmed not despite but *because of* the circuits of exchange and mutual obligation in which it seems inevitably to be inscribed. Charity can thus be understood, using Bataille's terms, as a mutual imbrication of the restricted and general economies, in which the former is in every way privileged.

Marvin Olasky and Gertrude Himmelfarb

We can now understand how this ambiguous logic underlies the thought of contemporary conservative writers, who, in any case, always remind us of their own position within a historical tradition. Both Marvin Olasky and Gertrude Himmelfarb, in particular, use their own histories of charitable relief in England and America respectively to underwrite their polemical arguments about contemporary welfare reform. "The key to the future," writes Olasky, "is understanding the past" (*Tragedy* 5). Indeed, everything these two writers positively advocate in terms of welfare policy (America must cut benefits and force recipients to work) follows from what they claim are *negative* truths about human nature that emerge from the study of history. Thus, the projects of both writers are necessarily circular; for the people whose ideas and actions they celebrate in their historical narratives—the people who wrote about or tried to alleviate poverty in America or England—were, on their own evidence, always making precisely the very same case that Olasky and Himmelfarb reiterate today. Accordingly, this discourse can do nothing more than endlessly reaffirm the most impotent of conclusions: that, as Murray puts it, "the underclass we have always had with us" (xiv) and that, as Kristol asserts, "we are not going to abolish" poverty, injustice, or "any of those things" ("A Capitalist Conception of Justice" 294). Such writers thus turn to history in order to learn, so to speak, that there is nothing to be learned from history.

For example, Olasky discusses how leaders of the scientific charity movement in nineteenth-century America, such as Lowell and S. Humphreys Gurteen, campaigned against the practice of "outdoor" relief (i.e., cash paid to support people in their own homes, as in modern welfare) in favor of the so-called workhouse or poorhouse. Such a policy is, of course, entirely faithful to the theoretical arguments put forth by the contemporary Right. As Himmelfarb summarizes elsewhere, the workhouse "offered a means of determining who was a 'pauper' and thus eligible for relief," and as she memorably puts it, it physically separated the pauper from "the working poor, thus preventing him from 'infecting' them." And, most of all, the humiliating and draconian conditions of the workhouse ensured that all but the truly desperate "would be loath to apply for relief." Thus, the workhouse was an essential component of what Himmelfarb frankly and admiringly describes as a strategy of "separation, segregation, differentiation," and "deterrence" ("Moral Responsibility" 4).

The work of these Victorian welfare reformers had a significant effect on American social policy of the time: "By the mid-1880s, outdoor relief was out and the works of Gurteen and Lowell were in the bookstores" (Olasky *Tragedy* 80). And yet, in Olasky's own account, Americans at the turn of the century, following decades of such separation, deterrence, and putting-to-work of paupers, were still repeatedly warning, just as he continues to do today and in almost exactly the same words, against the indiscriminate charity that rewarded immorality and fostered poverty (e.g., *Tragedy* 109). Thus, Olasky describes a history in which everything is always changing and everything is always the same. In his account, people are always practicing exactly what he preaches and yet also always decrying, exactly as he still does, that there was and is too little moral discrimination in charitable relief.

Himmelfarb, similarly but even more strikingly, moves via a trilogy of scholarly books—*The Idea of Poverty* (1984), *Poverty and Compassion* (1991), and *The De-moralization of Society* (1995)—from a detailed historical account of nineteenth-century English social theory to a fierce moral critique of contemporary American society. She too, however, manages to disguise the self-canceling quality of her own argument only by staying one step ahead of herself at each moment and by mobilizing alternating narratives of decline and progress, success and failure. In the first of these books, she questions Weber's celebrated vision of a socioeconomic rupture at the time of the Reformation, insisting that "even the briefest account" of the period before the industrial revolution "suggests the inadequacy of one of the most influential theories that have shaped our thinking about this period, the theory of a Puritan ethic imbued with the values of capitalism and profoundly subversive of the society and the ethos which had traditionally given sustenance to the poor" (*Idea of Poverty* 40). And yet, in the historical account that follows, Himmelfarb maintains two absolutely contradictory theses at once. First, in opposition to Weber, she argues that the Puritan ethic, far from being a historical ally or causal factor of capitalism, has always been a genuine alternative to the capitalist values of thrift and profit. At the same time, however, she also argues that those capitalist values are themselves, in any case, always-already profoundly moral both in principle and in their social effects, and thus in need of no supplement from either religion or ethics.

When Himmelfarb discusses Adam Smith, for example, she asserts: "A close reading of *The Wealth of Nations* itself suggests that political economy as Smith understood it was part of a larger moral philosophy, a new kind of moral economy" (*Idea of Poverty* 48). Still, she also concedes that Smith's famous image of the "invisible hand" (an impersonal economic mechanism by which private acts of self-interest are harmonized into collective wealth) made it possible for many of his followers to efface the moral core of his vision and simply stress the value of self-interest. Then, about a hundred years later, as she argues in the second book of the series, Alfred Marshall's neoclassical synthesis in economics "restored [its] original moral dimension" and "'moralized' both society and political economy" (*Poverty and Compassion* 303). But Marshall evidently fails in this moralizing project, much as Smith apparently failed to convey his underlying moral intentions to his readers. Today, a little more than a century after Marshall, and even though his neoclassical model of economics still dominates the field, society has once again been, as Himmelfarb claims in the title of her next book, "de-moralized." In this volume, Himmelfarb also presents her version of the argument I have been considering, contending that the system of welfare fosters "dependency," encourages sexual immorality, and undermines the "work ethic" among the poor. "Having made the most valiant attempt to 'objectify' the problem of poverty, to see it as the product of impersonal economic and social forces," Himmelfarb now argues, "we are *discovering* that the economic and social aspects are inseparable from the moral and personal ones" (*De-moralization of Society* 242; emphasis added).[6]

But what she calls here a discovery is, if one accepts her historical narrative, really a *recovery:* of neoclassical economics in its essence, of Smith in his misunderstood moral intentions, or even of the good old-fashioned prescriptions and prohibitions of the early-modern moral economy that preceded both of these. In the last analysis, and despite her own critique, Himmelfarb's argument at last converges perfectly with the Weber thesis. The "moral economy" of early-modern Puritans did indeed cooperate with capitalism in that both shared the same moral vocation: indeed, political economy and moral economy are coterminous, and capitalism itself is, so to speak, simply morality in action. But this alleged moral economy that underlies and saturates capitalism seems, in Himmelfarb's account, to be at one and the same time always both succeeding and failing, being ignored or forgotten and yet being industriously revived. This happens one more time in Himmelfarb's own prescriptive conclusions, which themselves revive, restore, and rejoin not just the ideas of her beloved Victorian reformers but also the sermonists and pamphleteers of early-modern England; and thus, at the end of her long road of historical scholarship, Himmelfarb has herself learned precisely *nothing,* for she is still preaching exactly the same thing that they did.[7]

Tocqueville on Pauperism

It remains unquestionably true, however, that the work of Olasky, Himmelfarb, and other conservative scholars had a significant effect on the debate preceding the welfare reform bill. In the year following the bill's passage, Himmelfarb published an edition of a previously little known text, Alexis de Tocqueville's *Memoir on Pauperism* (1835), clearly intending it as a further intervention into the contemporary policy debate. This text argues, in brief, that poverty is inevitable in industrial societies and that, to relieve such poverty, private charity is always preferable, both morally and practically, to any form of organized public welfare. In her introduction, Himmelfarb approvingly summarizes how the recently passed welfare reform bill eliminates "relief as a national, legal entitlement" and moves responsibility for its administration from the federal government to the states. She also argues that we should continue this process of devolution even further, "from the states to local governments," and then further still, to "charities, churches, community groups . . . and above all, families" (Introduction 31). Such proposals remain high on the national agenda at the time of this writing, via President George W. Bush's socalled faith-based initiative, which will potentially transfer a whole range of federally administered social services to private and religious charities. One therefore must agree with Himmelfarb that, in such a context, "Tocqueville's discussion of private charity as opposed to public relief takes on added significance" (31).

Let me pick up Himmelfarb's challenge by acknowledging how Tocqueville's text, which I will consider in some detail, both epitomizes the arguments I have considered in this and the previous two chapters and, perhaps, puts pressure on my schematic summary of them. I have suggested that the conservative approach to welfare constitutes, on the most basic theoretical level, an annulment of the gift in the name of work. And yet it might be objected that Tocqueville, like contemporary conservatives, does not so much *annul* the gift as *insist* upon it by privileging the social efficacy of charity. Indeed, whereas most contemporary ideologues sooner or later fall back into the crudest sort of social Darwinism, Tocqueville himself goes so far as to renounce the very possibility of distinguishing between the "deserving" and "undeserving" poor (Tocqueville 56) and denies as unrealistic the idea that work should be required as "the price of relief" (57).

To consider Tocqueville's argument a little more closely, however, is to see how it operates not merely by what Himmelfarb calls "a series of paradoxes" (Introduction 21) but, once again, by juggling sequential contradictions. In the first half of his essay, Tocqueville presents a quasi-anthropological summary of human history, which he envisions as a teleological process moving from primitive subsistence to developed civilization. He envisions the origin of all human society in primitive bands of "wanderers and hunters" who "have very few desires" and "the means of satisfying them with the least effort" (Tocqueville 40). In this imagined moment before the onset of civilization, life was evidently lived as a pure calculus of needs and exertions. Indeed, Tocqueville observes: "I have lived among the barbarous tribes of North America; I pitied them their destiny, but they do not find it at all a cruel one. Lying amidst the smoke of his cabin, covered with coarse clothes—the work of his hands or the fruit of the hunt—the Indian looks with pity on our arts, considering the refinements of our civilization as a tiresome and shameful subjugation" (44).

This striking moment—in which we glimpse from afar Marshall Sahlins's "first affluent society," evoked vividly with this image of the Indian lying comfortably at rest from the previous "work of his hands"—indicates that this is one more argument absolutely grounded in an anthropological narrative of origins. In this case, Tocqueville suggests that the development of organized agriculture produced both private property and social class, because "individuals arose who accumulated more land than they required to feed themselves and so perpetuated property in the hands of their progeny" (41). These developments, in turn, "increase the desires and the power of man," and "to satisfy these new needs, which the cultivation of the soil cannot meet, a portion of the population leaves agricultural labor each year for industry" (45).

Thus, both capitalist economics and a progressive increase in the number of people engaging in industrial labor are claimed to be the inevitable consequence of civilization itself.

In Tocqueville's account, however, there seem to be no entrepreneurs, no capitalists, no captains of industry; rather, his rhetoric seems to suggest that the industrial worker is himself the sovereign agent of production, someone who, as Tocqueville puts it, "speculates," because he now produces solely to meet "secondary needs which a thousand causes can restrict and important events completely eliminate" (47). The progressive creation of new needs and new products at once increases the economic vulnerability of the industrial workers themselves (by subjecting them to the inevitable fluctuations of the market for industrial goods) and increases their susceptibility to the misery that comes from their own growing and potentially unmet needs. As Tocqueville puts it: "the richer a nation is, the more the number of those who appeal to public charity must multiply, since two very powerful causes tend to that result. On the one hand, among these nations, the most insecure class continuously grows. On the other hand, needs infinitely expand and diversify, and the chance of being exposed to some of them becomes more frequent each day" (50). In this account, the working class literally produces the conditions of their own subjugation and privation, almost as they are said to do in the classical Marxist account, except that in this case they are constrained to do so, not by the economic structure of capitalist production, but simply by the determinative force of civilization in general, which is here understood as an inescapable teleology.

But this dismaying vision—that an ever-increasing number of social subjects will inevitably be doomed to pauperism and misery—coexists in Tocqueville's text with a contradictory vision of incremental social progress. A few pages earlier, he had asserted:

If one looks closely at what has happened to the world since the beginning of societies, it is easy to see that equality is prevalent only at the historical poles of civilization. Savages are equal because they are equally weak and ignorant. Very civilized men can all become equal because they all have at their disposal similar means of attaining comfort and happiness. Between these two extremes is found inequality of conditions. (42–43)

But the all-important gap or transition designated by the word "between" in the final sentence seems to refer both to a movement of historical progress and to a spectrum of social distinction in the present moment. If it is taken as the former, which would seem to be Tocqueville's explicit intention, the equality achieved by "civilized men" reveals itself, not as some potential equality of *condition* that would logically oppose the inequality said to exist in the historical interim, but at most an equality of *opportunity* (in which "all" have "similar *means* of attaining comfort and happiness").

Tocqueville also leaves unanswered what should be the crucial question: how and when do the intrinsically insecure conditions of industrial laborers turn into this civilized equality? Is it particular *individuals* who make this transition at particular moments of history, or is it human society as a whole? In fact, as Tocqueville will shortly suggest, there is neither any such possible transition for *all* individuals nor any foreseeable moment of overall historical rupture. "As long as the present movement of civilization continues," he suggests, "the standard of living of the greatest number will rise," but at the same time, "we must look forward to an increase of those who will need to resort to the support of all their fellow men to obtain a small part of these benefits" (50). Civilized men thus have an *equality* which is not in fact *equal*. True enough, those who need the support of their fellow men are not said to be morally responsible for their own poverty; rather, it is simply that their condition is intrinsically "insecure." But this means that Tocqueville has been able to achieve his structural vision of poverty only at the cost of contradicting his optimistic affirmation of equality of opportunity. Those whose conditions are intrinsically less secure must surely be said to have less opportunity to better themselves; indeed, since the insecurity of the industrial class is a direct consequence of the inevitable fluctuations of the market for their products, no amount of personal exertion on their part can possibly overcome it.

All such objections, however, still only begin to indicate the multiple tensions that emerge beneath the surface of Tocqueville's elegant prose. The second half of the essay might be said to recapitulate in synchronic terms the diachronic argument of the first half. Tocqueville begins with a few words on the history of welfare in England: how, since the Elizabethan Poor Laws, a system of organized "public charity" came to replace mere "private virtue" (52–53). But the fundamental argument really begins only with the restatement, one more time, of a quasi-anthropological vision of determinative human nature:

Man . . . has a natural passion for idleness. There are, however, two incentives to work: the need to live and the desire to improve the conditions of life. Experience has proven that the majority of men can be sufficiently motivated to work only by the first of these incentives. The second is effective only with a small minority. Well, a charitable institution indiscriminately open to all those in need, or a law that gives all the poor a right to public aid, whatever the origin of their poverty, weakens or destroys the first stimulant and leaves only the second intact. (54–55)

And this means, by extension: "Any measure that establishes legal charity on a permanent basis and gives it an administrative form thereby creates an idle and lazy class, living at the expense of the industrial and working class" (58).

This, of course, is the conclusion that Himmelfarb cherishes and that is replicated in the work of the other contemporary writers I have discussed above. Let us consider this conclusion further, however, in the light of what we have otherwise learned from Tocqueville's own account. Only a small minority of people, he claims, can be motivated to work by the desire to improve the conditions of life. Thus, the majority must be forced to work, by ensuring that they are always at the mercy of scarcity, forever subject to the goad of subsistence and survival. And even as the endeavors of the former class proceed— that is, as life's conditions improve, as industrial labor gradually supersedes agricultural labor, and as the progress of civilization creates ever more needs— there will be more and more people who need some kind of economic assistance. This need brings forth a system of organized welfare, and that system, in turn, simply increases the numbers of the needy, for all the reasons previously alleged.

Tocqueville's solution for this dismal possibility is, of course, a return to private charity. In other words, the problem is that organized civilization (at least in England) always includes organized welfare, so that if we could just get rid of the latter, we could have the benefits of the former without the ever-increasing numbers of paupers. But does this mean that private charity *will* eliminate poverty, which organized welfare has been unable to do? Absolutely not. Let us be quite clear on this point: private charity is preferred precisely because it is *inefficient.* Private charity, as Tocqueville frankly argues, cannot be "relied on," because "a thousand accidents can delay or halt its operation" and because, as he memorably puts it, "one cannot be sure of finding it, and it is not aroused by every cry of pain" (69). This is the real crux of the argument, and let me phrase it with the bluntness that Tocqueville avoids. *Charity's value lies in its inability to end poverty.* What is good about charity is that, unlike organized welfare, it cannot in principle do more than *partially* relieve privation and therefore can never interfere in any serious way with the goad of subsistence.

Here again, there is a positive argument that corresponds to this negative one. Tocqueville also argues, again just as contemporary conservatives do, that private charity is preferable because of its benevolent moral effect on givers and recipients alike. In developing this argument, Tocqueville once again begins with a paradox. One would normally assume, he acknowledges, that organizing welfare as a guaranteed political right "places the one who claims it on the same level as the one who grants it" (59) and that, correspondingly, forcing poor people to rely on private charity is degrading to them. But this, claims Tocqueville, is an illusion:

The poor man, while turning to individual charity, recognizes, it is true, his condition of inferiority in relation to the rest of his fellow men, but he recognizes it secretly and temporarily. From the moment that an indigent is inscribed on the poor list of his parish, he can certainly demand relief, but what is the achievement of this right if not a notarized manifestation of misery, or weakness, or misconduct on the part of its recipient? (59)

Note, by the way, how Tocqueville here contradicts his earlier structural explanation for poverty with this passing reinsertion of "weakness" and "misconduct" as the definitive characteristics of those who seek relief.

Now, Tocqueville also concludes: "The poor man who demands alms in the name of the law is . . . in a still more humiliating position than the indigent who asks pity of his fellow men" (59–60). The rhetorical and theoretical inversion apparently performed by this conclusion is, however, incomplete. Tocqueville claims that public welfare, contrary to one's expectations, actually creates unequal relations between the givers and the recipients, but he does not make the symmetrically opposite claim about charity. Rather, he acknowledges that charity too creates unequal relations, though only "secretly and temporarily" (59). He also claims that charity establishes "valuable ties between the rich and the poor" and "involves the giver in the fate of the one whose poverty he has undertaken to alleviate" (60). Organized welfare, however, breaks the only link which could be established between "the rich and the poor"—these two groups or classes that he now refers to as "two rival nations, who have existed since the beginning of the world" (60). But if charity does create a genuine bond between giver and receiver, involving the giver in the recipient's very fate, then in what sense could the (unequal) relation between them be considered either "temporary" or "secret"? Correspondingly, the claim about welfare flatly contradicts the essay's opening section, which portrays the birth of class as a fundamental historical rupture. At the *beginning* of the world, Tocqueville previously had argued, people were united by their common needs and by their common struggles to fulfill them. Even after the birth of agriculture, there was evidently at least a brief historical moment in which "everyone . . . reaps enough to feed himself and his children from the field which happens to fall into his hands" (40). Here again, however, even this flagrant contradiction is finally outweighed by an even larger and more insidious one. This link that charity establishes between rich and poor—the only such link, he specifies, that could *ever* be established between these "rival nations"—what else could it possibly be but a relation of superiority and subordination?

To be sure, charity is allegedly given "in the name of He who regards all men from the same point of view and who subjects rich and poor to equal laws" (Tocqueville 60). This passing transcendental moment must be emphasized because, as we will see again in other contexts, the reference to some divine point of infinite plenitude is often employed to anchor the otherwise self-defeating economies of the Work and the gift. But even the divine Subject enforces no more than an equality of opportunity (governing rich and poor by "equal laws"), and, indeed, as the very naming of these classes *in* his name attests (and as earlier Christian writers frankly affirm), God literally creates and preserves poverty on earth precisely so there might be an opportunity for charity. The spiritual equality that one might claim to exist between rich and poor is, in the most literal sense, absolutely contingent upon their economic and material inequality on earth.

Consider, finally, how in the last few pages of the essay Tocqueville transcribes a passage from his diary written during a trip to England in which he stayed with "a great proprietor" who was also a justice of the peace and attended a session of court in which suits involving the Poor Law were settled. After hearing various cases and commenting on them, his host complains that welfare (or what he calls "public charity") has "lost all of its afflicting and humiliating character in the people's eyes" (65). Wishing to share, Tocqueville says, the "truth and simplicity" (68) of such observations with his reader, Tocqueville inadvertently reveals how his earlier point was entirely specious. He attacks public welfare not because it is degrading but because it is not degrading enough; and he praises charity not because it binds people together but because it can in principle do so only in terms of permanent, known, established, and expected relations of subordination. This, we recall, is precisely why Himmelfarb praises the workhouse: because its degrading conditions deterred most poor people from even asking for relief and because it shamed and stigmatized those who did ask.

The "New Philanthropy"

I have been suggesting that these past and present attempts to celebrate mere charity, mere generous giving, as the salvation of society really conceal a refusal or prohibition of the gift. Indeed, what always remains absolutely unthinkable in the discourse of charity is to relieve poverty all the way down, to expend wealth and privilege without return or reserve. In the literal practice of contemporary charity—and especially in the large-scale and much-publicized forms of giving that have been dubbed "the new philanthropy"—one sees this conclusion realized with almost parodic extremity. In the 1990s, as one reporter summarizes,

the tech boom made more people richer faster and at a younger age than at any time in history. And these new millionaires, many of whom are under 40, aren't waiting to dole out their fortunes. True to their work-as-life code, they are, as a group, highly engaged with their causes, which they research meticulously, often with the help of professional charity consultants. And . . . these new-economy donors are consumed with accountability and results. (Streisand 40)

Article after article in the 1990s and beyond make this same point: that "today's tech millionaires and billionaires are applying to philanthropy the lessons they have learned as entrepreneurs" (Greenfield 50) and that, as *Time* magazine declared on its cover on July 24, 2000, these new philanthropists "want results." In other words, the new philanthropy quite literally transforms the gift into a Work by managing and evaluating charitable practices like any other investment. President Bill Clinton, during the holiday season at the end of 2000, released a report boasting of a "record increase in charitable giving" and announced at the same time a new public-private partnership to encourage more of it. As he put it, "this is just a small investment with a potentially [large] dividend," one that will "help younger people . . . discover the rewards of generosity."[8] His words clearly indicate the logic at work in this manner of thought, in which the literal "dividend" produced in the material world by the charitable investment is understood as the precise correlate of the psychic or spiritual reward simultaneously enjoyed by the generous giver. Much as George Gilder understands capitalist investment as a kind of general economy of giving and sacrificing, so in this case, the act and idea of the charitable gift are doubly reinscribed within a restricted economy of investment and return. Such an attitude also finds its perverse realization in the fact that, as Janet

Poppendieck argues, the business of shelters, soup kitchens, and other emergency services provided to the destitute by private charities has now been institutionalized to such a degree as to encourage an indifference to poverty and homelessness on the part of policymakers.

The so-called new philanthropy thus operates by means of an impossible and ruinous combination of giving *and* working. In its practice, it displaces the possibility of more organized and effective means of comforting the afflicted; and in its implicit theory, it refuses to follow the gift to its limits by insisting that even charity be judged by its (psychic and material) returns. The extent to which working and giving are now disastrously entwined in the theory and practice of charity was acutely in evidence following the terrorist attacks on the World Trade Center in New York on September 11, 2001. These events provoked an unprecedented outpouring of charitable giving for the victims and their families; and yet that very generosity, as well as the impressive sums it produced, became quickly controversial. In particular, the Red Cross, one of the most respected charities in the world, figured in a scandal that produced a congressional investigation and eventually resulted in the firing of its director, Bernadine Healy. At issue was the Red Cross's decision to hold in reserve some of the nearly $600 million donated to their Liberty Disaster Fund in the weeks following September 11 in order to ensure their readiness for potential future terrorist attacks. Following this decision, both the families of the victims and lawmakers in New York and Washington attacked the organization's leaders in the strongest possible terms, accusing them "of cynically using the Sept. 11 tragedies to address long-term fund-raising goals and of siphoning tens of millions of dollars from widows and children" (Henriques and Barstow). Two months later, on November 14, the Red Cross reversed itself, and in a televised news conference promised to spend the entire fund for the exclusive benefit of the World Trade Center victims (see Sontage 52).

This incident forces us to confront a double conclusion. Was it not excessive, by any conceivable measure, to spend the huge sums collected in the wake of September 11 entirely on the families of the victims, many of whom were already affluent? And, by the same token, was it not merely prudent and responsible for the Red Cross to hold some of its resources in reserve for the inevitable future disaster, which will, of course, appear as desperate in its moment as this one did? And yet is it not equally clear from this whole incident that the philanthropic demand for "results" simply cannot extinguish a demand for the absolute gift, for a generosity so excessive that it undoes all calculation? Clearly, some nonutilitarian principle presents itself in these events:

some need to confront disastrous loss with an expenditure without reserve, a gift that refuses economy itself.

Let me recall once more the structure of displacement that I considered in chapter 5—in which the restricted economy of investment and return seems to reassert itself amid attempts to think or represent its antithesis, and in which capitalism itself, having conquered the world with its "restricted" instrumentality, now presents itself as a kind of general economy of risk and expenditure. The present example reverses that structure, and yet leaves us at a still more ruinous impasse. A moment of sublime horror and need put so much generosity in play that even the routine charity on which we allow ourselves to depend was put in jeopardy: just three months after the World Trade Center attacks, the *New York Times* was reporting that "food pantries find charity dwindling as need grows" (Feuer D1). Yet we are no nearer to that ultimate gift which also annuls and undoes itself but only, this time, as something other than mere generosity: as that incalculable excess that we sometimes dare to call justice.

THEOLOGIES OF CULTURE:
THE WORK AS GIFT

The Gift of Art

The varied debates I have considered so far, in which a quasi-anthropological concept of culture figures so frequently, at another level converge with rather different debates about culture in its humanist sense. The central terms and issues of this so-called culture war—high versus low culture, universal versus relative value, Eurocentrism versus multiculturalism, and so forth—have been considered and reconsidered in more than sufficient detail elsewhere and do not require a comprehensive summary here. It suffices to note briefly the general effort on the part of conservative thinkers to defend the idea of the Work against what are alleged to be the leveling or relativistic tendencies of contemporary literary theory. I invoke this debate in order to suggest that it is one more site where an economy of giving and working reveals itself, an economy that, once again, can be traced back through a labyrinth of discourse in which these two ideas have long maintained their obscure connection.

To that end, let me both begin a new line of inquiry and indirectly suggest its connection to the previous one by briefly considering remarks made by Gertrude Himmelfarb at a 1991 conference at Boston University and subsequently published. Himmelfarb's paper on this occasion follows and responds to a paper by Cleanth Brooks, who mounts what is now a familiar defense of "traditional" formalist modes of literary analysis and interpretation. "The newest critics," Brooks argues bluntly, "having rejected literary merit as the basis for any canon, frankly accept political concerns as the warrant for selecting our great books" (Brooks et al. 354). This, he claims, is a "ruinous mistake," a betrayal of "great literature" (359) and of "Matthew Arnold's . . . 'best that has been thought and written'" (353). In her ensuing remarks, Himmelfarb first reminisces about a formative moment in her own education when she was taught *Moby Dick* by being asked to prepare "a glossary of nautical terms" (361). Even though she and her classmates "knew at the time that this was not the right way to approach this book," nevertheless, "my first encounter with *Moby Dick* . . . was a salutary experience. For I, and my schoolmates, knew at that time that Melville was a great writer and *Moby Dick* a great book, even if we did not know why" (Brooks et al. 363–64).

In other words, Himmelfarb's youthful encounter with what one is tempted to call the Great White Book taught her that literary education as a whole should transmit, more than anything else, a certain "greatness." It is not really even a matter, say, of privileging (aesthetic) form over ("political") content. It is, rather, a question of affirming, bringing forth, or paying tribute to something that *exceeds* the Work, something that allows us to move, as Himmelfarb acknowledges, from "particular great books" to "the idea of great books" (361). As she goes on to explain: "In retrospect I can appreciate how important it was that the first books I knew to be great were the Bible and commentaries on the Bible, which were indubitably great because they derived from the divine author, god Himself. . . . While I have since lost my faith in that divine authorship, I have retained a faith, so to speak, in His creation, a reverence for the ancient texts that are deserving of the greatest respect" (363).

This passage could not betray more clearly the metaphysical or theological framework within which Himmelfarb's argument operates. At the same time, a certain symbolic economy begins to reveal itself here via a sequence of related terms which denote, by turns or at once, the Work and the subject's approach to the Work. As imagined here, the "important" literary Work engenders in the reading subject a particular response that is said to be all-important. But this response is not a knowledge of the Work in its particulars or even a knowledge of the Work's own particular "greatness"; it is, rather, a kind of second-order knowledge: an appreciation of the "importance" of knowing the Work *in* its greatness. Having achieved such appreciation, one can then reaffirm that "great" Works in general "deserve" the great "reverence" and "respect" with which they are approached. Further, the transcendent Author's formerly presumed presence in the Work continues to be, even in its own absence, the very sign of the Work's greatness; and the knowing or appreciating subject thus holds faith in reserve despite her manifest loss of faith.

I am suggesting, in other words, that such rhetoric implicitly evokes Bataille's opposition between restricted and general economies, terms that here, however, diverge from the theoretical valence they have in Bataille's own texts to delineate the imagined encounter of a self-present but finite subject with the alleged self-presence and infinite plenitude of the Work. As Himmelfarb makes clear elsewhere in her paper, the absent place of the divine is now occupied by what she calls "collective opinion" and "the judgment of posterity" (Brooks et al. 364). The latter she describes in the revealing words of Edmund Burke, from a passage defending the value of "received opinion" as "an essential adjunct to reason": "We are afraid to put men to live and trade each on his own private stock of reason; because we suspect that this stock in each man is small, and that the individuals would do better to avail themselves of the general bank and capital of nations, and of ages" (quoted in Brooks et al. 364). Here again, the reasoning subject is envisioned as governed by its own scarcity and constituted by its productive investment of the "general" stock of reason. There is a certain slippage in Himmelfarb's argument as a whole, which seems to affirm both a singular and quasi-divine authority believed to be manifest in the literary text itself and a collective literary value determined by the accumulated judgment of the ages. In either case, however, she envisions an encounter of finite ("restricted") being with some absolute plenitude or ("general") excess embodied in, or at least mediated by, the Work.

The logic I am sketching here is a particularly common one in critical discourses addressing Shakespeare, who obviously serves, across a wide range of popular and learned discourses, as the very figure of high culture. In this case, and although the defense of traditional literary value typically portrays itself today as a beleaguered minority position, one must concede that this vision of a "universal" Shakespeare survives despite all the many salutary efforts to place him within his own period and document the historical construction of his cultural status. Indeed, such projects themselves are often merely viewed as "a testimony to Shakespeare's intrinsic strength" (Kirsch 421). Correspondingly, any particular theoretical approach to Shakespeare, such as Marxism, feminism, or the like, may be seen as merely striving "to appropriate Shakespeare for its own ideology" and thus subordinating him "to the imperialism and self-advancement of the particular group" (Vickers x–xii). In such rhetoric, any particular approach to Shakespeare occupies the place of the restricted economy and, indeed, exemplifies the self-interest and calculation, the *economism,* that Weber famously identifies as the organizing "spirit" of capitalism itself. This criticism suggests, in other words, that those whom Cleanth Brooks wittily calls the "newest critics" strive to make Shakespeare their own property and exploit Shakespeare in the expectation of "self advancement." Correspondingly, Shakespeare himself becomes the site of a kind of general economy of abundance, infinite variety, and a surplus of value that overflows any attempt to harness or contain it.

Harold Bloom exemplifies precisely this strategy in *Shakespeare: The Invention of the Human* (1998), a lengthy paean to the Bard as a transcendent source of universal value.[1] Here, Bloom argues, on the one hand, that after every specific interpretation of Shakespeare, "there is always a residuum, an excess that is left over," and, on the other hand, that those he calls the "ideologues" of the contemporary Academy "themselves are caricatures of Shakespearean energies" (718, 12). Or, as he puts it even more succinctly in a subsequent book, "Shakespeare speaks to as much of you as you can bring to him" and yet also "reads you more fully than you can read him" (*How to Read* 28). The relation of reader to Work is here understood as an asymmetrical circuit of exchange in which the "restricted" individual subject confronts a transcendent plenitude to which it will never quite measure up.

The logic at work here finally transcends any particular political or theoretical position within the contemporary culture wars. In *The Gift* (1983), a book frequently cited even by the kind of critics whom Himmelfarb and Bloom might well consider mere ideologues and relativists, Lewis Hyde brings an elaborate anthropological and theological apparatus to bear on these difficult questions of literary value. As Hyde observes in this book's opening pages, both ordinary language and a long-standing historical tradition of thought tend to envision the work of art in terms of gifts and giving. "A gift is a thing we do not get by our own efforts," Hyde argues; it is something that is "bestowed upon us." Therefore, he concludes, "we rightly speak" of artistic talent, intuition, or inspiration as "a gift," for "as the artist works, some portion of his creation is bestowed upon him" (xii). Similarly, he asks us to "extend this way of speaking . . . to the work after it has left its maker's hands," for the work of art "is received by us as a gift is received" (xii). Hyde concedes that works of art nearly always also function as commodities, but this means merely that they "exist simultaneously in two 'economies,' a market economy and a gift economy. Only one of these is essential, however: a work of art can survive without the market, but where there is no gift there is no art" (xi).

This argument is also explicitly grounded in what Hyde calls "the work that has been done in anthropology on gifts as a kind of property and gift exchange as a kind of commerce" (xiv). Indeed, it is quite precisely the hypothesis of an archaic gift economy that allows Hyde to move so freely from the anthropological to the aesthetic sense of culture. Because gift exchange precedes the literal market and yet, as Mauss argues, is itself simply a more "generous" or "noble" form of market exchange, then the evident fact that works of art today figure as particularly valuable commodities merely confirms art's primal or fundamental status as a gift. These anthropological gestures cannot conceal, however, what the language I have cited also reveals so clearly: that this whole way of conceptualizing the Work as gift is ultimately theological. Art is "bestowed" upon us from beyond, Hyde says, the product of an "inspiration" that is almost literally an inflowing of a divine *spiritus*—what he also calls (citing D. H. Lawrence) a "wind that blows through me" (xii).

It is at this conjunction of materialism and spiritualism that Hyde's vision takes the shape of a mysterious unity of the Work and the gift. He celebrates the "labor" that takes place when "our gifts rise from pools we cannot fathom" (20), "the inner gift that we accept as the object of our labor," and, finally, "the outer gift that has become a vehicle of culture" (xvii). The paradoxical figure that underlies Hyde's thought is thus at once theological and anthropological. Work is understood as the employment of gifts that come both from within and from without, gifts that serve at once as the *source* and the *reward* of the work that produces and expresses them. By extension, that ultimate social gift called art or culture is at once the vital source of the subject's self-development and the manifestation of the subject's "creative spirit" (xvii): in other words, a sign both of the subject's potential plenitude *and* of its perpetual incompletion.

On the "Work Ethic"

To consider more closely the theological structure underlying this figure of culture-as-gift will require me to return, one more time, to that alleged moment of economic and discursive rupture at the dawn of modernity most famously described in the Weber thesis. As I suggested in the previous chapter, this hypothetical early-modern birth of a "spirit" of capitalism transforms in particular the ideas of working and giving. With regard to the gift, such transformation itself has two contradictory movements. On the one hand, a medieval ideal of charity and holy poverty is superseded by a demand for discrimination in charitable giving and a moral division between "deserving" and "undeserving" poor. On the other hand, Reformation theology goes in the opposite direction by opposing the Catholic doctrine of justification by "works" with a new doctrine of justification by God's "free gift" of grace. In the first case, a kind of general economy comes under the sway of a restricted economy of calculation and investment; and the gift, no longer an end in itself, is reimagined as no more than a deliberate means to a calculable end. In the second case, by contrast, a kind of spiritual economism, a belief that salvation is the reward of one's works, encounters an attempt to think of divinity as a general plenitude whose gifts exceed all calculation.

It is now possible to extend the same line of thought to the idea of the Work by recalling once again how the single most celebrated doctrine of the early-modern moral economy is its so-called work ethic. This term remains even to-day the rubric for a whole range of personal and social significance that, at least according to Weber, was first invested in the idea of work at the historic moment that witnessed both the ascendancy of capitalist production and the rise of Protestantism. As Weber observes, in both classical and medieval thought, labor is considered to be "only necessary *naturali ratione* for the maintenance of individual and community," so that "where this end is achieved, the precept ceases to have any meaning" (Weber 158; see also Tilgher 30, 41). By contrast, early-modern homiletic writers seem to invest the idea of work with a new level of intrinsic meaning, seeing it as the quintessen-tial human vocation or "calling" and as "in itself the end of life, ordained as such by God" (Weber 158). The historical trajectory of the idea of work re-verses that of the gift. In this case, an earlier vision, in which work is no more than an instrumentality, a means to the end of "daily bread," is superseded by a new religious and social vision of work as the very vehicle of spiritual and personal fulfillment. And yet this new vision of work also coincides with the ascendancy of wage labor as the standard model of economic organization and with a pervasive new instrumentalization of material production. In other words, precisely when Western culture was beginning to develop the striking "division of labor" that Adam Smith celebrates in the opening pages of the *Wealth of Nations,* and even as industrial labor was increasingly being sub-jected to the structures of routine and calculation, a certain mode of homiletic discourse was, by contrast, imagining labor not as a rational means to a calcu-lable end but rather as an absolute end in itself.

Such symmetries once again raise suspicions that what is at issue is not some moment of positive historical rupture but simply a kind of refolding or rearrangement of a discursive structure. Indeed, Weber's is hardly the only such attempt to locate a fundamental rupture somewhere in the history of work: the birth of work in some allegedly proper sense has also been placed (by anthropologists such as Marshall Sahlins) at the period of transition from primitive nomadism to agriculture or (by Deleuze and Guattari) at that elusive moment of the "semiotization of activity by writing" (*Thousand Plateaus* 401).

One can even suspect that these alleged shifts in the social existence and meaning of work remain conditioned, however indirectly, by an ancient discursive opposition descending from the Judeo-Christian scriptures. In Genesis, divine creation is described as a work or labor, from which God himself requires "rest," and humanity is first placed in the Garden of Eden with the command to "till it and care for it." Then, Adam and Eve's subsequent punishment for eating the fruit of the tree of knowledge is a changed relationship to work in two senses: the woman is condemned to have pain in the labor of childbirth and both are condemned to grow their food by "the sweat of their brows." The biblical account thus portrays work in two radically incompatible ways, seeing it both, as Jaroslav Pelikan summarizes, as "a commandment, indeed an imitation of the very activity of God," and also as "a curse, a punishment from the same God" (10). Further, as has also been frequently noticed, the Ten Commandments do not restate the curse of work but rather require a weekly rest from labor.

The construction of a work ethic in early-modern Europe might thus be understood as little more than a shift in emphasis from "curse to calling" (Ciulla 5). And in any case, the underlying structure of this opposition always leaves available a kind of double bind in which humanity is constrained to labor both by the forever-unfinished coercion of scarcity *and* by some indefinable transcendent value invested in the act of labor and endlessly re-created in the laboring subject. The various theoretical maneuvers performed by early-modern writers in the face of this double bind are also illuminating. Luther suggests, for example, that if "Adam had remained in the state of innocence, he would have tilled the earth . . . not only without inconvenience but, as it were, in play and with the greatest delight." It is only after the Fall, therefore, that "work, which in the state of innocence would have been play and joy, is a punishment" (Luther 1:102–3). One might also reference here Milton's famous refusal to accept that there was literally no work in Eden, imagining rather that Adam and Eve

> labour still to dress
> This garden, still to tend Plant, Herb and Flour,
> Our pleasant task enjoyn'd. (*Paradise Lost* 9:205–8)

The doctrine of the calling constrains the Protestant reformers of the early-modern period to argue that even though work is no longer "pleasant," even though labor is no longer merely "play and joy," we must still find "in the humble tasks of daily duty an authentic vocation from God" (Pelikan 18). The fulfillment of the painful curse of labor is somehow to be understood as also an end in itself, and its own reward.

These observations rejoin my opening remarks on the subject of culture via another scriptural text which also addresses this strange double necessity of work: the parable of the talents. This brief text, in its long history of warring interpretations, not only figures in the historical transition from moral to political economy but also continues to serve, in some elusive way, as a kind of immense retrospective justification of the division of labor itself. The parable appears both in the Gospel of Saint Matthew and, in slightly different form, in the Gospel of Saint Luke. In it, Jesus compares the kingdom of heaven to a master who travels to a far country, leaving with each of his three servants five, two, or one "talents" respectively, and then demands an accounting on his return. The first and second servants double their talents by "trading" with them, but the third hides his talent so as, he later claims, to be able to return it safely. To this third servant, the master replies: "Thou evil servant, & slothful . . . Thou oughtest therefore to have put my money to the exchangers, and then at my coming should I have received mine own with vantage" (Matthew 25:26–27, cited from the Geneva Bible of 1560).

In the patristic period, the divine gift of "talents" was usually understood specifically as referring to the revelation of the divine Word to apostles and ministers, who are then obliged to transmit and communicate it. In the third century, for example, Origen thinks of the parable of the talents while commenting on a passage in Exodus in which the Israelites are commanded to "take from yourselves an offering for the Lord" (Exodus 35:4–10). "I am chagrined to attempt an explanation of this," says Origen at first, but then acknowledges that

since you earnestly expect that something be discussed from these words which have been read, and my Lord commanded me saying, "You should have given my money to the bank and at my coming I should have exacted it with interest," I shall ask him that he might see fit to make my word his money, that I might not lend my money, nor my gold to you, but his, that I might speak to you with his word and his "mind" and bring these things to the bank of your hearing. You who receive the Lord's money have already seen how you should prepare its interest for the Lord when he comes. (Origen 376)

In what would become an entirely conventional rhetorical strategy, Origen positions his own interpretation of the divine Word as itself an instance of the general interpretive "return" which both the text in question and the parable of the talents are understood to enjoin. Similarly, in the fourth century, Saint John Chrysostom understands the parable to be enjoining: "He that hath a gift of word and teaching to profit thereby, and useth it not, will lose the gift also; but he that giveth diligence, will gain to himself the gift in more abundance" (Chrysostom 472).

In the early-modern period, this meaning was gradually generalized, so that the talents come to refer to any of the personal "gifts and graces" entrusted to an individual by God, and especially to an individual's vocation, or "calling." However, interpreters of the parable also felt called upon to defend the text against its own manifest content, for in this period some writers apparently interpreted this passage, not unreasonably, as expressing a divine sanction for the general idea of usurious profit, the receiving of a financial "vantage" upon one's "own." For example, George Downame in his *Lectures on the XV Psalme* (1604)—in which, the author boasts, *the question of Usurie is plainely and fully decided*—cites what seems to be a defense of usury then circulating in manuscript:

But (say they again,) *What if our Savior Christ be so far from condemning usury, that he approveth it: for when as he condemneth that slothful servant because he had not occupied his talent, he saith, that he should have put forth his money to the bankers, that at his coming he might receive his own with usury, Mat. 25.27. Where (say they) our Savior speaketh of usury as of a lawful gain: and withal signifieth, that it is better for a man, who hath no other lawful trade to gain by, to put forth his money to usury, than to have it idle by him.* (284)[2]

The standard way to refute this literal interpretation of the passage was to insist on a strictly figural interpretation. Unlike the master in the parable, Jesus is not referring to money at all but to what Downame calls "spiritual gifts and graces," and the parable thus enjoins, not financial usury, but the profitable employment of one's personal skills, characteristics, and abilities.

But this division between literal and figural readings seems, in the various articulations of this conventional argument, to have a sort of inevitable discursive effect. Here, for further example, is how the popular Puritan sermonist Henry Smith phrases his version of this conventional point:

He which used his Talent, doubled it; and he which hid his Talent, lost it: even so to every man God hath given some gift, of judgment, of tongues, or interpretation, or counsel, to employ and do good; and he which useth that gift which God hath given him, to the profit of others, and Gods glory, shall receive more gifts of God, as the servant which used two Talents, received two more: but he which useth it not, but abuseth it, as many doe, that gift which he hath, shall be taken from him, as the odd Talent was from the servant which had but one: showing, that one gift is too much for the wicked, and therefore it shall not stay with him. One would think it should be said, Whosoever hath not, to him shall bee given: and whosoever hath, from him shall bee taken: for God bideth us give to them which want. But this is contrary: for he taketh from them which want, and giveth to them which have. It is said, that our thoughts are not like Gods thoughts: and so our gifts are not like Gods gifts: for he giveth spiritual things, and we give temporal things. Temporal things are to be given to them which have not, but spiritual things to them which have. (*Sermons* 321–22)

The opposition between the literal and the figural, seen as essential to the proper interpretation of the parable, seems then to carry this writer by its own rhetorical momentum toward an analogous opposition between the temporal and the spiritual. This shift, however, slightly alters the logical terms of the argument. With the original opposition, the literal reading (God permits or even enjoins the putting out of money for "vantage") must be *rejected* in favor of the proper figural reading (God requires the profitable employment of personal "gifts" and "graces"). With the new opposition, conversely, the temporal simply *accompanies* the spiritual, as a distinct mode of practice. This new experiential division is necessary not only to explain the apparent injustice of the parable's conclusion, which then really refers to how personal gifts should be used to produce spiritual profit, but also to eliminate any possible interpretation that might question the idea of *charity:* the giving of "temporal things . . . to them which have not."

The earlier figure, in which the Word of God is a gift that must be repaid in kind, survives alongside the more general understanding of the "talents" as any kind of human skill or capacity. Thus, early-modern writers also often suggest that the work of preachers and moralists themselves was the very paradigm of this profitable employment of spiritual gifts, which Smith envisions as "of judgment, of tongues, or interpretation, or counsel." In 1536, an ordinance for the Paris Faculty of Theology asserts that "the knowledge acquired by the doctors in the Faculty is a gratuitous gift for the edification of the Church and ought not to be hidden away" (quoted in Davis 47). An anonymous English writer from the 1580s suggests that the talents refer to "such gifts" as can benefit other people "either in science or knowledge" and stipulates that "those which are learned" must not "hide the gift of learning (which might profit), the which not being uttered profiteth nothing" (*Ruinate Fall of the Pope Usury* A5r–v). One of the emblems in Geffrey Whitney's well-known compilation (1586) depicts two scholars reading and enjoins:

We may not haste, our talent to bestow,
Nor hide it up, whereby no good shall grow. (177)

In producing the moral economy, then, these writers were practicing what they preached; and the act of reading this discourse is, correspondingly, the locus of the "profit" that justifies its production. Both in the Middle Ages and in the early-modern period, it was also commonly assumed that, to cite Natalie Zemon Davis's summary, "[k]nowledge is a gift of God, and cannot be sold" (44). Medieval canon law prohibited, at least in theory, the sale of scribal manuscripts or the taking of fees by professors (44), and in the Renaissance, "printed books operated under the sign both of sale and gift," for they always bore a dedication which inserted the book "into a gift relation" (Davis 46). Even today a book is hypothetically offered, presented, or "dedicated" to someone, and we continue to assume that a book's content, considered as an intellectual or aesthetic value, is irreducible to its price as a physical object.[3] A general association of knowledge and gift also survives, of course, in the colloquial use of words such "gifted" or "talented."

In any case, what happens in this discourse is evidently a kind of splitting, an assumption of two distinct modes of social practice: one subjective, concerned with a work of personal self-development; the other objective, concerned with work as a material obligation in the "temporal" sphere. Thus, in the Geneva Bible, the version of the parable of the talents in Luke is explained as teaching: "They that suppresse the gifts of God, and live in idlenesse, are without all excuse" (note on Luke 19:22); while of the version in Matthew, it is claimed: "This similitude teacheth how we ought to continue in the knowledge of God, and doe good with those graces that God hath given us" (note on Matthew 25:14). Thus, this discourse mandates above all that personal talents must be developed and employed; indeed, human beings are typically *permitted* what is often called a "moderate" profit in the temporal sphere but are *obligated* to perform a work understood as a development of a gift previously given, a work whose supreme example would be a kind of spiritual self-development. As Milton writes, "God even to a strictnesse requires the improvement of . . . his entrusted gifts" (*Complete Prose* 1:801).[4] And these divine gifts of knowledge and "talent" must be developed and employed in a manner entirely other than, and yet precisely analogous to, financial profit.

The idea of work is thus doubly linked to the idea of the gift: first, because work is the necessary means by which divine gifts are developed and employed; second, because one's vocation in this specific sense is also conceptually linked to charity as an analogous form of what is sometimes called "spiritual usury." Or, to put it another way, the *injunction* to labor (the "work ethic") that lies at the core of the early-modern moral economy is inextricable from the same discourse's *prohibition* of other practices. Historically speaking, in fact, the most striking thing about this discourse is that the practices it most vehemently prohibits are the very constitutive elements of the so-called political economy that emerges after Adam Smith and still dominates both public policy and the academic discipline of economics. The obvious example is usury itself, which, even as the publication of anti-usury tracts accelerates around the turn of the seventeenth century, was already becoming widespread and more or less socially acceptable. The other practices commonly denounced in the moral economy include "regrating," "forestalling," and "engrossing" the market, which all involve buying commodities that one has not produced in order to resell them at a profit—and which are today no longer even recognizably distinct from what we would call simply "business" or "commerce."[5] To buy cheap in order to sell dear, or to buy "here" in order to sell "there," is, in the terms of the moral economy, to conjure up an illegitimate profit in excess of the intrinsic value of the commodity and to intervene illegitimately in a commodity chain that is envisioned as directly linking the farmer and the consumer (see Thompson "Moral Economy" 193–94).

But even from *within* this archaic economic logic, how might one define or label the *general* offense of which the despised "middlemen" of exchange are guilty? One might be tempted to call it "investment": that is, the acquisition of "stock" intended solely for exchange. But this word, although beginning to be used in official documents of the East India Company around the turn of the seventeenth century, had not yet gone into general circulation—for example, Shakespeare never uses this word in its financial sense (see *Oxford English Dictionary*, s.v. "invest," 9; "investment," 5). The word "venture" also suggests itself, since in the early-modern period this word could refer, as it still does, to the investment of mercantile capital for profit. But this word could not in principle be applied categorically to the improper mode of value creation because, as many texts make clear, it refers precisely to that *risk* which allegedly makes "honest" trade the moral equivalent of labor. And if "usury" itself could sometimes serve as a virtual euphemism for economic immorality in general (see, e.g., Vaughan P4v–P5r), its root meaning as simply "the process of use" allows the word, as several commentators point out, to refer equally to "spiritual usury"—that is, the multiplication of God's gifts through prayer, meditation, or even labor itself, the very thing which the moral economy explicitly commands.[6] Thus, just as economic terms such as "forestalling," "regrating," and even "usury" itself have more or less passed out of general usage today, so early-modern English did not quite have a word for the mode or category of social practice whose prohibition was a central project of the moral economy. Precisely because the discourse is willing to approve, and even celebrate, "intercourse of merchandise," "bargaining," and "trading betwixt man and man" (T. Wilson 249)—activities that, as some contemporaries recognized, were strikingly similar to those it prohibits—its prohibitive force falls, instead, on an elusive category of action that might be considered the logical inverse of the gift: that is, an expropriation of a value produced by someone else.

In this, I suggest, these writers were groping somewhat awkwardly toward a related but different moral opposition, this one between what Marx would later define as two forms of appropriation: labor itself as "an appropriation of what exists in nature for the requirements of man" and a capitalist production founded on "the appropriation of surplus labor by capital" (*Capital* 289, 326; see also Balibar in Althusser and Balibar 213–16). Thus, the moral economy makes a fundamental distinction between the intimate personal propriety of human labor and some nameless other process based on investment and expropriation, *mandating* the first and *prohibiting* the second. This means, however, that the moral economy's attempt to control the exploitative excesses of usury and commercial fraud also turns itself inside out: that is, this discourse can turn against the second mode of appropriation (in which one person lives on other people's labor) only by mandating the first mode (everyone must labor). Thus, for example, the moral economy paradoxically tends to conflate the usurer and the beggar and to define idleness itself as *theft*.[7] George Downame (1604) refers to usurers as "drones" who are "given to idlenesse" and who "live of the sweat, yea blood of other men" (258); while John Dod and Robert Clever (1630) denounce the so-called sturdy beggar in almost exactly the same terms: "An idle person is a thief. He that doeth nothing, hath right to nothing, he hath no bread of his own to eat. He putteth stolen meat into his mouth every bit he eats. He cannot say, Lord give me this day my daily bread, for it is none of his" (305–6). Therefore, even as the moral economy frankly acknowledges the profit that labor potentially creates—that is, placing it under the Law of Value—it necessarily also places all potential laborers under the Law of Command.

Implicit within the structure of thought we have followed are therefore two different social subjects: the one perpetually needy and therefore forever subject to necessity; the other a subject for whom even the very realm of freedom (i.e., personal or spiritual self-development) must also be confronted as an obligation. It is here that the dilemma of *a work that is not work* finally rejoins the dilemma of *a gift that is not a gift.* The divine "talents" given "freely" by the divine are absolutely impossible to reciprocate and yet, precisely as such, function in the individual subject as no more than an implacable injunction to produce.

This vexed paradox reveals itself perhaps even more clearly in another well-known example of early-modern discourse. In this case one must recall early-modern Protestantism's rejection of the Catholic doctrine of salvation by "works" in favor of a new doctrine of salvation by God's "free gift" of grace. This famous theological innovation seems to reverse the economic shift more commonly ascribed to the period, reaffirming salvation, and even divinity itself, as a kind of "general" plenitude outside every conceivable economy of exchange. Reformation discourse as a whole might even be described as a kind of obsessive attempt to imagine the absolute Gift, which, however, absolutely fails in every moment of its own expression. The fundamental idea, of course, is that God's grace can never be earned or deserved by a human subject. If we receive grace, it is not a reward for our deeds; rather, as William Tyndale describes it in a celebrated passage, our good deeds merely indicate or express a grace already given: "I do good freely for so is my nature as a good tree bringeth forth good fruit and an evil tree evil fruit. . . . Whatsoever good thing is in us that is given us freely without our deserving or merits" (Tyndale C5r–C6r).[8]

In this model, we receive as a gift a kind of second "nature," which becomes our own, and then express that nature in the form of good deeds, which, most typically, are themselves understood to take the form of gifts. As Henrie Smith puts it, writing half a century after Tyndale and echoing the same scriptural image: "the kingdom of heaven belongs unto those that harboreth strangers, cloatheth the naked, feedeth the hungry, comfort the sick, and doth perform such charitable acts of compassion: yet not as the papist doth to account it meritorious, but as a faithful Christian to do it in faith. . . . It is not enough for us only to bear fair leaves, but we must also bring forth good fruit" (*Poore Mans Teares* 4–5).

In one sense, then, God's gift of grace is understood to produce, as its proper effect, a typological repetition of itself. As Tyndale writes, "By faith we receive of God and by love we shed out again. And that must we do freely" (C2v–C2r). Nevertheless, as may be illustrated once again with any number of texts, the charitable giving with which humanity echoes and confirms the divine plenitude must only be given to *worthy* objects. (This, of course, is the obvious point at which contemporary conservative attacks on welfare echo early-modern discourse.) Thus, the famous Protestant reformer Martin Bucer enjoins that, in giving charity, one should carefully distinguish between those "who lack indeed, and be not able to relieve their own lack," and those "who, when they may by their own honest labour maintain themselves, will not labour" (Bucer 12, 10).

In all this, however, this discourse reveals (as Jean-Luc Nancy observes in another context) how the logic of the absolute violates the absolute (*Inoperative Community* 4). No one can *deserve* God's grace; therefore, God gives *only* to the *undeserving*. Of human charity, however, the reverse is true. To be *like* God, to express by one's own gift the free gift of God's grace, is also to be precisely *unlike* God. We *must* and *must not* give "freely." These contradictions also indicate how, as Derrida has argued, a pure or "free" gift in the strict sense is rigorously impossible—for even to think the idea of giving is necessarily to enter into a cycle of exchange and circular "return." Tyndale's counterintuitive logic—his ingenious attempt to explain why good people still perform good deeds even outside every conceivable *economy* of salvation—also reveals itself obliquely in contemporary discourses on welfare and work. As we have seen, in the discourse of "welfare reform," it is always assumed that the performance of work produces the moral subject and that the moral subject expresses or manifests itself (or, most precisely, *indicates its presence*) by its willingness to work. Thus, participants in so-called workfare—like prisoners condemned to "hard labor" as a rehabilitative and punitive end in itself—are denied literal wages for their work, so that, in working, they do not primarily produce or earn but, rather, merely *signify* their potential for "personal responsibility."

Consider, finally, how the Geneva Bible misses no opportunity to translate or interpret virtually any reference to an offering or sacrifice in the Hebrew scriptures as a "free gift." When Moses enjoins the children of Israel to "[t]ake from among you an offering unto the Lord" (Exodus 35:5), the running head on the page paraphrases this line as "The free gifts are required." But a gift required cannot, in principle, be "free," so that this commandment inescapably neutralizes itself in the process of its own expression. In another similar passage, the children of Israel are enjoined to "keep the feast of weeks unto the Lord thy God, even a free gift of thine hand, which thou shalt give unto the Lord thy God, as the Lord thy God hath blessed thee" (Deuteronomy 16:10). The Hebrew word translated as "free gift" is a term in Jewish law denoting something "which is given of one's own accord when there is no obligation to do so, as would be the case in tithes, vows, sacrifices prescribed by the law" (Hartman 819). Tyndale translates the word as "frewilofferinge," and most subsequent English translations retain this unusual adjectival sense of "free will." The Good News Bible, for example, has "Celebrate the Harvest Festival, to honor the LORD your God, by bringing him a freewill offering in proportion to the blessing he has given you." The relative clarity of this recent translation emphasizes, by contrast, the ambiguity of the Geneva version. In the latter, the gift or offering is enjoined to be "as God blessed thee," a phrase which seems to denote both causality and proportion, and by which we are enjoined to give both *because* the Lord has blessed us and *in the same amount* that the Lord has blessed us. A contemporary Jewish translation has "Then you shall observe the festival of Shavuos for HASHEM your God; to the extent of what your hand can offer, HASHEM your God will have blessed you" (Herczeg). Here, the use of the future perfect tense in the final clause indicates the same ambiguity in a slightly different way, expressing in terms of *time* a calculation of *quantity*. One can compare this passage in its various translations to another marginal annotation in the Geneva Bible, this one attached to 1 Corinthians 16:2, a well-known passage in which Paul enjoins a weekly gift of charity. "Every one of you," says Paul, should "lay up as *God* hath prospered him," which the editors paraphrase: "That every man bestow according to the ability that God hath blessed him with." Let me mark for future reference how this recurrent figure construes the charitable gift as an ambiguously proportionate response to one's personal abilities and achievements, while also understanding the latter as always-already a divine or spiritual "gift." In the present context, it is enough to observe how such passages also describe two acts of giving linked in a closed circle of exchange and proportional reciprocation, and thus command something (a "free" gift) which the act of commandment itself makes impossible.

Kant and Beyond

I have been trying to sketch some of the theological and quasi-anthropological foundations of that insidious double bind in which one must labor to live and yet also live to labor, subjected to the claims both of a political economy of self-interest and scarcity and of a moral economy of generosity, self-fashioning, and spiritual plenitude. As a few more brief examples will indicate, this structure of thought persists across a wide range of discourse all the way to the present moment. Indeed, to shift from the early-modern moral economy to one of the quintessential expressions of Enlightenment philosophy, it is striking to find the same two social subjects identified above—that is, the subject bound to a (negative) work of pure survival and the subject enjoined to a (positive) work of self-development—serving, for Kant, as paradigmatic illustrations of morality. In his *Groundwork of the Metaphysics of Morals,* Kant attempts to define an absolute principle of morality rigorously distinct from every economy of instrumental self-interest. At one point, almost in passing, Kant cites the example of a shopkeeper who refrains from overcharging even an inexperienced customer. In this case, "people are served *honestly,*" but this does not mean that "the shopkeeper has acted in this way from duty," nor even that he has "an immediate inclination towards his customers, leading him, as it were out of love, to give no man preference over another in the matter of price." Rather, "the action was done . . . solely from purposes of self-interest" (65). This example corresponds to the almost exactly contemporary vision of Adam Smith, in which, to quote one of the most famous sentences from *The Wealth of Nations* (1776), "it is not from the benevolence of the butcher, the brewer, or the baker, that we expect our dinner, but from their regard to their own self interest" (15). For Smith and a whole tradition of subsequent thought that remains within the same horizons, the moral value of the market transcends the actions of any of its individual agents and inheres solely in the system as a whole. For Kant, by contrast, the shopkeeper's actions are in no sense moral ones, since morality refers to action done exclusively for *"the sake of duty"* (65). I observe this here merely to highlight how Kant's thought rejoins the tradition of moral economy—from which it otherwise departs in almost every conceivable way—in understanding morality as something rigorously distinct from all instrumentality, and which in particular has nothing whatsoever to do with the merely practical ethics of commercial exchange.

Later, Kant gives four concrete examples of the concept of moral duty. The second is that of a man who "finds himself driven to borrowing money because of need" even though "he well knows that he will not be able to pay it back" (89). The third is that of a person who "finds in himself a talent whose cultivation would make him a useful man for all sorts of purposes," but who, being "in comfortable circumstances, . . . prefers to give himself up to pleasure rather than to bother about increasing and improving his fortunate natural aptitudes" (90). The needy subject, Kant suggests, remains capable of moral reflection, recognizing both a "demand of self-love" (which induces him to promise to pay back the money even when he knows he cannot) and the claim of what Kant famously calls the categorical imperative, of universal moral law. When he submits his potential actions to the latter, he sees that making a promise that he will be unable to keep "can never rank as a universal law of nature and be self-consistent, but must necessarily contradict itself. For the universality of a law that every one believing himself to be in need can make any promise he pleases with the intention not to keep it would make promising, and the very purpose of promising itself, impossible" (90).

In such an argument, however, the exercise of the categorical imperative preserves not just the possibility of promise making but also the original need-iness that set the whole example in motion. How or where is such need to be answered? As against, for example, the homiletic moralism of early-modern writers—who would enjoin the other hypothetical player in Kant's drama (the potential giver of the loan) to "[l]end to . . . poor neighbors in time of their great need," looking neither for "vantage" nor even "so much as for the principal again" (T. Wilson 189-90)—Kant seemingly strives to intercept in advance the very possibility of such a "free" gift.

As for his next example, the talented but idle subject, Kant suggests that he must choose between giving in the form of a cultivation of the talents given him by nature (or by God) and the giving over of himself to an unproductive pleasure. In this case, the categorical imperative as such does not quite apply:

Yet he asks himself further "Does my maxim of neglecting my natural gifts, besides agreeing in itself with my tendency to indulgence, agree also with what is called duty?" He then sees that a system of nature could indeed subsist under such a univer-sal law, although (like the South Sea Islanders) every man should let his talents rust and should be bent on devoting his life solely to idleness, indulgence, procreation, and, in a word, to enjoyment. (90)

One can hardly fail to notice the anthropological gesture that anchors Kant's acknowledgment of the hypothetical or actual possibility of a primitive society with no apparent need for either duty or work. As we have seen, the an-thropological Other seems almost inevitably to surface in any attempt to think or question work's necessity, a necessity that Kant proceeds to reaffirm in the strongest possible terms: "Only he cannot possibly *will* that this should be-come a universal law of nature or should be implanted in us as such a law by a natural instinct. For as a rational being he necessarily wills that all his powers should be developed, since they serve him, and are given him, for all sorts of possible ends" (90).

The necessity so strongly announced here locates itself paradoxically out-side the moral system itself, as a kind of metaphysical excess that cannot even be accommodated by universal law and that is grounded, instead, in the absolute exigency of the divine or natural gift. The apparent autoteleology of self-development is "given him," but only in the very shape of obligation; and the apparent injunction to the Work as an end in itself is revealed instead as a nonnegotiable instrumental necessity to be exercised "for all sorts of possible ends."

This two-sided figure—work as at once a (negative) response to need and as a (positive) obligation of self-development—obviously corresponds to what I have called the double necessity of work. One can cite any number of examples to illustrate its remarkable staying power across a wide range of discourse. For example, John Wesley—who revives the moribund tradition of moral economy at the very moment of the birth of political economy with Adam Smith—often implicitly alludes to the parable of the talents so as to analogize financial and spiritual value. Wesley repeatedly preaches that God has "committed to our charge that precious talent which contains all the rest, *money*," a talent that must be employed "for such purposes as our blessed Lord has commanded us" (2:285). God will ask each one of us at Judgment Day, Wesley warns: "Didst thou employ thy *understanding,* as far as it was capable, according to those directions, namely, in the knowledge of thyself and me?" (2:293).[9]

About half a century later, in *Past and Present* (1843), Thomas Carlyle would celebrate how "[f]rom the inmost heart of the worker rises his god-given Force, the sacred celestial Life-essence breathed into him by Almighty God; from his inmost heart awakens him to all nobleness,—to all knowledge, 'self-knowledge' and much else, so soon as Work fitly begins" (235). And Matthew Arnold in *Culture and Anarchy* (1869), similarly, defines culture as an "inward *working*" (16), something that involves "*developing* all sides of our humanity [and] all parts of our society" (8) and "the general harmonious expansion of those *gifts of thought and feeling* which make the peculiar dignity, wealth, and happiness of human nature" (32–33; emphasis added). What is always most at stake for Arnold is a "total spiritual growth" of the individual, which involves "his bringing to perfection the gifts committed to him" (21). Such formulations also indicate something that has often been noticed about Arnold's project as a whole: how a quasi-anthropological concept of "culture" is allowed to serve as a stand-in for theology. "Religion says: "*The kingdom of God is within you,*" Arnold writes, "and culture, in like manner, places human perfection in an *internal* condition, in the growth and predominance of our humanity proper" (32). Even in Soviet Russia, as we have seen, what was called a "liberation" of work was always typically defined as a condition in which, as Maxim Gorky puts it, "[e]very citizen has full liberty to develop his capacities, *gifts* and *talents*" (255; emphasis added).

Let us finally acknowledge, one more time, that these familiar Victorian and modern celebrations of the Work of culture do not and cannot in principle escape the exclusionary impulses that inevitably cling to an ethos of labor and production. "All true Work is Religion," writes Carlyle; but this means, as he frankly attests, that "whatsoever Religion is not Work may go and dwell among the Brahmins, Antinomians, Spinning Dervishes, or where it will" (Carlyle 239). Arnold, similarly, tries his best to insist that culture "seeks to do away with classes; to make all live in an atmosphere of sweetness and light" (Arnold 48); and yet he repeatedly also contrasts the "finely tempered nature . . . who tends towards sweetness and light" with the Philistine, with his "coarsely tempered nature" (37). In other words, to celebrate an ideal of cultural "perfection" which is "not a having and a resting, but a growing and a becoming" (33), is necessarily to divide those who grow from those who merely rest. Such acts of division and exclusion are inevitable in any thought grounded in a so-called culture understood as a realm of self-development whose two poles are to be found in work and the Work.

Perhaps the most perfectly concise instance of this conclusion may be cited from a poem that William Butler Yeats, by his own account the "last of the romantics" (240), explicitly intended to serve as his artistic testament. In one passage, Yeats begins by enjoining "Irish poets" to "learn your trade" and "Sing whatever is well made." He then goes on to add to this positive injunction its inevitable negative corollary:

> Scorn the sort now growing up
> All out of shape from toe to top,
> Their unremembering hearts and heads
> The base-born products of base beds. (343)

Hayek on "Liberty"

As such examples suggest, the ancient figure of work-as-gift, as it filters through a variety of other texts and thought, finally returns us to more or less the same dilemma that we reached in part 1: in which, to phrase it once again in schematic terms, the only freedom from the curse of daily labor lies, with profound paradox, in a new Law of Command enjoining us to the Work. This endlessly renewed aspiration to *a work that is not work* produces not only a politics of exclusion but also, as I shall argue one more time in closing this chapter, *a freedom that is not free.* As a limit case of this enduring conceptual structure, I consider the thought of F. A. Hayek, the Nobel Prize–winning philosophic celebration of the market after Adam Smith.

Although his career spans over half a century and encompasses a wide range of texts and topics, Hayek's thought shows remarkable consistency throughout, and his basic arguments can be simply stated. First, in an argument drawn in part from his mentor Ludwig von Mise, he argues that socialism is literally impossible, a mere "fatal conceit" that was always "wrong *about the facts*" (*Fatal Conceit* 6), because a centralized knowledge about material production (what and how much to make) can never be attained. Only "the price system" of the market, he writes, "enables entrepreneurs, by watching the movement of comparatively few prices as an engineer watches the hands of a few dials, to adjust their activities to those of their fellows" (*Road to Serfdom* 49). Second, only a market economy and the existence of private property can ensure, to use his favored term, the "liberty" of individuals. The two points are themselves interrelated and join to form what he explicitly summarizes as "the central concept of liberalism," namely, "that under the enforcement of universal rules of just conduct, protecting a recognizable private domain of individuals, a spontaneous order of human activities of much greater complexity will form itself than could ever be produced by deliberate arrangement" (*Studies in Philosophy* 162).

Both of Hayek's two basic arguments (the impossibility of centralized knowledge and the consequent necessity of individual achievement) invite a variety of critiques, not least of which would be that this whole critique of socialism applies in the first place only to a Soviet-model "command economy." Here, the crucial point is that both arguments are also wholly grounded in an ethos and an ontology of production whose theological underpinnings are once again evident. The individualism for which Hayek argues descends, as he acknowledges in his famous book *The Road to Serfdom* (1944), "from elements provided by Christianity and the philosophy of classical antiquity," and it is grounded in "the belief that it is desirable that men should develop their own individual *gifts* and bents" (14; emphasis added). Hayek's liberty, he explicitly argues, is a historical stand-in for, and necessary supplement to, the Christian doctrine of free will. To the Christian doctrine that man "must be free to follow *his* conscience in moral matters if his actions are to be of any merit," liberalism simply adds "the further argument that he should be free to make full use of *his* knowledge and skill" (*Individualism and Economic Order*

14–15). Conceding that he is himself "not prepared to accept the anthropomorphic conception of a personal divinity" (*Fatal Conceit* 137), Hayek still insists that his particular brand of liberalism is "reverent of tradition" and therefore also "not incompatible with religious beliefs" (*Studies in Philosophy* 161)

Correspondingly, Hayek's thought also grounds itself, as explicitly as possible, in an anthropological vision of human evolutionary development. Himself following the formula defined above, Hayek relies on an assumed anthropological knowledge of the origins of man as a stand-in for the theological faith that is no longer tenable in its own right but that "provided mankind of a powerful support in the long development of the extended order that we now enjoy" (*Fatal Conceit* 137). In many different texts, he repeats an idiosyncratic argument about the evolution of human morality from its earliest stages. As against the more familiar belief that civilization *creates* altruistic or communitarian behaviors that eventually put an end to the Hobbesian war of all against all, Hayek argues something like the reverse:

There can be no doubt that our innate moral emotions and instincts were acquired in the hundreds of thousands of years—probably half a million years—in which Homo Sapiens lived in small hunting and gathering groups and developed a physiological constitution which governed his innate instincts. . . . For the small hunting and gathering band, consisting of twenty-five to fifty people, there were two overriding moral conceptions which today we describe with the terms "solidarity" and "altruism." Solidarity means common purposes pursued together with our fellows. We all know the elation which we experience in the present day when we find ourselves joining in the pursuit of common purposes with our friends. . . . Yet, there can be no doubt that while in the small group it is a necessity that all the members spontaneously pursue the same ends in a commonly known situation, obedience to this instinct would have prevented any expansion of society. . . . The same applies to the second traditional "good instinct," which still governs our emotions, but which had to cease to be obligatory to make the great society possible . . . altruism can extend only to the known needs of known other people; it cannot lead to the growth of a society which depends on our serving the needs of people of whose very existence we have no idea. (*Knowledge, Evolution and Society* 29–30)

Solidarity and altruism, far from being the products or defining features of civilization, are merely primitive instincts that must be put aside in order to create a civilized economic or political order.[10] This astonishing argument, so unlike most other forms of conservative thought, functions to set up Hayek's positive vision of the market, a vision that, as he would doubtlessly concede, is finally no more than an elaborated version of Adam Smith's. Countering our alleged primeval tendency to engage in common efforts, the market motivates us to make individual efforts—which lead, however, to positive common ends. And countering our instinct to serve the visible needs of known friends, the market allows us—or, rather, *forces us*—to serve the invisible needs of unknown friends.

I have summarized this feature of Hayek's thought in some detail because it represents a quintessential instance of the process I described in chapter 5, by which the contemporary discourse of capitalism appropriates and defuses the potential of both "general" economics and the very idea of the gift. Hayck's basic argument, which at one level celebrates capitalism for bringing to birth a "restricted" economy of rational self-interest and utility, also celebrates its irrationality, its embrace of chance, its alleged willingness to invest and produce without certain return. Hayek insists again and again that "by following the spontaneous generated moral traditions underlying the competitive market order . . . we generate and garner greater knowledge and wealth than could ever be obtained or utilized in a centrally directed economy whose adherents claim to proceed strictly in accordance with 'reason'" (*Fatal Conceit* 7). As opposed to some who attack Marxism as a kind of secular religion, Hayek argues on the contrary that socialism epitomizes an instrumental rationality that must be rejected in favor of the intuitive, instinctual, and finally inexplicable order of market exchange. To put this slightly differently, and to use the terms that have governed my argument here: Hayek announces the impossibility of that ultimate Work called *society*—that is, "the belief that it is both possible and desirable to reconstruct all grown institutions in accordance with a preconceived plan" (*Studies in Philosophy* 161)—and yet such renunciation of the Work of society is to be performed precisely in the name of the Work called culture or, to use his preferred word, "civilization." Civilization is, par excellence, the very product of those "individual gifts" that the market allegedly allows—or again, more precisely, *forces*—individuals to develop. "It was," he writes, "men's submission to the impersonal forces of the market that . . . has made possible the growth of a civilization . . . that is greater than any one of us can fully comprehend" (*Road to Serfdom* 204).

All this also leads to one more essential conclusion. Hayek's thought is based on a kind of metaphysical paradox: our "submission" to the market is the absolute condition of our freedom. One does not even need to question this formula in itself to see the further conclusion to which it inexorably leads: that this freedom of the market is always and merely a freedom to *produce*. In 1944, Hayek argues that, in a wealthy society such as ours, it might be possible to guarantee "a given minimum of sustenance for all," but then immediately stipulates that doing so will leave us with "the important question whether those who thus rely on the community should indefinitely enjoy all the same liberties as the rest" (*Road to Serfdom* 120). In 1988, similarly, he attacks socialism for teaching people that "they possess claims irrespective of performance, irrespective of participation," and argues, "We may be able to assist the weak and disabled, the very young and old, but only if the sane and adult submit to the impersonal discipline which gives us means to do so" (*Fatal Conceit* 153).

So let us be quite clear: under the regime of the market as Hayek understands it, there can be in principle no right to be lazy, no freedom *not* to produce. Hayek can imagine only a kind of entrepreneurial freedom, a freedom to make and grow; and as any entrepreneur will readily acknowledge, you can make and grow anything (including money) only by having other people work *for you*. This means that the whole impressive edifice of Hayek's thought is built on an absolute contradiction: on the one hand, *work makes you free;* on the other hand, there will never be freedom either *in* or *from* work. And for Hayek himself, as for so many others stranded within the same horizons of thought, to justify, confirm, and propagate this Law of Command remains itself an unending Work.

9

ARTS AND ENDS

Reopened Questions

My attempt to trace the thought of the Work and the gift has arrived repeatedly at a kind of impasse that can be described in any number of ways but that I have indicated under the paradoxical formulations of *a work that is not work* and *a gift that is not a gift*. By the same token, what lies ahead is the task that is not a task, the project of thinking the impossibility of project, the labor of a thought that begins again at the very point of its recognition of its own limit. Such formulations, it may be objected, seem to betray themselves by announcing, in their own structure, an impossibly difficult labor of thought or, even worse, by heralding a merely paradoxical vision that could be, as such, no match for the implacable demands of the workaday world. But whatever theoretical and practical difficulties still beckon, an *opening* question now presents itself that is in no way difficult to frame and that indeed might best be phrased with absolute simplicity. This question would be: what are we doing?

Not even what *should be* our work, but simply *what is it?*

It is persuasively argued today that we are *over*worked; but even if such observations are exaggerated—if in fact we still work "only" the forty-hour week (with a bit of "overtime") that has seemed reasonable in industrialized nations for nearly a century—it must nevertheless be asked: what are we making or achieving with all that work?[1] The claims of a Morris or a Ruskin that we should labor collectively to make the world more beautiful seem merely quaint today. The Marxist dream of a community made possible by its own productivity and in which true individuality would therefore be possible has been relegated by many to the dustbin of the history of ideas. It has even been famously suggested by Francis Fukuyama (as he attempts to "reclaim" the legacy of Hegel from its Marxist inversion) that it is no longer possible even to imagine a world significantly different from this one and that the very telos of human knowledge and politics is already in our hands. But let me ask then, and in particular of those who still believe in the Work: what is ours?

The only answer that comes readily to mind is technological innovation. Doubtlessly, no one would wish to underestimate the extent to which technology has revolutionized transportation, communication, medicine, and so forth and, by so doing, often improved the material lives of human beings in strictly incalculable ways. But whatever technoparadise may be believed to lie ahead, relatively few of us directly contribute to its progress: most of us merely procure or manage, facilitate or coordinate—or, worse, merely stitch and carry and load—for increasingly anonymous organizations whose own future appears increasingly precarious and which yet ask us to embrace our new insecurity as our freedom. To answer my initial question this way is thus to do no more than raise it again. In other words, if technology is our project, then what is technology's project? Is not the dream of laborsaving devices, of a world less onerous, precisely what has always been at stake in technology? If technological progress itself becomes its own telos, then has it not betrayed its own logic and promise?

At the very heart of the unyielding world of work is therefore a ghostly acknowledgment of that which must finally disturb that world. Even as the technical developments of the much-heralded "information economy" disturb "the methods of traditional calculation and the conceptual opposition between work and non-work, activity, employment, and their contrary" (Derrida Specters 75), so too in the world of the Work we are constrained to recognize that there may be nothing more to produce, that the grand project of the West as a demand for meaning has been interrupted. Even Fukuyama suggests that in the great homogeneous political formation that he claims as our final destination, there will soon be no more art, no more philosophy, and, indeed, nothing more that we really have to do.

At the heart of the thought of the gift as well, I now suggest, is that which must fundamentally disturb and displace that thought. As even its defenders must agree, the very essence of capitalism is an atomistic privatization of social exchange. When we exchange commodities in the marketplace, it is fundamentally understood that the seller retains no claim upon the object sold. This is precisely the characteristic of capitalist exchange that Marcel Mauss contrasted with the Maori idea of the *hau,* a kind of presence or quality that remains immanent in the gift even after it is given. Under the regime of capital, by contrast (to paraphrase Adam Smith's famous formula), it is not from the benevolence of the baker that I should expect my bread; but by the same token, if I do buy bread and decide (say, like a conceptual artist) to paper my walls with it instead of eating it, that can be no concern of the baker's. This is even more true with regard to the "universal equivalent," money. It is perhaps possible to imagine situations—for example, with extreme luxury goods like fine cuisine or vintage wine—in which the seller of some commodity might concern himself to some extent with the specifics of its use and appreciation. But it would be the height of absurdity to imagine a potential *buyer* of any commodity saying to the seller: "I will buy what you have to sell, but only if you promise to do something worthwhile with the money." And yet that, of course, is precisely what we do say with regard to the charitable gift, which must never be given, we are repeatedly told, except to those who "deserve" it and unless one is sure to "do some good." How strange it is to recognize that a kind of general economy has always been inscribed at the very heart of the restricted economy of capitalism! In other words: we always buy and sell without thought; and perhaps one need only observe so much to begin, at least, to think the impossible possibility of giving that way.

At any rate, what evidently now remains is a kind of negative work: a work that must be, on the one hand, simply a clearing of our heads and a clearing of the decks and, on the other hand, something that I will now begin to call the *unworking* of our works and gifts.

Unworking the Work

The term "unworking" is one of several possible translations of the French words *désoeuvrement* or *désoeuvré,* which take on a particular theoretical valence in the texts of Maurice Blanchot. Among other possibilities of meaning, the term indicates a process by which all forms of art and literature constantly aspire to the stature of the Work only to fail by succeeding (or vice versa). The implications of Blanchot's term are, however, by no means trivial or merely existential. Unworking also has an "exacting political meaning" (Blanchot *Unavowable* 56), which has been further drawn out by Jean-Luc Nancy in his *La communauté désoeuvrée* (1991), a book that will be of particular interest in the final chapter. Peter Connor translates Nancy's title as *The Inoperative Community,* but in the present context it will be preferable to adopt the more literal translation as an acknowledged neologism and understand the phrase as *the community of unworking*—or, perhaps, *the community which is not a Work.*

All these terms, titles, and translations have complexities that I will try to bring out in the pages that follow, first by indirection, through a selective survey of the themes of work and gift in the avant-garde traditions of the last century, and then directly, to indicate an opening of thought that begins on the other side of a limit at which such traditions repeatedly arrive. This will, in a sense, involve a consideration of twentieth-century art as a "history." And yet we must also acknowledge at the outset that, as Nancy argues, art has a history at all only "in a radical sense, that is, not progress but passage, succession, appearance, disappearance, event," and all cultural production tends to withdraw itself "from the history or the historicity that is represented as 'progress'" (*Muses* 87). Nevertheless, the art of the last century and our own seems almost irresistibly to evoke at least a quasi-progressive narrative of sequential and ever more radical destabilizations of the "objet d'art." Although, for example, the celebrated avant-garde movements of the century's first half (Futurism, Dada, and Surrealism) present themselves in retrospect primarily in the form of canonical objects and paintings, some of their successors in the second half of the century (Situationism, Fluxus, "Neoism," and so forth) scarcely produced anything that can be called "Works" at all. In a whole series of well-known gestures of aesthetic negation—for example, Marcel Duchamp's "readymades" (in which the artist simply titled and signed mundane objects such as a bottle rack and a urinal); or Yves Klein's "zones of immaterial pictorial sensibility" (works that exist only in the form of their conditions of sale); or Guy Debord's *Screams in Favor of Sade* (a movie consisting almost entirely of dark film stock)—representation itself reaches what has long been recognized as a certain limit or crisis point after which would appear to be only two possibilities: either absolute cessation (the abolition of art) or a simple rebeginning, as though, so to speak, *nothing* had happened. All this is entirely familiar today, in an era in which broad questions of aesthetic ontology ("that's not art!") seem to govern the most casual conversations on the subject.

In these myriad attempts to rethink art's privileged status as the very sign of the Work—once again to observe no more than the obvious—aesthetic, economic, and political questions are inextricably linked. To throw out (or to throw *into* play) the characteristics always assumed to define the Work of art—beauty, coherence, durability, originality, and the like—is also to question whether such Works remain necessarily appropriable by the market and thus by the Law of Value itself. Such questions have been raised in particular by those whom Iwona Blazwick calls that "legendary series of avant-garde artists and groups whose path [intersects] with popular revolutionary movements at emblematic moments" ("Bitter Victory" 10), but they might also be seen as necessarily implied by the project of aesthetic modernity itself. And in this, the history of art in our times can be understood, using the terms that have governed my argument here, as a repeated attempt to rethink the gift as a Work and the Work as a gift. The *negative* assault on the Work that so defines twentieth-century art has always been accompanied by a related, *positive* attempt to achieve some new mode of purely gratuitous expression: something that might take its place outside every market, outside even the object or the sign in their durable and recuperable meaning.

Today, however, a curious duplicity haunts the very project or prospect of the aesthetic. On the one hand, art seems commonly to announce or indicate in every possible way its own historical exhaustion; on the other hand, cultural production continues with a variety and a volume unsurpassed at any previous historical moment. Art, music, film, literature, imaginative representation and expression of every kind, clearly continue to figure in the popular and institutional imagination as the absolute paradigms of the Work, as the very figures of achievement and value, of autoteleology and self-fulfilling freedom. And the object of art assuredly retains, as Nancy suggests, its age-old ability to "exhorbit value itself" (*Muses* 83) and still correspondingly appears as the very site in which social distinction and class are relentlessly constructed and endlessly reinscribed.

In what follows, I consider in turn the two aspects of twentieth-century art that center on my titular terms. In other words, the aesthetic ferment of our times might best be understood as a constant disturbance of the opposition of work and the Work that never succeeds in displacing it. This is the first of the dilemmas to which the enigmatic nonconcept of unworking offers itself as a theoretical negation and reopening. The various avant-garde groups of twentieth-century art, whatever their other differences, meet on the ground of a double critique defined, on the one side, by the Dada slogan "No more masterpieces!" and, on the other side, by the Situationist slogan "Never work!" The difficulties that attend this two-pronged assault on culture and the work ethic are, however, by no means limited to the obvious recuperation of such groups by an academic "history of art." Indeed, sometimes this double critique seems to present itself with an all-too-obvious symmetry that will allow me to recall previous arguments and hazard another schematic summary. I argued in part 1 that many contemporary thinkers, especially on the Left, question the social necessity of work only to reaffirm the Work, grasping the latter either as the source and expression of an individual or group identity or as some (residual or emergent) form of authentic creativity and (self-)production. Now I observe, correspondingly, that the attempt to destabilize the Work in the theory and practice of twentieth-century art often comes full circle to arrive back at a simple reaffirmation of work.

An inevitable opening example of this process is F. T. Marinetti's celebrated Futurist manifesto of 1909, a text commonly seen as the inaugural gesture of an avant-garde tradition continuing at least through Surrealism or beyond (e.g., Blazwick "Bitter Victory" 10; Marcus 197). Here, Marinetti outlines an audacious cultural reversal in a text that, nearly a century later, has perhaps not quite lost all of its ability to shock: "Come on! Set fire to the library shelves! Turn aside the canals to flood the museums! . . . Oh, the joy of seeing the glorious old canvases bobbing adrift on those waters, discolored and shredded! . . . take up your pickaxes, your axes and hammers, and wreck, wreck the venerable cities, pitilessly!" (Marinetti and Flint 43). The symmetry of Marinetti's gesture is obvious: he calls for an ecstatically violent negation of the objects and institutions of traditional culture and exalts the processes and products of industrialism ("good factory muck," "metallic waste," "energy," "action," and "the beauty of speed"; 41). Futurism will "sing of great crowds excited by work, by pleasure, and by riot," of "polyphonic tides of revolution in the modern capitals," and of "factories hung on clouds by the crooked lines of their smoke" (42).

In another manifesto from 1910, the initial group of Futurist painters promise to "sweep the whole field of art clean of all themes and subjects which have been used in the past" and "support and glory in our day-to-day world, a world which is going to be continually and splendidly transformed by victorious Science" (Apollonio 26). The Futurists thus envision a kind of "general" aesthetic economy in which industrial labor and artistic achievement, work and the Work, would complement rather than oppose one another and unfold together in a renewed energy of mutual production. "Italy is being reborn," write the Futurist painters; "in the land where doing nothing in the sun was the only available profession, millions of machines are already roaring; in the land where traditional aesthetics reigned supreme, new flights of artistic inspiration are emerging" (Apollonio 25). Here, the end of classicism is understood as the beginning of a new "artistic inspiration," and, as many have argued, an emergent quasi-fascist nationalism merges seamlessly with a visionary rethinking of art's value and purpose.[2]

What most compels our attention about this characteristic Futurist position, however, is an unavoidable sense that it exalts work only by almost completely effacing it. Speed, energy, power, and the like are envisioned only in a kind of splendid and impossible isolation—as what Marinetti calls "the ideal life of lines, forms, colors, rhythms, sounds, and noises combined by genius" (Marinetti and Flint 154)—or else as the pure product of abstractions such as "science," which thus serve as discursive stand-ins for industrial labor in some more concrete sense. The racing car is celebrated for beauty, the factory for its power; and what is always erased in all these celebrated figures is any recognition of the effort and utility that would seem to define the very concept of work itself. The Futurists affirm once more a *work that is not work* or perhaps, more precisely, *a Work of work:* something that is claimed to be interchangeable with either "pleasure" or "revolution" (Marinetti and Flint 42), with either art or politics, and which is thus, one can only conclude, at once everything and nothing. Leaving aside any aesthetic judgment of their surviving corpus of painting (long ago recuperated for an academic history of art), it remains evident that the Futurists achieve no more than a kind of double *theoretical* failure: a negative critique of the Work which devolves into a merely abstract positive celebration of the products and processes of industrial work.

This point can be clarified by juxtaposing Futurism to a populist mode in American art of the 1930s, an art that would seem at first glance to be, either in its representational style or in its political and theoretical commitments, as different as possible. I refer in particular to the celebrated murals produced either by the Federal Art Project, established in 1935 under the auspices of the Works Project Administration (WPA), or by the Treasury Department's Section of Fine Arts, which commissioned a variety of paintings and sculpture for public buildings between 1934 and 1943. Here too a manifest attempt to question the cultural status of the Work leads directly to a reaffirmation of work. Holger Cahill, director of the Federal Art Project, repeatedly argues at the time for the program's wider importance as part of a radical democratization of the arts: "The organization of the Project has proceeded on the principle that it is not the solitary genius but a sound general movement which maintains art as a vital, functioning part of any cultural scheme. Art is not a matter of rare, occasional masterpieces. The emphasis upon masterpieces is a nineteenth century phenomenon. It is primarily a collector's idea and has little relation to an art movement" (*New Horizons* 18). To that end, as is well known, this public art of the 1930s embraced, as its quintessential theme and subject, what has been aptly described as "the simple dignity and worth of labor and the common man's contribution to building his community" (O'Connor Introduction 22), a "laissez-faire world in which enterprising people work singly and together to build America" (Park and Markowitz 29–30).

This so-called New Deal art was promoted by the federal government both as a literal form of economic relief for cultural workers and as a kind of ideological boosterism for the nation as a whole. Accordingly, such art would renounce any avant-garde pretensions. Indeed, the WPA and the "Section" sought to promote the arts, as it were, on the plane of both the restricted and general economies, claiming at once to be preserving a national culture threatened by economic depression and to be leveling or disseminating culture in an unprecedented way. Thus, on the one hand, Cahill argues that the central goal of the program was "the conservation of artistic skills and talents" (*New Horizons* 17), and on the other, he denounces those "persons in the art field" who "cannot get away from aristocracy in matters of aesthetic selection" because they believe that art is too good to share with the masses (Cahill "American Resources" 36). The mural itself, that most familiar form of WPA and Section art, directly responds to the demand that artists should "talk to the people in a language they could readily understand"—a demand that, in its turn, was claimed to have done "more to awaken an art interest in the masses than could possibly have been calculated" (Norman 52). Thus, New deal art both conserved culture and fostered its production and consumption, claiming for itself a central role in an incalculable, "general" movement of cultural abundance.

It is evident, however, that this purported democratization of art in no way escapes from the system of "high" and "low" culture, and thus from the opposition of work and the Work. Cahill, for example, has no sooner denounced the idea of the "masterpiece" as a mere invention of art collectors than he begins to undermine his own argument by observing:

When one goes through the galleries of Europe . . . one is struck by the extraordinary amount of work which was produced in the great periods. During the early part of the twentieth century it is said that some forty thousand artists were at work in Paris. It is doubtful that history will remember more than a dozen or two of these, but it is probable that if the great number of artists had not been working, very few of these two dozen would have been stimulated to creative endeavor. In a genuine art movement a great reservoir of art is created in many forms, both major and minor. (*New Horizons* 18; see also "American Resources" 35)

As such comments indicate, Cahill does not finally reject the idea of a self-fulfilling masterpiece but, rather, envisions a broad field of cultural production in which "minor" art is to be encouraged as a first step in the production of "major" art. As he puts it elsewhere: "Though we cannot tell whether our day has produced masters, or masterpieces, I think we can say that we have a situation in this country which makes it possible for both to appear" ("American Resources" 35).

In the end, a purported democratization of art is valued only insofar as it provides the underlying conditions of possibility for the master Work. In this sense, as Marlene Park and Gerald E. Markowitz argue, New Deal art simply "traded in reversals"; whereas an avant-garde artist such as Duchamp places "a urinal for exhibition in an art gallery," the WPA and the Section "placed art in post offices" (181). In such art, therefore, work and the Work, the "blissful diligence" of the common man (O'Connor Introduction 22) and the potential masterpieces that both depict such diligence and are themselves, however indirectly, *a product of it,* remain locked in a closed system of mutual definition and hierarchical value.

It is equally obvious that even the characteristic theme of New Deal art—the exaltation of work and workers—remains itself in service of a broader project of national identity. As Cahill puts it: "It is to the creative talent of our own day that we look to provide us with the fresh and unfolding revelation of our country and our people, for the expression of those qualitative unities which make the pattern of American culture" ("American Resources" 44). Or as John Dewey writes in 1940, "the murals which are now to be found in public buildings . . . strengthen that legitimate pride which enables one to say, 'I am an American citizen'" (quoted in Marlene and Markowitz v). Thus, New Deal art both *depicts* the literal building of America and is *valued* precisely insofar as it contributes to the Work of an American national identity.

To return from this brief-lived aesthetic populism to the avant-garde tradition that follows Futurism in a sequential chain of groups and movements is to observe a more complex but similarly unfinished attempt to disturb the opposition of work and the Work. Dada, for example, more or less begins and ends with a relentless critique of aesthetic value whose quintessential gesture might be Marcel Duchamp's penciling of a moustache on a reproduction of the *Mona Lisa.* Such gestures, writes a contemporary observer, "are no innocent games" but rather a "usurping of the masterpiece's privileges . . . aimed at destroying its prestige" (Motherwell xxxiii). Tristan Tzara, in his Dada manifesto of 1918, calls for "a great negative work" (Motherwell 81) to be accomplished by a movement that would "recognize no theory" (Motherwell 77) and that would exist solely in the form of "a protest with the fists of its whole being engaged in destructive action" (Motherwell 81). Yet Dada's negative and destructive "disgust" for aesthetic value remains in principle inseparable from a kind of master critique of Value in any of its political or economic guises. In narrowly political terms, Dada would always be characterized by a certain cosmopolitanism, moving sequentially from Geneva to Berlin to New York, its participants men from various countries fleeing the trenches of the First World War because, as Richard Huelsenbeck writes memorably in 1920, they lacked "the kind of courage it takes to get shot for the idea of a nation which is at best a cartel of pelt merchants and profiteers in leather, at worst a cultural association of psychopaths who, like the Germans, marched off with a volume of Goethe in their knapsacks, to skewer Frenchmen and Russians on their bayonets" (Motherwell 23). As Tzara puts it, Dada sought to "bedeck the artistic zoo with the flags of every consulate" (Motherwell 75). Beyond such mere cosmopolitanism, however, Dada also rejects all aesthetic or political discourses of either origin ("abolition of archeology") or *telos* ("abolition of the future") and is thus, as Andre Breton concludes, neither "a school of painting" nor "a political movement" nor even so much as what Huelsenbeck calls "an idea in the 'progressive cultural' sense" (Motherwell 81, 203, 32).

Nevertheless, either in the explicit discourse of its participants or in the retrospective judgment of art history, Dada was quite unable to maintain this pose of consistent negation. "Dada has often been called a purely negative movement," writes William S. Rubin (at the time the chief curator of the Painting and Sculpture Collection of the Museum of Modern Art in New York), but "nothing could be further from the truth," since in fact "Dada fostered real contributions to art, poetry, music, and even politics" (*Dada and Surrealist Art* 10). The quasi-economic figure in such an observation evokes that familiar progressive narrative of twentieth-century art in which artistic innovation steadily accumulates and brings ever-greater returns: so that Dada produces Surrealism, and then Surrealism, in its turn, produces Abstract Expressionism, and so forth. But even in the explicit discourse of its participants, Dada typically grasps its own negative work only in the form of aesthetic and political *exclusions* of the most conventional kind. Thus, Tzara, for example, calls for the "abolition . . . of every social hierarchy" but also, in the very same passage, mocks and denounces "those who are impotent to create," and even goes so far as to affirm that only "those who are strong in words or force will survive" the destructiveness of Dada itself (Motherwell 81).

Such gestures correspond closely to the political program outlined in another Dada manifesto, coauthored by Huelsenbeck and Raoul Hausmann, which demands "the introduction of progressive unemployment through comprehensive mechanization of every field of activity," "the immediate expropriation of all property," and "the communal feeding of all" but makes all such demands subordinate to an "international revolutionary union of all creative and intellectual men and women" (Motherwell 41). That the two texts I have just cited should meet on the ground of an essentially similar ethos of creativity and production is particularly striking given that Huelsenbeck would later denounce Tzara for "trying to bind Dada to abstract art" (Motherwell 31) and thus allegedly losing faith with its impulse of aesthetic negation.

Dada is also one more case, as many of its surviving "Works" clearly suggest, where a critique of the prestige and privilege of the masterpiece leads to a celebration of the techniques and imagery of industrial labor. In well-known paintings and drawings by Francis Picabia such as *Very Rare Picture on This Earth* (1915) or *Amorous Parade* (1917), in Duchamp's *Chocolate Grinder No. 1* (1913) and other of the preparatory studies for his *Large Glass* (1915–23), and in the objects and photomontages of Hausmann such as *The Spirit of Our Times* (1919) or *Tatlin at Home* (1920), an insistently mechanistic iconography both recalls the Futurists and consolidates what would eventually be recognized as a central motif of twentieth-century art.[3] In Dada, however, all that remains of the positive Futurist embrace of technology appears to be an entirely negative critique of aesthetic value by which the artist simply proclaims, as Huelsenbeck puts it, that he will "paint no more men, women, donkeys and high-school students, since they partook of the whole system of deception" (Motherwell 36).

Dada painting and sculpture thus retain, I suggest, an unresolved tension between work and the Work that reaches an absolute limit with Duchamp's celebrated "readymades." This small group of objects has produced a voluminous literature of interpretive response, far more than can be summarized here; so I will observe simply how they have been commonly taken as a sort of unsurpassable gesture of aesthetic negation. "When Duchamp signs mass-produced objects . . . and sends them to art exhibits," writes Peter Bürger in a well-known study of the avant-garde, he "not only unmasks the art market where the signature means more than the quality of the work" but also "radically questions the very principle of art in bourgeois society according to which the individual is considered the creator of the work of art" (51–52). Both Rubin and Motherwell define the readymades, similarly, as "man-designed, commercially produced utilitarian objects endowed with the status of anti-art by Duchamp's selection and titling them" (Rubin *Dada and Surrealist Art* 36) and as "manufactured commercial object[s] . . . that [Duchamp] selected and exhibited under his own name, conferring on [them] the status of 'sculpture,' an anti-art and consequently dada gesture" (Motherwell xxiii).

And yet, as is clearly suggested by the strikingly similar terminology shared by all three of these descriptions, a readymade exists at all only in and as the conceptual aftermath of its literal production as a "commercial" or "mass-produced" object. A readymade is a Work that appropriates work: either phase of this double production is equally necessary to the anti-art gesture. The readymade therefore cannot in principle challenge the various opposi-tional systems (work versus the Work, aesthetic versus utilitarian, and so forth) whose discursive power it claims to unmask. In this sense, the ready-made also exists only in the form of a kind of circular paradox in which work and the Work do no more than endlessly change places. Robert Motherwell claims, for example, that a readymade is "a subtle solution to an essential dada dilemma, how to express oneself without art when all means of expression are potentially artistic." And yet, in the very same passage, Motherwell also claims "that the bottle rack [Duchamp] chose has a more beautiful form than almost anything made, in 1914, as sculpture" (xxiii). Thus, Motherwell simultane-ously *repeats* the original Dada gesture (undermining the Work by ascribing beauty to a mass-produced object) and *neutralizes* it (employing his aesthetic judgment in a manner that confirms that all means of expression are indeed potentially "artistic").

In his own famous remarks on the subject, delivered in 1961 at the Museum of Modern Art in New York, Duchamp asserts that his intention with these objects was "to expose the basic antinomy between art and 'readymades'" (Duchamp 142). As he goes on to explain, however, this act of exposure is rad-ically paradoxical, for it both requires and renounces repetition. For example, Duchamp claims that he "realized very soon the danger of repeating indis-criminately this form of expression and decided to limit the production of 'readymades' to a small number." He did this because "for the spectator even more than for the artist, *art is a habit-forming drug* and I wanted to protect my 'readymades' against such a *contamination*" (142). Yet he also acknowledges that he allowed subsequent replicas of the "original" readymades to be manu-factured and exhibited and claims, in fact, that the one absolutely crucial char-acteristic of the readymade "is its lack of uniqueness" (142). In other words, the readymade is said to inhabit a sort of limbo between a bad uniqueness (i.e., the originality or unitary value which it intends to destabilize) and a nec-essary repetition that is always in danger of recrystallizing the value of origi-nality.

Duchamp also mentions that he has "imagined a 'reciprocal readymade': use a Rembrandt as an ironing board!" (142). To consider this symmetrically reverse anti-art gesture more closely, however, is to see once again how neither

it nor the readymade proper can ever extricate themselves from the antino-
mies in which they are inscribed. The readymade is constituted by a positive
movement intended to negate itself: that is, a merely utilitarian object puts on
the mask of the Work in order to unmask the Work. Conversely, to apply a hot
iron to a Rembrandt (or even, shall we say, to urinate in Duchamp's *Fountain*)
would be to bring down a transcendent aesthetic Work to the level of the
merely utilitarian. In this case, even more than with the readymade itself, the
gesture would seem to require infinite repetition, for only at the point when its
significance had been entirely exhausted—when a urinal was finally just a urinal and a Rembrandt literally no more than any other piece of canvas—would
the gesture have actually done its intended work. In this sense, the reciprocal
readymade's vocation is to make itself (retrospectively) impossible. For the
basic readymade, however, something more like the reverse seems to be the
case. It is clear enough that the bare handful of readymades and "assisted
readymades" that Duchamp did produce and reproduce have in fact now
been fully recuperated (and thus, in his sense, contaminated) by art. But if
Duchamp had made more of them, would not the readymade at some point
lose its ability to satisfy our craving for the aesthetic drug? For that matter,
would not their unlimited reproduction simply dissolve the readymade back
into that realm of commercial or mass production from which it had pointedly
distinguished itself at first? The readymade's vocation thus can only be *to
make itself possible*. Rather than protecting a gesture of aesthetic negation
from contamination by aesthetic value as Duchamp claims, the readymade in
fact strives to protect the sovereignty of the Work from contamination by repetition and mere utilitarian value.

In the end, Duchamp's whole career seems similarly to evoke this kind of
circular paradox, in which the idea of the Work is simultaneously both questioned and reaffirmed. "I don't believe in the creative function of the artist,"
Duchamp tells Pierre Cabanne in 1966:

He's a man like any other. It's his job to do certain things, but the businessman does
certain things also, you understand? On the other hand, the word "art" interests me
very much. If it comes from Sanskrit, as I've heard, it signifies "making." Now everyone makes something, and those who make things on a canvas, with a frame, they're
called artists. Formerly, they were called craftsmen, a term I prefer. We're all craftsmen, in civilian or military or artistic life. (Cabanne and Duchamp 16)

Here again is the familiar strategy in which one celebrates work in order to critique the Work. Just so, Duchamp celebrates every kind of positive creation

(doing, making, crafting), but only so as to reduce the particularity of conventional art within the full spectrum of creativity. In his remarks from 1961, similarly, Duchamp ends by famously reminding his audience: "Since the tubes of paint used by the artist are manufactured and readymade products we must conclude that all the paintings in the world are 'readymades aided'" (142). Whereas at one moment he implicitly concedes the special status of those who "make things on a canvas, with a frame," here Duchamp reduces the field of production in a different way by observing that all Works remain necessarily dependent on prior work. One could easily take the same insight even farther by observing, for example, that artists too must eat, have shelter, and so forth, so that all the pretensions of the aesthetic—in fact, *all* pretensions of any kind—must always rest on a substratum of labor. As Walter Benjamin famously observes, all "cultural treasures . . . owe their existence not only to the efforts of the great minds and talents who have created them, but also to the anonymous toil of their contemporaries" (256). But here again, the unspoken final question would be: if all Works are in some sense readymades, then are *all* objects, all products of any kind, potentially Works? The deliberate symmetry with which Duchamp joins his two distinct but analogous gestures of aesthetic desecration (readymades and "reciprocal" or "aided" readymades) would seem to suggest precisely this conclusion, even as those gestures still wholly depend, for their own aesthetic force, on the very categories they otherwise seem to challenge.

Elsewhere in the 1966 dialogues, however, Duchamp also confesses that "deep down I'm enormously lazy. I like living, breathing, better than working. I don't think that the work I've done can have any social importance whatsoever in the future. Therefore, if you wish, my art would be that of living: each second, each breath is a work which is inscribed nowhere" (Cabanne and Duchamp 72). One must linger for a moment to admire this passing vision of a work which itself merely passes: a work that is literally utopian in that it is present only "nowhere" and that would no longer claim to express the imagined *spiritus* of transcendent Being but, rather, reside in the merely corporeal breath of mortal being. Of course, Duchamp's claim is in fact utterly belied by what he acknowledges to be his "constant preoccupation: to collect [his] work and preserve it" (78)—a preoccupation both exemplified and parodied, for example, by famous meta-works such as the *Boît en valise,* a suitcase containing tiny handcrafted replicas of all Duchamp's works, including the readymades. Further, Duchamp's "art of living" might be understood as no more than a work of self, a Work of self-production and self-presence, something that (like the readymade or like all art) would necessarily see itself as vulnerable to repetition and inscription—and that would thus risk the reinscription of everything otherwise renounced under the categories of work or art or "social importance."

Nevertheless, such an admission at least exemplifies what Breton calls Duchamp's pose of "truly supreme *ease*" (Motherwell 209) and also heralds an opening of thought that will eventually take us beyond the circular paradoxes I have described here. A few subsequent examples will further suggest how, in the continuing avant-garde tradition, and especially in groups such as the Letterists and the Situationists in postwar France, an attempt to destabilize the opposition of work and the Work remains absolutely fundamental. Indeed, the central project of these groups is something later described by Raoul Vaneigem with the famous title *The Revolution of Everyday Life* and summarized by Guy Debord as "a systematic questioning of all the diversions and works of a society, a total critique of its idea of happiness" (Knabb 29). This revolutionary transformation would begin "with the management of production and work" (Knabb 308), proceed to transform the domain of the Work (art and culture), and finally arrive at the ultimate Work of subjectivity itself, so that people will finally be allowed to "reinvent their own unique fulfillment" (Knabb 308–9).

In this, Situationist thought seems, at least in part, to anticipate the contemporary critique of work that I discussed in part 1 of this book, despite the fact that relatively few contemporary theorists engage explicitly with Situationist texts. Among other things, the Situationists resemble many of the writers considered earlier in their similar reliance on an implicit anthropological history. What Debord famously calls "the society of the spectacle" is understood to emerge historically in the wake of some fundamental moment of sociocultural rupture coinciding with the primeval division of labor (Debord *Society* 180; see also Jappe 74). After this rupture, human society no longer had any common language or real community (*Society* 186). Indeed, the fact that culture itself now exists only as an independent and uniquely privileged sphere of creative activity is the most obvious consequence of this "lost unity" of life and work. All such unities and communities, however, are now about to be restored. Debord suggests (here anticipating the arguments of contemporary "autonomist" Marxism) that the conditions of possibility for a reborn human community are already present in the technological achievements of industrial labor. The revolution of everyday life will begin with a "transformation of the nature of work and the development of a new technology tending to ensure the worker's domination over the machines" (Knabb 308). Such a transformation has finally become possible because society has reached the "level of knowledge and technical means" that will make possible a *"direct* construction of all aspects of a liberative affective and practical existence" (Knabb 31).

Such an argument appears to be more or less the same as that of the contemporary theorists of "general intellect." For the Situationists, however, an explicitly Marxist critique of the conditions of industrial labor merges seamlessly with a more conventional avant-garde assault on the Work. Liberation will first emerge in the former and then reunite with the latter. But since all actually existing culture is no more than the direct sign and consequence of our former social unity, any and all contemporary participation *in* culture involves an absolute paradox. On the one hand, "culture is the locus of the search for lost unity"; yet, on the other hand, "in this search for unity, culture as a separate sphere is obliged to negate itself" (*Society* 180). Therefore, the Situationists would actually find themselves forced to claim that "we are artists only insofar as we are no longer artists" (Knabb 139).

As such formulations indicate, however, the Situationists extend this negative strategy to more or less everything but the idea of creativity itself and continue to affirm strongly what I have elsewhere described as an ethos of *homo faber*. They repeatedly argue that contemporary capitalism has "from the workshop to the laboratory emptied productive activity of all meaning for itself" (Knabb 307). In the wake of this lost plenitude lies only the spectacle, in which people must now discover "the meaning of life in leisure activities," replace "authentic desires" with "artificial needs," and find in mere consumption the self-fulfillment they ought to find in production (Knabb 307). The spectacle is thus the very site at which the double Situationist critique (of work and the Work) finds its most obvious application; and the emergence of new relations of production in the literal workplace will, it is argued, liberate both the production and the consumption of Work in its developed cultural sense. That is, "the struggle of the proletariat for the actual domination . . . of production and work" will inexorably lead to a "shifting of the center of interest of life from passive leisure to the new type of productive activity. This does not mean that overnight all productive activities will become in themselves passionately interesting. But to work toward making them so, by a general and ongoing reconversion of the ends as well as the means of industrial work, will in any case be the minimum passion of a free society" (Knabb 308–9). Here again, we must linger momentarily to admire this audacious vision of a grand collective Work of (reworking) work, in which a productive "passion" will be experienced—and therefore achieved—in the very process of producing itself.

Nevertheless, this quintessential Situationist argument necessarily raises a version of the same question that was constantly at issue in part 1: namely, how are we to understand this new productive activity that will be neither traditional labor nor traditional art, this new mode of passionate creation that somehow exists in the form of a working-toward its own self-fulfillment? The Situationist answer to these vexing paradoxes rests on the crucial idea of a *supersession* (*dépassement*) of both work and the Work. Both the original French term and the English word commonly used to translate it retain a subtle ambiguity. The term seems to refer to a process by which both labor and art can be declared obsolete and then displaced or replaced by something else that exceeds or surpasses them. Indeed, the Situationists presumably call for a supersession of work rather than simply an end of work precisely so as to convey this double motion of initial negation followed by reaffirmation on a higher level. For example, Anger Jorn, one of the other central Situationist figures, argues that automation in the industrial workplace has both positive and negative aspects: although it "deprives the individual of any possibility of adding anything personal to automated production," it "saves human energy by massively liberating it from reproductive and uncreative activities." Therefore, Jorn concludes, "the value of automation thus depends on *projects that supercede it* and open the way for expression of human energies on a higher plane" (Knabb 46; emphasis added). Indeed, the leisure made possible by automation will serve as "the basis on which can be built the most magnificent cultural construction that has ever been imagined" (Knabb 46). In this case, automation contributes to something that supersedes or surpasses it; and yet automated work presumably will continue, precisely so as to make possible this continuing supersession of itself. In other words, automation's value depends on its contribution to projects that go beyond it, but it remains the absolute condition of possibility for such projects.

But the idea of a supersession of art is somewhat more difficult to imagine, particularly since, as we have seen, art in the modern world *already* exists only within a kind of dialectic of negation and (re)affirmation. Indeed, for Debord, contemporary art can be nothing else but "a negative movement which seeks the supersession of art." In an often-cited passage, Debord also suggests that Dada and Surrealism marked the end of modern art precisely insofar as each one personified either one side or the other of a double critique: "Dadism wanted to *suppress* [*supprimer*] art without realizing it; surrealism wanted to *realize* [*réaliser*] art without suppressing it. The critical position later elaborated by the Situationists has shown that the suppression and the realization of art are inseparable aspects of a single *supersession of art*" (*Society* 191). But how is one to conceive, in any practical or material sense, of this new unity of aesthetic suppression and aesthetic realization, this art that exceeds or displaces itself?

There would appear to be two possible answers. The first would proceed from Debord's point that "art in the epoch of its dissolution" can be nothing other than "a march toward its self-suppression (*Society* 180) and conclude that art realizes itself by abolishing itself. In this case, we would have to understand that the art of the past and present contributes, via its various gestures of negation and self-critique, to the nonproject that follows in its wake, but artistic production, in the period of its supersession, will literally cease and desist. This possibility has been, as it were, represented (if not literally realized) by any number of avant-garde artists and groups. One might reference here, for example, Marcel Duchamp's famous gesture of abandoning art to play chess after the "definitive incompletion" of his *Large Glass,* or the "autodestructive" objects of Gustav Metzger and Jean Tinguely, works of art designed to destroy themselves. Even more broadly, one can cite Metzger's call for an "art strike" between 1977 and 1980, a gesture later repeated on a larger scale by Stewart Home and others in the Neoist group, who called for artists to "put down their tools and cease to make, distribute, sell, exhibit or discuss their cultural work for a three year period beginning on 1 January 1990" (Mannox et al. 1),[4] and yet again echoed by Jimi Cauty and Bill Drummond of the pop music group the KLF (Kopyright Liberation Front), who in 1992 retired from music at the height of their commercial success, deleted their catalog of recordings, and bought a series of newspaper ads commanding the world to "Abandon All Art Now."

Such gestures, however, quite apart from their obvious practical failure to suppress or even curtail cultural production in any significant way, would appear to have certain limitations built into them from the start. For the Situationists, the supersession of art and culture coincides with—and, indeed, is a kind of effect or consequence of—the supersession of industrial labor. As I summarized above, the Situationists understand contemporary labor to have both a positive and a negative aspect, in that labor-saving technology both alienates workers from production and yet makes possible new modes of creativity by affording workers more leisure. The supersession and realization of work are to be found in the triumph of its positive aspect; for when the workplace is transformed and human energies are finally free to express themselves on a higher plane, then even automation will presumably no longer deprive the individual of his or her opportunity to contribute something personal to industrial production. But the relationship between industrial and cultural production thus involves an absolute contradiction, in that the liberation of labor succeeds by making labor "passionately interesting" and by saving time spent at labor so that "magnificent cultural constructions" might be brought forth. The liberation of literal production (work) will facilitate the production of culture (the Work). But if the supersession of work lies in the Work, how can the supersession of the Work lie in its abolition? The success of the first project would render the success of the second impossible—or vice versa, depending how one looks at it.

Art's supersession can also be grasped, however, in another way: as simply a radical transformation of art's social significance and status. In this case, art will not simply cease but will, rather, become a part of life, no longer distinguishable from any other activity. This possibility has also been a persistent theme throughout the twentieth-century avant-garde. One thinks here, for example, of Arthur Cravan, boxer, art critic, occasional publisher, and prototype "of pure Dada behavior" (Rubin *Dada and Surrealist Art* 11), who writes in 1913 that "painting is walking, running, drinking, eating and fulfilling your natural functions" (Motherwell 12). One will, here again, recall Duchamp, whose serene vision of an art of living was cited above and for whom, as Andre Breton puts it, "the question of art and life . . . does not arise" (Motherwell 211). To be sure, these cases may seem merely to exemplify a kind of *pose*, and a pose, moreover, characterized by a certain quasi-aristocratic superiority to all manner of organized production and exchange. The Dadaist, writes Huelsenbeck, "is the man who rents a whole floor at the Hotel Bristol without knowing where the money is coming from to tip the chambermaid" (Motherwell 28–29). Duchamp himself was always famously reticent about how he managed to make a living during the many years following his claimed retirement from artistic production.

Yet the other side of this coin, and the attitude to which it is always conceptually linked, would be an aspiration to radically democratize the field of cultural production. Such aspirations, which I briefly considered with regard to American "New Deal" art, are one more obvious feature of the postwar avant-garde. The COBRA group, one of many avant-garde movements that coalesced in the wake of Surrealism, writes in its manifesto (1948):

It is clear that what is called "genius" is nothing but the ability of personality to break away from the ruling aesthetics, so to speak to rise above it. Genius must be common to all when this aesthetics has lost its hold on us. . . . This does not mean that the statements of all people are to have the same general validity, but that everybody will be given the possibility of being heard. The genius of the people, the source where all may slake their thirst, takes the place which in former times was occupied by individuals. (Olasen, unpaginated)

The Dutch painter Constance, a member of COBRA, writes, similarly, that "a new freedom is about to be born," in which "the profession of artist will cease to occupy a privileged position" (quoted in Home *Assault on Culture* 9). With the Situationists, even more broadly, this leveling of the field of aesthetic creation finally rejoins the revolutionary transformation of everyday life, so that, as Mustapha Khyati writes, "the realization of art—poetry in the situationist sense—means that one cannot realize oneself in a 'work,' but rather realizes oneself, period" (Knabb 172). Thus, what I have briefly sketched as two possible ways to imagine the supersession of art finally become one. With its supersession, art disappears—only to reappear as what Stewart Home describes (and dismisses) as "a poeticized construction of daily existence" (*Neoism* 32). Art reaches its absolute realization by relocating itself in the self-development or self-fulfillment of the creative Subject.[5] In this, the Situationists, like the whole twentieth-century avant-garde tradition of which they remain a quintessential instance, arrive at precisely the same place as the contemporary theorists of work discussed in part 1. The crucial notion of *supersession* reveals itself at last as in no way a rejection or abolition of either work or the Work but at most a kind of infinitely drawn-out deferral of both.

Plagiarism and Potlatch

The twentieth-century avant-garde thus seems repeatedly to founder at precisely the point of opposition between work and the Work whose displacement it seeks. An ideal of the self-fulfilling Work is systematically destabilized and yet always allowed to reappear in the shape of the self-realization and fulfillment promised to the individual subject. In the present context it will not be surprising that such gestures and their attendant paradoxes are also bound up with the question of the gift. We have already glimpsed some of the ways in which Dada, either in its impulse of aesthetic negation or in its corresponding fascination with an art of living, refuses to subject itself to any rational economies of production or exchange. Dada aspired to exist in *acts* rather than in *works;* and such acts, as Rubin suggests, "may take any form as long as they remain *gratuitous*" (*Dada and Surrealist Art* 11). Breton, similarly, writes that "Dada gives itself to nothing, neither to love or to work. It is inadmissible that a man should leave any trace of his passage on earth" (Motherwell 203).

As Breton's figure suggests, however, an attempt to divorce art entirely from economy compels Dada both to embrace and to reject the gift—to give itself to "nothing" precisely so as to be able to give at all. Such a figure also indicates, even if unwillingly, how the kind of traceless, negative gift of which Breton speaks (a gift untouched by all emotional or utilitarian concerns) is strictly impossible, at least insofar as it remains under the sign and governance of the given name. Indeed, in this case that strange aleatory hobbyhorse of a name, Dada, was in fact never merely *given* (*dare, datta*), for it still remains enmeshed in well-known disputes (between Tzara and Huelsenbeck in particular) about who is owed the credit for having coined it (Rubin *Dada, Surrealism, and Their Heritage* 189–90). The all-too-obvious recuperation of every conceivable trace of Dada by an academic history of art must therefore be understood to spring from a certain double necessity inscribed in the very gesture of avant-garde negation itself, which in this case evidently both insists upon and refuses that very gratuitousness on which its very definition depends.

The figure of art-as-gift would reemerge even more explicitly in the postwar avant-garde. The free newsletter of the Letterist movement in 1950s Paris was called *Potlatch*, a title explicitly inspired by the writings of Mauss and Bataille (Home *Assault on Culture* 20; Jappe 148–49) and with which the Letterists would claim to be restoring, at least discursively, a kind of gift economy. In 1959, after the Letterist movement had been more or less subsumed into Situationism, Debord writes in one of the last issues of *Potlatch* that "the non-salcable goods that a free bulletin such as this is able to distribute are novel desires and problems; and only the further elaboration of these by others can constitute the corresponding return gift" (quoted in Jappe 148). Both the Letterists and the Situationists also attempt to destabilize the conventional economies of artistic authorship and consumption with the strategy they called *détournement*, which involves appropriating and altering preexisting texts or images so as to alter their meaning (see Knabb 9). A strategy of appropriation is, they claim, the only "appropriate" way to pursue art in the aftermath of the Work. As Debord and Wolman write: "All aware people of our time agree that art can no longer be justified as a superior activity. . . . Since the negation of the bourgeois conception of art and artistic genius has become pretty much old hat, [Duchamp's] drawing of a mustache on the *Mona Lisa* is no more interesting than the original version of that painting. . . . In fact, it is necessary to finish with any notion of personal property in this area" (Knabb 8–9).

Given that even Duchamp's readymades, otherwise the very model of aesthetic negation, must now be superseded, the only practice that remains available even to the avant-garde is a kind of deliberate plagiarism performed in the name of a more collective model of authorship. No longer a mere desecration of masterpieces intended to diminish their prestige, *détournement* would aspire, by contrast, to announce and itself constitute a system of exchange without individual givers or receivers, a system in which works would apparently give themselves without reserve in an endless process of mutual dissemination.

In one aspect, therefore, this characteristic strategy itself supersedes the mere aesthetic negation that, as the Situationists often acknowledge, was always characteristic of their avant-garde predecessors (see Knabb 55). The unexpected combinations and juxtapositions that result from *détournement* are also understood to produce, as it were, a negation of this negation: "The mutual interference of two worlds of feeling, or the bringing together of two independent expressions, *supercedes* the original elements and *produces a synthetic organization of greater efficacy*" (Knabb 9; emphasis added). Thus, *détournement* may be considered the methodological correlative of the general idea of a *supersession* of art; and as such, it retains the same conceptual problems. The Situationists continue to envision their negative appropriation of other works as positively *productive* of a more intense "efficacy," a higher level of aesthetic organization and meaning. Here again, in other words, the Situationist negation of art loses faith with anything like Bataille's vision of loss without reserve (see chapter 5). The remainder or excess that is understood to emerge from the practices of *détournement* (like the "progress" that Lautremont declares, in an epigram frequently cited by the Situationists, to be the goal and effect of plagiarism) inevitably threatens not merely "the closed circle of exchangist rationality" but also the "expenditure, without return, of a gift that forgets itself" (Derrida *Given Time* 47). Whatever aesthetic excess emerges from these practices of plagiarism and misappropriation is always intended for reinvestment.

Such dilemmas continue to be evident in the contemporary avant-garde, for example, in the extensive writings and various other avant-garde provocations of Stewart Home, whose involvement with the Neoist group's Art Strike of 1990 has already been briefly mentioned. Both in his survey of the twentieth-century avant-garde, *The Assault on Culture* (1988), and in other manifestos and occasional writings, Home often denounces the Situationists as "poor theorists" who merely repeated earlier avant-garde ideas and "dressed [them] up in surrealist clichés" (*Neoism* 161–62). But it is hard to see what is different about his own definition of plagiarism as "the conscious manipulation of pre-existing elements in the creation of 'aesthetic' works," which "enriches human language" and "leads to progressive social transformation" (*Neoism* 51). Later, after his break with Neoism and now writing as an ostensible member of the Praxis group (a kind of semiparodic, one-man avant-garde movement), Home still celebrates plagiarism in more or less the same terms as the Situationists had done several decades earlier: seeing it, for example, as the only conceivable aesthetic technique in an era in which "everything has been done" and "nothing can be taken seriously" (*Neoist Manifestos* 32).

Home's pose of relentless parody, along with the sheer profusion of his declarations and manifestos, makes his whole project, as he acknowledges, more or less "undefeatable, self-refuting and incomprehensible" (*Neoist Manifestos* 28). Yet Home's aggressive assault on the values and institutional structures of art still collides headlong with an all-too-familiar limitation of aesthetic negation: "Today, we are no longer stupid enough to imagine that what we do is new, or even that such an assertion does not imply a progression—and hence a certain amount of 'originality' " (*Neoist Manifestos* 33). One can no more fail to admire these self-canceling paradoxes than one can ignore the ingenious syntactical stutter by which the renunciation of all aesthetic progress still accords a certain pride of place to "originality" itself. Praxis itself, Home also claims,

abolishes the divide between theory and practice by defining itself in terms of the tautology "I am what I am." That is to say that whatever we are or do is PRAXIS.

Where previous avant-garde movements sought to define themselves through the exclusion of ideas, PRAXIS finds coherence in the totality of human endeavour and particularly in the endeavour to seek definition through exclusion. (*Neoist Manifestos* 34)

In this case, similarly, it is impossible to ignore the declension by which an announced radical immanence (grasped specifically as an *abolition* of distinctions) finally arrives at a new positive project of "definition" whose very vehicle is a process of exclusionary distinction. Of course, it is by no means certain that the text just cited, which so expertly mimics the rhetorical rhythms of other twentieth-century avant-garde manifestos, is intended to be anything more than a satire. Such uncertainty, however, itself indicates that same residuum of "originality" that Home always seems both to renounce and to announce. In other words, the characteristic evasions and ironies of Home's text seem still to leave us stranded at the same limit point—art as life and vice versa—at which so many of the other figures briefly discussed here seem repeatedly to arrive.

The concrete practice of *détournement*, or creative plagiarism, might be considered to have reached its fruition with contemporary popular music, particularly in the practice known as "sampling," in which small or large parts of previously existing recordings are incorporated into a new piece of music. This is not the place for a detailed history of this intriguing practice, which seems to have begun with DJs mixing music live for the dance floor, and which has always been conditioned by the evolution of electronic technology for musical performance. At one end of the spectrum, sampling has today produced the phenomenon known as the "mix-up" or "mash-up," in which two or more different pop songs are superimposed using computers to microsynchronize their rhythms (see Strauss). The other end of the spectrum is occupied by a varied group of musicians who employ sampling in the service of rather more pronounced political, satiric, or aesthetic projects. One can reference here experimental musicians such as Negativland, the Tape Beatles, the KLF (Kopyright Liberation Front), and John Oswald (who calls his work "plunderphonics"), all of whom in their separate ways combine snippets of previously recorded music into elaborate sound collages, and all of whom have been frequently embroiled in legal battles over their use of copyrighted materials.

Even these fruitful experiments with creative plagiarism, however, would seem merely to further illuminate the peculiar irony that has been inscribed in the very idea of aesthetic plagiarism from its inception. On the one hand such practices—acts of appropriation that present themselves as acts of giving—remain wholly dependent on the broader sociopolitical goals with which they have been invested: namely, the destabilization or abolition of individual authorship itself. Only from the point of view of such a potential emptying out of aesthetic authority could plagiarism claim to figure within a hypothetical new economy of art.

In fact, however, it is easy to show that the assault on authorship in which the artists I have named and many others are currently engaged remains in service of an utterly conventional system of aesthetic value. In their book *Fair Use,* for example, the members of Negativland detail at length their various struggles against the prevailing laws of intellectual property but in the end claim only that such laws have "deleterious effects on culture itself" (Negativland 90). Indeed, their specific proposal for revising the laws of copyright is simply: "Ownership should extend to the entire *work* only. In other words, copyright and ownership of a song means that no one else can use that song, or cover that song, without paying the artist—because that's the artist's *work,* that's the artist's entire *work*" (90; emphasis added). What is called for here is simply a lightening of copyright protection, in which sampling—that is, "any fragmentary use" (90)—will be permitted, but only provided that "the material used [is] *superceded* [emphasis added] by the *new nature* of the usage itself" or, in other words, when "the new whole [is] more than the sum of its parts" (154). In fact, the work of musicians like Negativland must finally be recognized, not as an attack on, but as a wholehearted *embrace* of the society of the spectacle. It is precisely because we are always now inundated with sounds and images, Negativland argues, that artists must be allowed to sample some of these—so long as they only take something less than "the complete self-contained creation of another" (155), and so long as they use such fragments to create a new instance of aesthetic value.

Similarly, an exhibit entitled *Illegal Art: Freedom of Expression in the Corporate Age* in New York and Chicago in 2002–3 showed a variety of musical, video, and visual works, including those of Negativland, that in various ways appropriate previously existing materials without regard for their legal status. All these works, as the exhibit's press release suggests, are intended as a deliberate provocation against the laws of copyright and "intellectual property law," because such laws have "a silencing effect, discouraging the creation of *new works.*"[6]

Now, it remains only to consider a few final examples in which, rather than gestures of appropriation and creative plagiarism, the avant-garde embraces instead the figure of *potlatch:* a sort of destructive conflagration of signs and values. Here I will reference in particular Yves Klein, another avant-garde artist of the 1950s and 1960s in France who has been understood to have broad affinities with the Situationists insofar as he too attempts, in a variety of ways, to rescue art from the encroachments of "the spectacle" (see Buchloh; cf. Charlet 17–18). Klein himself specifically defines his own project in terms of an "overcoming" (*dépassement*) of "the problematic of art" (Perlein and Corà 71). Yet as Benjamin H. D. Buchloh argues, Klein's work must also be seen as "distinctly apolitical and anti-social" (258) and, at least as retrospectively constructed in the writings of critics such as Pierre Restany, often seems to celebrate, rather than critique, "the new techno-scientific society of consumption, spectacle, and control" (259). Klein himself frankly acknowledges that his experiments with pure monochrome paintings and "immaterial" objects were intended to achieve or manifest what he calls, intending the word in all its senses, a personal *property:*

Space consented to manifest its presence in my paintings in order to constitute them as notarized acts of ownership, my documents, my proof, my diplomas as conquistador. I am not only the owner of Blue, as one might believe today, no, I am the owner of

"COLOR," for it is the terminology of the legal acts of space. Of course, my incommensurable property is not "only colored," it simply "is": my paintings are there only as my visible deeds of property. (Perlein and Corà 71)

Klein repeatedly claims, as he does here, that the literal objects or paintings that constitute his "works" represent merely the traces of his art the way a deed is merely the trace of a building. The true "being" of that art, he asserts, "is found beyond the visible, in pictorial sensibility in the raw material state"—or, more precisely, and as the metaphor of the deed suggests, in the artist's declared *appropriation* of space and color. Klein thus might be said to reiterate the Situationist project through inversion: that is, he seeks to destabilize aesthetic value and "private property" by obsessively embracing both.

Klein's project becomes of particular interest in the present context with the famous set of rules he establishes for the sale and exchange of what he calls *zones de sensibilité immatérielle.* Klein seems to imagine the sale and transfer of these literally immaterial works at once as a commercial transaction, a eucharistic sacrifice, and a gift exchange; and his carefully described procedure for such sales is worth considerable scrutiny:

The zones of immaterial pictorial sensibility by Yves Klein the Monochrome are sold for a certain weight of fine gold. . . . For each zone sold, a receipt is delivered which indicates the weight of fine gold, the material value of the acquired immateriality. The zones are transferable by their owners. . . .

If he wishes the fundamental immaterial value of the zone to belong to him definitively and to be one with him, he must solemnly burn his receipt, after having written his family name, proper name, address and the date of purchase on the stub of the receipt book.

In the event that he wishes to fulfill this act of integrating the work to himself, Yves the Monochrome, accompanied by a museum director, a well-known art dealer, or a critic, plus two witnesses, must throw half the weight of the gold received into the ocean, or into a river or into any place in nature where this gold cannot be recovered by anyone.

From this moment the zone of immaterial pictorial sensibility belongs absolutely and intrinsically to its owner. The zones sold in this way, after the purchaser has burnt his receipt, are no longer transferable by their owners. (Perlein and Corà 223–24)

What immediately strikes one about this set of procedures is the way gestures of utter renunciation and meticulous preservation are combined. To possess the zone of sensibility, the record of its purchase must be destroyed, but only after leaving a record *of* this record: so that the immaterial property must remain forever linked to the proper name of its buyer.[7] The apparent moment of gift exchange or potlatch is sealed by a mutual relinquishing of both the Work and its recompense, which instantaneously produces, however, an absolute self-present property and an "owner." Finally and most obviously, Yves the Monochrome is required to throw away not *all,* but merely *half,* of the gold presented to him. He must do so, further, in the presence of representatives of the artistic establishment, who would seem to be there both to certify with their authority that a genuine work of art is being bought and sold and to witness the subversion of the conventional ontological status of the aesthetic enterprise itself.

One recent critic of Klein, Nicolas Bourriaud, suggests that "the creative instant when the work is charged with the immaterial sensibility of the artist could . . . be compared to the poetic effusion that Bataille calls 'sovereignty': the deployment of a project that aims at the destruction of every project" (37). But in fact, Klein's ritual, like his art as a whole, clearly eschews even the slightest possibility of a loss without return or reserve and is, rather, grounded in certain inviolable assumptions of calculation and exchange, however unorthodox. Such assumptions are clearly instantiated, for example, in Klein's decision to keep half the gold, an inescapably obvious gesture that remains a sticking point for even the most celebratory readings of his ceremony as a whole. To be sure, Klein claims that no financial value is at stake in the transaction at all. "Pictorial sensibility in the raw material state," he says elsewhere, cannot be paid for by "money," only by "gold" (Charlet 92). The demand for payment in gold also vaguely suggests some notion of alchemical transmutation (in which, rather than lead being turned into gold, gold is somehow sacrificed in order to make the immaterial object appear).[8] Nevertheless, one might surely have imagined the ceremony with complete, mutual sacrifice on both sides; and Klein's curious insistence on retaining half the gold all too clearly reveals an underlying assumption that a remainder or surplus, a wage or price, is indeed owed to the artistic master of ceremonies who mediates between the transcendent sensibility and the literally sensible.

To observe this is not, however, to allege some contamination of an otherwise perfect ritual; it is, rather, to observe how a quasi-theological vision of aesthetic self-presence underlies Klein's seeming assault on the ontological status of art. In another context, Klein frankly concedes:

Good businessmen are alchemists in their way, just like artists. Everything they approach, touch, everything they are interested in, becomes, produces, or earns silver or gold. It's a sort of philosopher's stone which they have developed themselves. . . . This philosopher's stone, this *personal gift,* is what would allow us to convert or transmute into gold any well-defined state of the things of nature, exterior to the self but made precisely for the self. . . . The essence of painting is that "something," that ethereal glue, that intermediary product which the artist secretes with his entire creative being, and which he has the power to place, incrust, impregnate in the pictorial material of the painting. (Perlein and Corà 82–83)

Here, the comparison of businessmen and artists as creators of value is perhaps less striking than the naive affirmation of the artist's "creative being." The latter is obviously envisioned here in terms of that quasi-theological structure I have previously discussed, in which all forms of production and self-production are understood as a reciprocation of a "personal gift" that arrives in the subject from some transcendent source. Restany, with a frankness that rivals Klein's own, suggests that the remainder of the gold in the ceremony "returns momentarily to Yves Klein, who is only its guardian," because ultimately "this gold, the product of God's fire, belongs to God" (Restany and Loselle 35). Indeed, after Klein's untimely death it was learned that he had privately presented to the Augustinian nuns of Cascia, Italy, what Restany describes as "an *ex-voto* dedicated to Saint Rita," in the shape of a box with four compartments. The lower compartment "contains three gold ingots resting on a bed of blue pigment" and a manuscript which explains that the gold is "the product of the sale of the first four zones of immaterial pictorial sensibility" (Restany and Loselle 35–36; see also Charlet 236–37). Klein's immaterial art thus replicates with astonishing fidelity the most conventional of aesthetic economies in which, as I suggested in chapter 7, all human creativity is understood as a necessary reciprocation of a transcendent gift. Perhaps needless to add, this is thus one more case in which the absolute gift as a dissemination without return or reserve is by no means embraced but, rather, in every way limited and proscribed.

Let me finally add two brief examples that will, respectively, bring to our full gaze that terminal limit of aesthetic negation we have repeatedly been glimpsing and indicate, with necessary indirection, a certain opening or rebeginning beyond that limit. I have already had occasion to mention Bill Drummond and Jimi Cauty, who brought their own remarkably successful careers as pop music stars (performing variously as the Timelords, the Justified Ancients of Mu-Mu, and the Kopyright Liberation Front, or KLF) to an abrupt end in 1992. As Stewart Home observes in a brief appreciation of the group, Drummond and Cauty obviously share a general interest in plagiarism and a general impulse of aesthetic provocation with the whole tradition of twentieth-century avant-garde art (*Neoism* 102–3). Their 1987 album *What the Fuck Is Going On?* for example, is a collection of satiric collages of pop music heavy with samples of copyrighted material; the record was, accordingly, suppressed by legal action.

The end of their career as pop stars was also accompanied by a series of outrageous attacks on the commercial music industry, including firing blanks from a machine gun at the audience of a British music awards show and having the carcass of a dead sheep delivered to the hotel where the show was taking place. Two years later, now operating as the K Foundation, they exhibited an artwork that was entitled *Nailed to the Wall* and that consisted of £1,000,000 in cash nailed to a wooden board; then, on the island of Jura, with a journalist and a cameraman as witnesses, they filmed themselves burning the money (Brook 5). This astonishing potlatch—in which, quite literally, it becomes no longer "a question of giving and returning gifts, but of destroying" (Mauss 37)—might at first be thought to demand a certain reticence on the part of any commentator, a principled refusal of even the slightest discursive recuperation. In fact, however, Drummond and Cauty themselves had already invited and ensured such recuperation by filming their actions, pressing the ashes of the burnt banknotes into a brick, and publishing an illustrated account of the event under the title *The K Foundation Burn a Million Quid*.

What we can say is that such an act, by shifting the focus of avant-garde negation from aesthetic value to the Law of Value itself, at least illumines with peculiar vividness the absolute limit of the Work as self-fulfilling freedom. Drummond and Cauty returned to the island of Jura on August 23, 1995, to show the film in the village hall; a transcript of an ensuing discussion with the townspeople is included in their book. An unnamed member of the audience articulates what must be considered an absolutely inevitable and unanswerable political critique of their actions:

You have destroyed notes with a monetary value of £1 million. . . . what you burnt was proceeds which represent the resources that you have burnt. . . . It's not your money, it's society's money. You had no right to destroy it. . . . The value of money is why we're all sitting here with clothes on—you have a responsibility when you have money and you haven't used that responsibility . . . at all. If you'd invested it in the economic structure of some underprivileged country—not by giving them rice but by giving them the resources to produce their own rice—you would see, eventually, thousands upon millions. What you've done is deprived people of life by burning that money. (Brook 18–20)

True enough, at the heart of the potlatch is also a refusal of the gift, an absolute betrayal of the Other. Yet it remains equally unanswerable to point out, as Drummond and Cauty do, that if they had simply spent the £1 million on themselves (the way any number of other successful artists have done), there would be neither any recuperation nor any opportunity for anyone to reproach them. In other words, it is as necessary to commend the unsurpassable extremity of Drummond and Cauty's gesture as it is to denounce it in the name of that same Law of Value whose impossible negation it announces. This terminal undecidability of value, this absolute (non)gratuitousness, is perhaps the very thing which the whole avant-garde tradition that is here at once mocked and fulfilled was always striving to achieve. Drummond and Cauty's fire had a place foretold for it from the beginning; and if it had not happened, it would have been necessary to invent it.

Or, to put all this another way, the unforgettable manner in which Drummond and Cauty demonstrate the limit of art as *self*-fulfillment will also serve with uncanny efficacy as the absolute figure of art as unfulfillment and incompletion—and therefore, in another, more rigorous sense, of freedom. Let me finally discover the same paradoxical figure in one more contemporary work: Félix González-Torres's *Untitled (Portrait of Ross in LA)* (1991), which takes the form of 175 pounds of hard candy wrapped in colorful wrappers and deposited in a corner of the room. A posted legend informs the spectators that they are invited to take a piece of the candy, that the candy is "always replenished" to exactly 175 pounds, and that this figure was the "ideal body weight" of the artist's lover, who died of AIDS.

To take a piece of the candy is to experience, perhaps, a certain *frisson* of subversion, a palpable negation of what Walter Benjamin famously calls the "aura" of a work of art. And in this, before anything else, González-Torres's work initially conveys a sort of levity or effervescence, a sense of relief as of a task made needless or a burden lifted. In its full context, however, the work also closes on the viewer with the implacable force of allegory and tragedy. One can only assume that the artist's lover had dwindled, under the progressive effects of this most cruel of diseases, to something less than the figure specified as his "ideal" weight (as he had also, perhaps—who knows?—in his health sometimes exceeded it). The indirection with which the installation merely *indicates* such suffering while *representing,* by contrast, an emblem of the lover as a limitless supply of sweetness is perhaps the principal source of this work's extraordinary pathos.[9]

And yet, tasting such pathos to the fullest, the installation seems, at the same time, to offer something else. Indeed, it exists precisely in the form of an *offering*.[10] Not merely an emblem, it is rather a performance in which an evocation of mortal finitude merges with something open-ended and inexhaustible. Its litany is not "Ask and it shall be given" but rather "Take—and it shall be given back." And in this, the work gestures toward something that is hard to name, something that is at once a gift and the loss of a gift or, perhaps, most precisely, *the gift of loss*.

Maurice Blanchot and "Unworking"

I suggested at the outset of this chapter that what Maurice Blanchot calls the *unworking* of art will indicate the opening of thought occasionally glimpsed across this astonishingly varied history of aesthetic experimentation. But this term denotes neither a concept in itself nor some positive aspect of art that might accordingly be defined, made present, or recuperated as some supersession of an obsolete problematic. I accordingly try to approach it by turning away from the aesthetic itself and returning to the more explicitly political questions that, as we have seen, also pervade the various avant-garde traditions of our times. This will indeed be no more than a rearticulation of that inevitable process by which the demands of work always interpose themselves against the airy pretensions of the Work at the very moment when the latter represents itself as the former's aspiration and fulfillment. Such a reunion of mere labor and aesthetic achievement can take shape either as fatal conjunction of two obligations, lived by the working subject as a perpetual reproach, or as that mutual absence and displacement indicated by Blanchot's elusive term.

Let me sketch the first alternative by briefly juxtaposing two polemical texts issued by an organization calling itself the American Council of Trustees and Alumni (ACTA), a conservative advocacy group. The first report, "The Shakespeare File: What English Majors Are Really Studying," was issued in December 1996; the second report, "Defending Civilization: How Our Universities Are Failing America and What Can Be Done about It," was originally issued in November 2001 in response to the terrorist attacks of the previous September 11.[11]

In the first report, ACTA alleges that Shakespeare has been dropped as a requirement in many American university curricula in favor of classes in popular media and cultural studies. As has been documented elsewhere, this charge itself is largely unfounded; but in the present context I focus instead on the report's explanation of why such curricular changes are worth concern in the first place. Even if Shakespeare were to fade from the curriculum of English studies in favor of other writers, why would it matter? According to the report:

It matters . . . to employers, especially to the school systems, newspapers, publishers and others who hire English majors. . . . for English majors not to read Shakespeare . . . is like an M.D. without a course in anatomy. . . . This country cannot expect a generation raised on gangster films and sex studies to maintain its leadership in the world. Or even its unity as a nation. Shakespeare has shaped our language and our culture. His works provide a common frame of reference that helps unite us into a single community or discourse. (Martin et al. 10)

In other words, the question of Shakespeare evokes a triangle of interrelation between work, the Work, and questions of national identity. Shakespeare is necessary for the individual as he or she prepares for professional employment; and Shakespeare is also necessary collectively as the self-present center of our common being, the "common frame of reference" around which our community defines its own assumed world preeminence. The argument is thus grounded in a certain paradox: Shakespeare is himself an absolute autoteleology, a cultural ideal who gives himself freely to be known; but he is to be fostered and propagated in purely instrumental terms.

The more recent report shifts the focus of such an argument to specific political concerns. It consists of a brief statement and then 117 numbered quotations from named and unnamed professors and students, which are intended to indict the American academy for its alleged failure to support the war on terrorism. This document invites a variety of critiques, not least for the astonishing speciousness with which it attacks academic freedom in the name of academic freedom. Here, I make only a single observation regarding the report's approach to the question of historical memory. The text literally begins and ends with the same passage, citing, both as epigraph and in its final lines, the words of Lynne Cheney, former head of the National Endowment for the Humanities and a founder of ACTA, from a speech delivered on October 5, 2001. Cheney argues: "At a time of national crisis, . . . we need to encourage the study of our past. Our children and grandchildren—indeed, all of us—need to know the ideas and ideals on which our nation has been built" (Martin et al. "Defending Civilization" cover and 8).

This affirmation of national memory, however, proves to be at most a partial one, for the report itself makes clear that ACTA does not advocate the study and preservation of *all* memories of the American past. Let me mention just two of the 117 brief quotations that the report uses as illustrations of what is fundamentally wrong with American education. Citation 12, for example, is ascribed to "Dean of the Woodrow Wilson School at Princeton University": "There is a terrible and understandable desire to find and punish whoever was responsible for this. But as we think about it, it's very important for Americans to think about our own history, what we did in World War II to Japanese citizens by interning them" (13). Citation 102 is ascribed simply to "Group at Amherst College": "The United States of America is built upon a history of violence and repression. This began with the genocide of Native Americans . . . and it continued as Black people were brought here as slaves" (27).

If comments such as these, which do little more than mention familiar and well-documented events of American history, are so unacceptable as to constitute a threat to civilization itself, then it means that this text's *injunction* to cultural memory is inseparable from an *interdiction* of such memory. We are asked to remember only what Cheney calls "ideas and ideals," and to remember them specifically as formative or constitutive essences on which a nation, "our" nation, has been "built"; but we are positively warned against remembering specific *events* in the history of that nation whose knowledge might contaminate the purity of those ideals. It is here that the nearly invisible connection between the two reports reveals itself, at the point of an asymmetrical intersection of work and the Work. In the first text, the Work of culture is said to be necessary for the creation of literal workers, whose efforts, in turn, will constitute the Work of America. In the second text, correspondingly, the Work of intellectual inquiry is asked to subordinate itself to a national Work understood at once as the pure expression of its own essence and as the aggregate of its labors in the simpler sense.

Here again, in other words, is the same triangle of concerns (art, nationalism, and labor) that repeatedly emerges in the modernist avant-garde—no less in the overt nationalism of Italian Futurism and American New Deal art than in the overt negation of it in Dada, Situationism, and others. I will argue here that the thought of Maurice Blanchot allows us to cut through this fatal triangle, whose structure evidently unites discourses on both the Left and the Right. Yet I can do so only via a brief consideration of the biographical scandal that surrounds Blanchot's own youthful association with a circle of ultranationalist journalists and literary critics in pre-war France. A political indictment of Blanchot's writings from this period was first presented in Jeffrey Mehlman's article "Blanchot at *Combat:* Of Literature and Terror" from 1980 (reprinted in his 1983 book *Legacies of Anti-Semitism in France*) and was continued by Steven Ungar in his *Scandal and Aftereffect: Blanchot and France since 1930* (1995).[12] Mehlman discusses in detail several otherwise forgotten articles written by Blanchot between 1936 and 1938. To repeat one sample of the passages cited by Mehlman (and in my opinion the worst of them), Blanchot in April 1936 denounces the French government for listening "to the appeals of unfettered revolutionaries and Jews," who in denouncing Hitler are trying "to precipitate young Frenchmen, in the name of Moscow or Israel, into an immediate conflict" (quoted in Mehlman 11). In such a passage, the apparent hope of peaceful coexistence with Hitler will, of course, strike one today as scarcely less deplorable than its obvious gestures of political and national exclusion.

Mehlman concedes that these early articles constitute "a fragment barely assimilable by the authorial *corpus* of which it nevertheless forms part." But he also aspires "to construct a logic of [Blanchot's] work that would restore the fragment to a position at the core of [his] *oeuvre*" (Mehlman 83). Now, as has been summarized at more length by Michael Holland and Leslie Hill, Blanchot after the 1930s avoids political writing in favor of literary criticism for many years, returning to politics only in the 1950s, in texts which now clearly associate themselves with left-wing positions.[13] Moreover, several of Blanchot's later texts engage rigorously with Jewish thought in a manner that one might be tempted to call philo-Semitic were it not that this same work includes a critique of philo-Semitism as no more than a displaced symptom of anti-Semitism. Among his last books are *The Unavowable Community* (1983), a text written in dialogue with Jean-Luc Nancy about the possibility of a community beyond all social exclusions; and *The Instant of My Death* (1994), a *récit* of an incident in which Blanchot himself was nearly shot as a member of the French resistance in the waning days of the war. Given all this, how and why would one understand Blanchot's writings of the 1930s, however deplorable their politics, as the "core" of his career?

At stake here, among other things, is precisely the question of the oeuvre, both in terms of Blanchot's literal biography and as a crucial sticking point in his theory of writing; to consider these biographical questions is thus by no means merely a digression. Mehlman's case for the centrality of Blanchot's right-wing journalism to his corpus primarily rests on a reading of his essay "How Is Literature Possible?" (1942). In this text, Blanchot discusses Jean Paulhan's *Flowers of Tarbes; or, Terror in Literature,* even as he also draws Paulhan's thesis to its limit. In brief, he asks how it is that modern writers, who begin with the impulse (as Ezra Pound famously puts it) to "make it new," to break free from all rhetorical commonplaces and "deal a mortal blow to all literary forms," nevertheless still produce literary forms and texts (*Reader* 56)?

Blanchot's answer points in the direction of a kind of deconstruction, a nascent awareness of that nostalgia for full self-presence (what Derrida calls logocentrism) that always haunts the project of writing. The writer approaches the work with what Paulhan and Blanchot audaciously call a "terrorism," aspiring to shatter all preexisting structures of rhetoric and literary form with the pure living presence of her own thought. But precisely when the writer shatters literary forms, thought necessarily takes shape in such forms; and precisely when the writer claims to look in his heart and write, what he finds there are "clichés, conventions, and the rules of language" to which his thought must, in principle, "yield" (Blanchot *Reader* 59). And in such yielding, the thought which seeks to unwork itself becomes—or at least disappears into—a Work.

For Mehlman, this argument should be read as "a coded farewell to plans for a French fascism in the 1930s" and as "Blanchot's own liquidation of an anti-Semitic past" (13, 16). But even as Mehlman acknowledges that deconstruction is "the heritage of the style of reading Blanchot was . . . initiating" (18) in this essay, he also asserts that his own reading *of* Blanchot is "of a piece with the general interpretive effort called 'deconstruction'" (84). This, to be sure, is a moment of strange interpretive vertigo. If Blanchot's work is to be understood as at once bequeathing a "legacy" of anti-Semitism and a "heritage" of deconstruction—the very method used to make this very point—then we would seem to be stranded in what Blanchot himself might call a vicious circle,[14] a manifestly self-defeating economy of poisoned legacies and competing appropriations. One can, however, cut through this circle by recognizing that Mehlman's reading is actually not nearly deconstructive enough. True, he brings something from the margins of a body of work back to its foreground, a practice often associated with deconstruction. But his conclusion is the product of a more or less traditional empirical hermeneutics—in which that which was occluded is now brought to light, in which right-wing politics are revealed, based on specific homologies and textual clues, as the interpretive "truth" of a text, and in which that textual truth is also taken as the "core," the determinative center, of an oeuvre. At work in Mehlman's analysis, then, is the causational and interpretive model that Althusser calls "expressive," which "presupposes in principle that the whole in question be reducible to an *inner essence*, of which the elements of the whole are then no more than the phenomenal forms of expression" (Althusser and Balibar 187).

This expressive and reductive reading is particularly insufficient given the later development of Blanchot's own theory of writing, for "How Is Literature Possible?" represents only the first stage in a theoretical trajectory that moves on to reverse the structure of Blanchot's initial question. In the early essay, Blanchot asks how writers who seek to destroy literature from within nevertheless end up producing literary Works. As Blanchot elaborates this already difficult question in other essays, it can sometimes sound as though he were making a kind of formalist argument—as though he were describing what the Russian formalists, for example, call the "estrangement" of meaning that takes place in literary texts, or affirming merely (to cite a celebrated and familiar motto from American New Criticism) that "a poem should not mean but be."[15] Several of his essays from the 1950s formulate, at times somewhat obscurely, insights that would eventually become the common parlance of contemporary literary studies. Blanchot insists, for example, on the radical *exteriority* of the text, on the inseparability of writing and reading (and thus of literary production and literary consumption), and on the impossibility of delimiting the text's interpretive horizon from the moment of its inscription. But Blanchot's approach to writing finally goes even farther, turning his initial question on its head in order to ask: how is it that the *work* of writing, the work manifest not just in an individual author's labors but also in *la chose littéraire*, in the whole institutional and discursive structure in which questions of rhetoric, genre, status, and signification alike interpenetrate—how is it that all of this produces only what he will eventually call a *work of the negative*, an *absence of the book?*

This is the paradox to which Blanchot's difficult texts constantly attend. If one asks, as critics commonly do, "Where is literature going?" one can answer only that "literature is going toward itself, toward its essence which is disappearance" (*Reader* 136). It is precisely because the text or work presents itself in sovereign "independence" from all of its determinants, including the author itself, effacing in its apparent completion and coherence all traces of the labor that produced it, that it falls short of the "proud transcendence" at which the author had aimed. The author's work disappears into the finished Work, from which, therefore, something always seems to withdraw into this very (dis)appearance. Thus, the Work "reverses the values we customarily accord to the words 'making' or 'doing' [*faire*] and 'being'" (137–38). "So it is," Blanchot also writes, "that the painter prefers the various states of a painting to the painting itself, and the writer often wishes to accomplish almost nothing" (140). The painter or writer knows precisely that her work can only proceed beyond itself "to a point where all that seems to speak is impersonal neutrality." These are "necessary contradictions" (141) that haunt every work of writing or thought. They problematize, above all, the idea of the oeuvre and the corresponding notions of intentionality and literary self-presence which are, as we have seen, central to Mehlman's critique.

The notion of unworking indicates or gestures toward, even if it cannot quite *name* (citing Nancy's summary) "that which, before or beyond the work, withdraws from the work, and which, no longer having to do either with production or with completion, encounters interruption, fragmentation, suspension" (*Inoperative Community* 31). As Leslie Hill also suggests, providing a certain colloquial clarity to what must otherwise remain an elusive and enigmatic nonconcept, *unworking* might be thought of as the curious double acknowledgment, following the apparent completion of any book, that one has always left something out, and that leaving something out "is what makes it possible to say anything at all" (Hill 222). Writing is here revealed, not as the autonomous production or expression of a self-present subject, but as that which conveys in its very essence only the finitude and fragmentation, the "breach and the fissure" (138), which is the very condition of singular being itself. This means, too, that the radical externality of the text is not to be grasped as a merely formal characteristic; rather, as Emmanuel Levinas summarizes, "Blanchot determines writing as a quasi-mad structure in the general economy of being, by which being is no longer an economy, as it no longer possesses, when approached through writing, any abode" (*Proper Names* 132–33). In writing, singular being is cast out from the *oikos* and exposed to what Levinas elsewhere calls "the plenitude of alterity" ("Trace of the Other" 345) and to what Nancy calls "being-in-common."

And therefore, most importantly, to thus determine writing as this "exteriority of absolute exile" (Levinas *Proper Names* 133), as the very site of our exposure to the Other, is also to grasp writing as the very site of ethics and of politics. By contrast, Mehlman and others who indict Blanchot's whole career on the basis of his pre-war writings are constrained to stand on the very ground of the Work as presence: they suggest, in effect, that Blanchot's attempt to think the negativity of writing was no more than an act of personal exoneration, an attempt to free himself from the political or ethical consequences of his own early texts. We would have to understand Blanchot, so to speak, as trying to liquidate his own writing by liquidating writing itself: a gesture of bizarre theoretical overkill that would seem, in any case, to have quite miserably failed, as the continuing controversy over his record attests. But such an argument, which finally rejoins a vulgar critique of deconstruction as mere political quietism, gets things backward. As Steven Shaviro argues, for Blanchot "it is precisely politics which haunts the strange, neutral space of writing," which means there is never a freedom "from complicity, from the demands of politics" (831–32). More specifically, as we shall see in more detail in the final chapter of this book, Nancy has discovered in Blanchot's *désoeuvrement* the nearly untranslatable rubric for a rigorous model of community itself: a community that, most of all, "takes place . . . not in a work that would bring it to completion . . . but in the unworking and as the unworking of all its works" (*Inoperative Community* 72).

We can now also conclude that the quasi-deconstructive vision of writing that begins in Blanchot's early literary criticism is necessarily also the critique of what Philippe Lacoue-Labarthe calls "nationalist-aestheticism," a position (to which the early Blanchot evidently succumbed) that sees all community as grounded in the pure self-presence of a national identity, and that identity, in turn, as quintessentially expressed by a national art (see Lacoue-Labarthe 61–76). In our times, such a position is perhaps most usefully exemplified, as Lacoue-Labarthe also suggests, by Martin Heidegger, with whom Blanchot's writings of the 1940s and 1950s are often in implicit dialogue, and who is himself at the center of an even wider controversy about his direct involvement with German National Socialism in the 1930s. This is not the place for a detailed exposition of that controversy, or of Heidegger's influence on Blanchot and contemporary theory. Nevertheless, in the present context, one can at least reject either of two common responses to the Heidegger problem. That is, one will neither wish to *defend* Heidegger by reference to some intrinsic value in his thought that can be separated from his political choices and so preserved from the contamination of retrospect, nor *condemn* him (following the same logic to an opposite conclusion) by reference to some immanent essence of his philosophy as a whole that is alleged to be unilaterally conducive to a fascist politics.

Otherwise, I suggest that Blanchot's "unworking" can be further understood as the precise theoretical obverse of a certain obsession with work that, as Werner Hammacher argues, was a central feature both of National Socialism itself and of Heidegger's deplorable attempt to philosophize its project. Hammacher suggests that the notorious and apparently cynical motto *Arbeit macht frei* (work makes free) actually sums up the essence of National Socialism, in which work "as the form of the self-appropriation of the 'being and life' of a people is simultaneously the form of its liberation from everything that is not itself, that is not proper to it" (28). At the heart of German fascism is thus a certain double affirmation of work, which is understood both as the self-appropriation by individuals of a national essence and as their production, via a Work of purification, of the national community. National Socialism is thus the nightmare fulfillment of the exclusionary tendencies that emerge from every politico-ethical system affirming work as the uniquely privileged bearer of social value.

Heidegger's political texts from 1933 to 1934, the period of his direct involvement with the Nazi party, are depressingly obvious in their deployment of such figures. In his Rectorship Address (1933), given when he had accepted the post of rector at Freiburg University, Heidegger asserts: "The German student's notion of freedom is now being returned to its truth," which will lie, he says, in "certain bonds and forms of service": "The first bond is the one that binds to the ethnic and national community [*Volksgemeinschaft*]. It entails the obligation to share fully, both passively and actively, in the toil, the striving and the abilities of all states and members of the Volk. This bond will henceforth be secured and rooted in student existence [*Dasein*] through *labor service*" (Wolin 35). The second bond "is the one that binds to the honor and the destiny of the nation" and is manifest in military service; the third bond "is the one that binds the students to the spiritual mission of the German Volk" and is manifest in "knowledge service" (35). These three bonds, and the three forms of work with which they are linked, are "aspects of the German essence" (36). In such passages, work is clearly being understood at once as the very *source* of an individual being (*Dasein*) and as the very *form* of that individual's obligatory contribution to the Work of a national community that, in its turn, can claim those developed individuals as *its* works.

This mirroring structure, in which the individual's labor and the grand Work of national "destiny" are doubly related, appears repeatedly in Heidegger's texts from this period. One might well pause briefly here to remark one last time on the remarkable persistence of this fatal triangle in which labor and art (work and the Work) are doubly linked as the source and expression of an essential national community: an ideological structure central to German fascism, to Soviet communism, and even to a certain mode of Western free-market liberalism. Thus, Heidegger, speaking to a group of National Labor Procurement program recruits in January 1934, sounds uncannily similar to contemporary critics of welfare when he insists that only through work can an unemployed individual "win back proper dignity and self-confidence in his own eyes and acquire proper self-assurance and resoluteness in the eyes of his *Volksgenossen*" (Wolin 56). This unity of work and national community is also assumed in Heidegger's rather more rigorous essay of 1935, "The Origin of the Work of Art." Here, Heidegger famously uses the image of the Greek temple to explain how "Art is truth setting itself to work" (Heidegger 165). It is only in the precinct of the temple, he argues, that the myriad events of human life "acquire the shape of destiny for human being," so that "[o]nly from and in this expanse does the nation first return to itself for the fulfillment of its vocation" (167). All art, "as the letting happen of the advent of the truth of being, is as such, *in essence, poetry*" (197)—that is, a making, a "being composed" (197), a setting-to-work. And this poetic work is precisely the site in which "the concepts of a historical people's essence . . . are performed for that people" (199).

We may even venture to identify this analogy of the Work and the State as precisely the blind spot of Heidegger's thought where it opens itself to its own unworking. At another point of his essay, Heidegger explains: "One essential way in which truth establishes itself in the beings it has opened up is truth setting itself into work. Another way in which truth occurs is the act that founds a political state" (Heidegger 186). The founding or establishing of the Work or the State is thus precisely an act of *sovereignty*. But in acknowledging this, we must also recall Bataille's redefinition of sovereignty as the confrontation of singular, "restricted" being with the general economy, a kind of opening up by which finite existence recognizes its own access to the global movement of limitless energy and irredeemable excess. To rethink Heidegger's vision of the work of art in such terms makes possible a radically different conclusion. The proper sovereignty of the Work lies not in its illusory and impossible completion or coherence but rather in an abandonment to its own dissemination; the proper sovereignty of the State, by the same token, lies not in the violent enforcement of some pure national presence but rather in its willful embrace of limitless inclusivity and being-in-common. The moment of greatest independence and power, for the Work or the State, is precisely when the boundaries of either reveal themselves in their inevitable and infinite openness.

Nevertheless, many commentators (including Blanchot) have denounced Heidegger for remaining silent after the war about his support of National Socialism.[16] Perhaps, similarly, one may wish to ask why Blanchot himself never explicitly apologizes for his own writing of the pre-war years, especially since his politics and thought seem to have transformed themselves so radically. Why did he choose to live his long life in nearly complete obscurity and personal silence? The question is perhaps both necessary and impossible: for to answer it can only involve a ransacking of texts for some "spiritual or ideal presence" that would have left some "mark or sedimentary deposit that would allow one to track it down, in other words to restore it—on the basis of that mark as deficiency—to its ideal presence" (Blanchot *Station Hill Reader* 475–76). I would add that an apology is something that one either "gives" or "makes" and that is thus intimately bound up in the questions of work and gift which are at stake in the present discussion. For Blanchot to give or make an apology would be, in effect, to enter a cycle of exchange, to seek to balance an account that his detractors, in any case, insist on keeping open—and thus also to ask for what Derrida aptly calls a "forgiveness which is anything but forgiveness" (Derrida *On Cosmopolitanism and Forgiveness* 49).

It will surely also be obvious, to return to my opening observations, that the injunctions of the ACTA report cited in the beginning of this section themselves epitomize a new version of that nationalist aestheticism from which Blanchot departs and which his subsequent thought seeks in every way to undercut. It is no coincidence, in other words, that the same organization that enjoins the study of "great" books—and commands us to study them simply *in* and *for* this greatness—should also enjoin the study of pure historico-social "ideals," and command that we study them, here again, only as the alleged founding principles of a history whose own particulars must be occluded lest they violate the purity of those ideals. Blanchot's vision of memory, though it too takes the shape of two contradictory injunctions, represents as it were the precise converse of the ACTA model. The latter says: remember, but not too much, and not everything. By contrast, Blanchot not only argues but also perhaps indicates—though only negatively or indirectly, and in part via the obstinate obscurity of his public image—that *every event* "interposes, through testimony, the indefeasible duty not to forget: remember, beware of forgetfulness and yet, in that faithful memory, *never will you know*" (*Reader* 247–48). The first model enjoins a perpetual production of banal abstraction, incapable even of silence. Blanchot, on the contrary, looks to writing and to memory as perpetually repeated transgressions of their own limits; in both of which, however, the return of barbarism and terror remains always possible, and in which, therefore, "the debt is our only lot," and we are never "acquitted of responsibility" (*Reader* 249).

One must finally stipulate, however, that what Blanchot attempts to indicate as this almost indescribable absence of writing is in no way merely the sign of some potential reproach that might be directed at the *limits* of a finite being (writer or Work) condemned to fulfill its destiny at those very limits. In his essay "The Narrative Voice," Blanchot sketches the paradox by which language, which alone can signify all ideas—including the very idea of limit itself—also indicates in its own process the inexhaustible connectedness of being:

I write (I pronounce) this sentence: "The life forces suffice only up to a certain point." As I pronounce it, I think of something very simple: the experience of weariness that constantly makes us feel a limited life; you take a few steps on a street, eight or nine, then you fall. The limit set by weariness limits life. The meaning of life is in turn limited by this limit: a limited meaning of a limited life. But a reversal occurs that can be discovered in various ways. Language modifies the situation. The sentence I pronounce tends to draw into the very inside of life the limit that was only supposed to mark it from the outside. Life is said to be limited. The limit does not disappear, but it takes from language the perhaps unlimited meaning that it claims to limit: the meaning of the limit, by affirming it, contradicts the limitation of meaning or at least displaces it. (Blanchot *Infinite Conversation* 379)[17]

Such observations lead Blanchot to a careful examination of the narrative voice in literature. He suggests, in brief, that the "I" of writing necessarily becomes an impersonal "he"—either literally, in the various strategies of narrative itself, or implicitly, in the text as read and interpreted. Blanchot calls this narrative "he" the "neuter," which, he further suggests, always "marks the intrusion of the other—understood in its irreducible strangeness" (385). This intrusion, here again, will not allow the Work to exist as such, as "a completed whole, once and forever accomplished" (386). Yet this incompletion itself is not the text's inadequacy or failure but the reverse. It is precisely at its limit that the Work achieves its limitlessness; it is precisely when writing reveals the impossibility of its closure and opens itself, as it must, to the intrusion of the Other, that the Work is most properly *itself* (cf. Hill 97).

Years later, Blanchot would himself employ this neutral voice of narrative to describe "a young man" who faces, and by chance escapes, an enemy firing squad. He writes:

I know—do I know it—that the one at whom the Germans were already aiming, awaiting but the final order, experienced then a feeling of extraordinary lightness. . . . Perhaps ecstasy. Rather the feeling of compassion for suffering humanity, the happiness of not being immortal or eternal. (*The Instant of My Death* 5)

The incompletion that haunts the project of writing is the incompletion of mortal being itself, which in confronting its own finitude most reaffirms compassion: the social bond that binds only by unbinding, that connects absolutely but only on condition of death (see also Derrida *Demeure* 60). This is the moment of ecstasy in which the restricted economy (scarcity) to which singular being is indeed absolutely bound is experienced *at* its limit, and thus precisely not merely *as* a limit but also as an access to the general economy of being-in-common.

In the next chapter, I will follow a different route to arrive at more or less this same formulation, in which the limitlessness inherent in language offers itself as both a figure and a source of what Blanchot calls the negative community and Nancy calls the community of unworking. Such phrases indicate, though only once again with a necessary indirection, a coming community that is "less a gathering than the always imminent dispersal of a presence," a community of "limitless power which, in order to limit itself, accepts *doing nothing*" (Blanchot *Unavowable* 32–33). This negative or unworking community, precisely when it is recognized as neither the State nor the *Volk* nor any group linked by a common identity or a common (self-)production, is, as Blanchot concludes, "rather similar to what could have been the gathering of the children of Israel in view of the Exodus if they had gathered while at the same time forgetting to leave" (33). I conclude this chapter by lingering over this memorable figure of a promised land achieved in its very forgetfulness of itself, this community that negates itself *in* and *as* the promise of its own being-in-common.

MARXISM AND THE GENERAL ECONOMY

On Means and Ends

We finally return, as of course we must, to economy itself: to the discursive domain that still so oddly straddles ethics and science. It is time to state in its most general form a point that has been implicit throughout this book. That which we call "economics," both inside and outside the limits of the formal discipline of this name, remains today fundamentally a thought of the Other, a mode of inquiry involving constitutive acts of division and exclusion: between manual and intellectual, productive and unproductive labor; between capitalist production and its hypothetical predecessors or successors; between the gift and the commodity, between work and the Work. In the end it is evident that such divisions constitute no more than a closed structure of thought in which different discourses simply reinterpret or reprivilege one side or the other of variously named oppositions that finally reveal or reduce themselves, as we have partially seen, to a broad opposition between instrumentality and autoteleology, between means and ends.

It is equally evident, however, that a kind of terminal instability haunts all these familiar divisions of the economic field, an instability I will trace here as another avenue leading toward a displacement of the terms and premises that have governed my discussion thus far. I necessarily begin by returning briefly to perhaps the most celebrated of all such economic divisions: Aristotle's distinction between two modes of acquiring wealth: *oikonomia,* household management, and *chrematistike,* business or moneymaking. As we have seen,

Aristotle seems to concede the irreducible necessity of both economic modes, which always overlap to some extent within social life, even as he privileges the former as both more "natural" and more conducive to individual and collective happiness. I note in passing that a different but analogous economic opposition is assumed within the body of ancient Jewish law known as the Mishnah, edited in the second century AD but drawing on a priestly code of the land of Israel from about the same time as Aristotle. The Mishnah distinguishes between a "distributive" economy, which involves the giving of material goods to the priesthood or to the poor in accordance with various ritual or symbolic obligations, and a "market" economy involving commercial exchange and driven by supply and demand (Neusner 10–11).

In both cases, economy in some higher, purer, or more proper sense is always to be distinguished from some other field of practice which it closely resembles and with which it must coexist. The Mishnah assumes the existence of a secular marketplace, even as it distinguishes it from and subordinates it to all forms of charitable and spiritual exchange. Aristotle, similarly, concedes that his two forms of economic behavior overlap each other and can be distinguished only by their purpose or end (see Shell 94). Economics concerns acquisition for use and consumption: that is (to cite a late-sixteenth-century commentator on Aristotle's *Politics*), "such manner of getting, tending to the attainment of a happy life." Moneymaking or business, by contrast, concerns the potentially limitless acquisition of wealth for its own sake, a process whose "end . . . is not use, but profit."[1] By defining his two modes of acquisition in terms of their respective ends, however, Aristotle introduces a certain necessary ambiguity into the division itself. From one aspect, Aristotle seems to understand business as a pure instrumentality: a set of practices whose only value is the profit it produces. Economy, conversely, would be a process whose every component—tilling the land, baking the bread, managing the *oikos*—joins with the rest to constitute the "happy life" that is the telos of the whole process. Seen this way, business would be a means to an end and economy would be an end in itself. Yet such a contrast might, with equal plausibility, be reversed. Economy, precisely in its harmony with the productive rhythms of nature, might be envisioned as a process of specific means leading to specific ends, in which you must sow that you may reap, and in which you may reap only what you sow. Business, correspondingly, in its limitless quest for a profit wholly unrelated to consumption, might be thought of as an end in itself—a vision illustrated, for example, in the conventional comic type of the miser.

This Aristotelian distinction seems to reemerge at least implicitly in an astonishing variety of subsequent thought. I have previously mentioned Marx's acknowledgment that his own opposition between two cycles of exchange (C-M-C versus M-C-M') largely mirrors Aristotle's opposition between acquisition for use or for exchange. In the present context, it is also striking that the familiar anthropological vision of an archaic "domestic mode of production" that precedes all subsequent regimes of economic organization also seems at least broadly homologous with Aristotle. Marshall Sahlins explicitly characterizes this archaic economy as "production . . . oriented to livelihood, not to profits," which, like *oikonomia* (and Marx's cycle of C-M-C), "envisions not only a moderate quota of good things, but these of a *specific useful character* responding to the producers' customary requirements." Sahlins also opposes this to a "production for exchange (value)" which, like Aristotle's *chrematistike* (and Marx's M-C-M'), "holds out the indefinite goal of 'as much as possible'" (Sahlins 83–84).

Aristotle's opposition also influences in complex ways the long subsequent tradition of moral economy, both in its major historical flowering during the early-modern period (just prior to the birth of capitalism) and in what I have suggested is its contemporary reemergence. The discourse of moral economy in its earlier period largely consists of a set of moral prescriptions and prohibitions for buying, selling, giving, working, and so forth. As I briefly considered in chapter 8, early-modern writers belabor a moral opposition between the process of producing tangible value through labor (especially agricultural labor) and the various financial or commercial practices which, like *chrematistike,* produce nothing but profit. In the present context I observe the evident instability of this opposition with regard to the question of means and ends. As with Aristotle, it would be entirely plausible to assert that the moral economy *mandates* economic instrumentality (sowing in order to reap) and *prohibits* moneymaking as an end in itself. The emblematic villain of moral economy discourse is always the miser or hoarder, a figure often conflated with the usurer and imagined as someone who "doth abound, yet starves and nothing spends" (Whitney 74), who gathers and accumulates and yet never enjoys the fruits of his own exertions. Yet by the very same token this discourse also demands that each human being must work (citing conventional phrases from various texts) for "his neighbors profit," "for the common good," for "the advancing of God's glory, and the benefit of men."[2] Thus, this discourse can be said to condemn the mere instrumentality of commercial calculation and profit, even as it celebrates true economy, paradoxically, as an instrumental process that nevertheless presents itself as an absolute moral end in itself.

By contrast, the discourse of "political" economy that emerges with Adam Smith might be thought to transcend such oppositions by claiming the whole field of the production and distribution of value as its object of knowledge. Yet political economy is itself founded on an act of division and exclusion, one that apparently reverses the general thrust of the moral economy and yet finally reveals a similar instability. As it develops as a formal discipline in the nineteenth century, economics found it necessary to portray itself as a field of empirical and scientific inquiry with its own rules, limits, and theoretical purity. For example, the economist John Neville Keynes (father of the more famous John Maynard Keynes) begins his one-volume introduction to political economy (1890) by declaring:

The function of political economy is to investigate facts and discover truths about them, not to prescribe rules of life. Economic laws are theorems of fact, not practical precepts. Political economy is, in other words, a science, not an art or a department of ethical inquiry. . . . It furnishes information as to the probable consequences of given lines of action, but does not itself pass moral judgments, or pronounce what ought or what ought not to be. (Keynes 12–13)

Paul Samuelson, in a recent edition of the most famous textbook of modern economics, reaffirms this distinction with similar bluntness. Although "the conflict between efficiency and fairness is one of the most profound questions of value that a society faces," Samuelson asserts, "positive economics cannot say what steps governments should take to improve equity" (P. Samuelson, Nordhaus, and Mandel 141). To be sure, a whole range of writers over the last two centuries and today contest this distinction between economics as science and economics as a normative moral or ethical discourse.[3] Nevertheless, the history of economic theory continues to be conventionally understood as a narrative of enlightenment, a progress from moral to political economy. Similarly, the status of economics as a science seems to remain, for the most part, contingent upon its renunciation of the moral and ethical project that had been central to the economic vision of ancient, medieval, and early-modern thought.

In this, classical economic theory seems to declare itself a science of *means* and to renounce the study of *ends*. As Keynes observes in the lines already quoted, economics can provide "information as to the probable consequences of given lines of action," and such information can presumably help social subjects make certain choices in certain situations. But economics cannot itself make the choices, because all such "normative questions," as Paul

Samuelson puts it, must be "answered in the political arena by democratic voters or autocratic planners" (P. Samuelson, Nordhaus, and Mandel 114). In other words, economics can be instrumental, but it cannot prescribe or prohibit. Yet here too, the logic of this opposition, pursued to its limit, finally collapses onto itself, for the same thought also portrays its own renunciation of normative morality as itself a position of the highest moral value. The model envisions society as constituted by private vices which are the means to public virtues, a society in which individual acts of self-interest are led (by an "invisible hand") to a greater good. Thus, the "freedom" of the market is understood to be not only the most effective method for attaining material prosperity but also an end in itself, something to be sought for its own sake.

In this sense, what Marx always argued of capitalism—that its final product is its own perpetuation, because each economic transaction empowers and strengthens the system by multiplying its constitutive unit, capital—is implicitly acknowledged by this familiar model of market morality. Let me briefly observe this model in a contemporary text, Senator Robert Dole's acceptance speech for the 1996 Republican presidential nomination. "The high office of the presidency," Dole declares at the beginning of one memorable passage, "requires broad oversight and attention to three essential areas—the material, the moral, and the nation's survival, in that ascending order of importance."[4] This formula suggests a transcendence of ends over means in that the nation's survival is a goal more important than, and therefore separate from, the moral. But then, Dole goes on to assert: "In the last presidential election, you, the people were gravely insulted. You were told that the material was not only the most important of these three but, in fact, the only one that really mattered. I don't hold that for a moment. No one can deny the importance of material well-being. And in this regard it is time to recognize that we have surrendered too much of our economic liberty."

Dole is here presumably alluding to how his opponent, President Bill Clinton, had in the previous election reminded himself of the central importance of economic issues with what became a celebrated aphorism: "It's the economy, stupid." By contrast, Dole argues that to reduce politics to mere life-and-death concerns (the material) is itself a "grave" error. Nevertheless, and precisely because this seems to be the fundamental point, one is brought up short by the last sentence. The rhetoric seems to require a concluding antithesis, something like: "no one can deny the importance of material well-being, but we must also never lose sight of our moral welfare." The present last sentence thus almost seems a mistake. Its only apparent logic would lie in an implicit but unstated point: that the realm of material prosperity is always-already the realm of "economic liberty," and vice versa. Dole goes on to declare: "I do not appreciate the value of economic liberty nearly as much for what it has done in keeping us fed as I do for what it has done in keeping us free."

But the alliterative parallelism in these lines conceals a dissymmetry with its own grave consequences. Dole asserts that the market both feeds us and makes us free and that being free is more important than being fed. But how are we to understand the practical relation of these three propositions? Although to be fed is always in some sense to be free (from material necessity), the reverse of this formula does not hold. As a matter of brute fact, and by the same logic that leads to the initial conclusion, freedom must always potentially be, as the song has it, just another name for nothing left to lose; even so confirmed a defender of the market as Hayek concedes that "to be free may mean freedom to starve" (*Constitution of Liberty* 12). Accordingly, and as Dole's rhetoric necessarily indicates, the ideology of the market always attempts to have it both ways. We are asked to be willing to *live free or die* and reassured at the same time that freedom is our best chance to live—so that a so-called economic liberty is understood at once as a means to the end of economic prosperity and as an absolute end in itself.

There is thus a paradoxical double logic at work here, a logic that finally resembles, for example, the mode of condensation and contradiction ascribed by psychoanalytic theory to the operations of the unconscious (as in the joke in which a defense lawyer claims he will prove both that a particular kettle was broken before it was borrowed *and* that it was in perfect condition when it was returned); or the specious duplicity of the early-modern moral economy, which asks us to give without looking "for reward in earth nor yet in heaven," even as it reassures us "that good deeds *are* rewarded both in this life and in the life to come" (Tyndale civ; emphasis added); or even Bataille's derisive vision of the Hegelian "master," who attains such status by "risking" his life in a battle he is always-already certain to win (see chapter 5). Such paradoxical double logic is also, as it were, merely the *positive* counterpart of that *negative* double-bind by which, as I have suggested throughout, the same ideology envisions labor both as curse and as commandment, insisting we must work to live and yet also live to work.

Marxism at Its Limit

Marx and Engels also portray their thought as representing a "scientific" socialism to be rigorously distinguished from mere utopianism; and many subsequent thinkers in their tradition similarly reject any attempt to understand the Marxist critique of capitalism as an essentially *moral* one.[5] Yet Marxism, in almost any of its varieties, refuses to renounce a concern for the ends of social practice in the manner of classical political economy. Indeed, even when it is shaken free from the more specific teleology indicated in Marx's schema of successive historical modes of production, most Marxist thought remains resolutely teleological in its vision of *work:* envisioning a future in which labor is "not only a means of life but life's prime want" ("Critique of the Gotha Program," *Collected Works* 24:87) and in which the evolution of material production finally makes possible "a "development of human energy which is an end in itself" (*Capital,* vol. 3, *Collected Works* 37:807). This aspiration seems to encounter a certain limit or impasse at every turn: this work that is not work, this labor that liberates itself from necessity and yet remains an absolute human vocation, must somehow be considered neither the simple antithesis of limitless, chrematistical production-for-exchange, a mere return to some archaic version of production-for-use, nor merely another version of the Work-as-gift (culture) that cannot be separated from hierarchies of social distinction and that accordingly (as apologists of the market are eager to remind us) thrives under the regime of capital as perhaps nowhere else. How, then, are we to understand this properly Marxist work, this absolute autoteleology, this blossoming of human force that is its own end?

To be sure, Marxism in any of its forms always seeks to grasp this historical fruition of work in the form of paradox. Marx and Engels suggest, in a famous dictum, "Only within the community has each individual the means of *cultivating his gifts* in all directions; hence personal freedom becomes possible only within the community" (*The German Ideology, Collected Works* 5:78; emphasis added). This formula, after a rigorous displacement of its central terms, will indeed indicate a way beyond the fatal conjunction of the Work and gift that has been my subject throughout. It must first be acknowledged, however, that when Marx and Engels envision community as the site where individual "gifts" are "cultivated," they risk contaminating their thought with the very problems they otherwise oppose. The issue is not merely the theological figure that haunts the rhetoric of personal "gifts" and "talents" (see chapter 8), nor that words such as "cultivated" and "cultured" (as Raymond Williams famously demonstrates) are indissolubly linked to their literal social origins in the accumulation of agri-cultural wealth and property (see Williams *Keywords* 87–89). It is, rather, the way these lines suggest—at least in one possible reading of them—that the community is merely the *ground* of a labor of individual self-development.

Implicit here would then be an ontology of production and creativity in which freedom itself could be grasped (in Jean-Luc Nancy's words) only as "a property of the subjective constitution of being, and as the property of an individual 'subject'" (*Experience* 7). In this case, the individual "gifts" that this subject would be allowed (or obliged) to cultivate would be anything but gifts. As the constituent elements of this subject's self-development, such gifts would present themselves in the very shape of obligation: they would be, in Kant's words, "given," but only "for all sorts of possible ends" (90). The subject self-constituted by these gifts that are not gifts, moreover, could then himself "never give anything without calculating, consciously or unconsciously, its reappropriation, its exchange, or its circular return—and by definition this means reappropriation with surplus-value, *a certain capitalization.*" Indeed, this restricted economy of investment and return, as I will follow Derrida in suggesting, "is the very definition of the *subject as such*" (*Given Time* 101–2).

To pursue this reading, therefore, is to discover at the conceptual core of Marxism at least a risk of that recurrent displacement I previously considered with regard to the "general" economy. Let me recall briefly Jean-Joseph Goux's analysis of a certain mode of "postmodern" capitalism that presents itself not as a restricted economy of investment and return but rather as a kind of general economy of ecstatic dissemination and extravagant expenditure (chapter 5). As I briefly mentioned in chapter 2, and as Thomas Frank observes at length, contemporary capitalist discourse also frequently appropriates the rhetoric and imagery of revolutionary struggle, using "vibrant knock-offs of Stalin-era Soviet art" and "images of statues being torn down by the righteous masses" (173) to celebrate a "business revolution," a "freewheeling, employee-worshipping world of work" (180) created by "'business activists' and 'corporate radicals'" (216).[6] One might go so far as to join Guy Debord in claiming that the "highest ambition" of the society of the spectacle is to "turn secret agents into revolutionaries and revolutionaries into secret agents" (*Comments* 11).

Thus, both Marxism and general economics remain, in their own force and principle, vulnerable to appropriation by the same (restricted) economy that each one, in their separate ways, addresses as the object of its fundamental critique. It would also appear that, just as general economics seems to fail at precisely the point when it is construed as the property of an individual subject (see chapter 6), so the belief in individual and subjective self-development that continues to pervade some versions of Marxism is the very point of its vulnerability to such appropriation. At the same time, the relationship between general economics and Marxism is itself characterized by a double mo-

tion of critique and convergence. As I also observed in chapter 6, general economics emerges from Bataille's fascination with archaic practices of gift giving
and sacrifice, but it finally encompasses an epistemological critique of the totalizing projects of Western thought. Such projects, Bataille argues, operate
by means of a restricted theoretical economy that assumes the progressive development and accumulation of knowledge and in which, accordingly, one
must always repress any awareness of "the baselessness of the nonmeaning
from which the basis of meaning is drawn" (Derrida "From Restricted to
General Economy" 257). Bataille's attempt to link material and theoretical
economies has, however, a particular consequence with regard to his relationship with Marxism. If capitalism (a system of material production fundamentally grounded in economistic "return") would be the obvious paradigm of a
restricted *material* economy, then Marxism (one of the last "classical" and
totalizing philosophic systems) would seem no less a paradigm of a restricted
theoretical economy. General economics would thus seem to locate itself in
opposition both to capitalism and to the preeminent theoretical critique of
capitalism.

Even Marx's career is marked by two absolutely opposed impulses: he always aspires, on the one hand, to produce the all-encompassing Work and, on
the other hand, he leaves a series of unfinished or unpublished texts (the 1844
manuscripts, *The German Ideology,* the *Grundrisse,* the later volumes of *Capital,* the ethnological notebooks), whose own incompletion implicitly indicates the impossibility of this absolute project. Further, general economics
joins with Marxism in its critique of that quite different alliance between epistemology and political economy that characterizes the ideologies of capitalism all the way from Adam Smith to the so-called neoclassical synthesis. This
tradition of economics, as Althusser has argued, takes certain economic
"facts" and a particular human subject as *given.* The conceptual "gift" at the
heart of this whole problematic finally refers back, as it must, "to God as its
founder, i.e. to the Given who himself gives himself, *causa sui,* God-Given"
(Althusser and Balibar 162–63)—and thus at once grounds all subsequent
disciplinary *knowledge* and figures an originary *value* transcending the cycle
of economic exchange on which the discipline focuses as its empirical object.
As has often been argued, economics, like all theoretical empiricisms, locates
itself in a space of knowledge inhabited and informed by the gaze of an absolute subject who is everywhere and nowhere and at the same time fundamentally divides social life between a sphere of "narrowly non-economic
interests" (culture) and a sphere of acquisition defined, as Bourdieu has mem-

orably expressed it, "by the fundamental tautology 'business is business'" (*Outline* 177).

Such insights shadow a necessary convergence of Marxism and general economics. The theoretical problem I have attempted to describe in either case might be portrayed as a recurrent displacement, in which the restricted economy, the economy of "return," is itself what returns, on the other side of any attempt to inscribe its opposite. Thus, Bataille's attempt to project a radically different political and theoretical economy adumbrates a particular mode of postmodern capitalist apologetics, and Marxism's radical critique of work seems potentially to reinscribe an ontology of *homo faber* that remains available for appropriation by the ideology of the market. A convergence of Marxism and general economics would have to present itself in the form of a different relation between the restricted and general economies—and hence also between the two constellations of ideas and practices that I have called here the Work and the gift. Derrida briefly indicates some directions for such a project in his seminal reading of Bataille, "From Restricted to General Economy." Summarizing the trajectory of Bataille's epistemological theory, in which the surplus energy in the terrestrial biosphere produces or indicates the excess of meaning at the heart of all knowledge, Derrida appends a note:

One would make a gross error in interpreting [Bataille's] propositions in a "reactionary" sense. The consumption of the excess of energy by a determined class is not the destructive consuming of meaning, but the significative reappropriation of a surplus value within the space of restricted economy. From this point of view, sovereignty is absolutely revolutionary. But it is also revolutionary as concerns a revolution which would only reorganize the world of work and would redistribute values within the space of meaning, that is to say, still within restricted economy. This last movement— only slightly perceived, here and there, by Bataille . . . is rigorously necessary, but as a phase within the strategy of general economy. ("From Restricted to General Economy" 337 n. 33)

Here one must note, first, the implicit critique of those who, in the manner of contemporary cyber-libertarians such as George Gilder, would appropriate Bataille's project (in a "reactionary" sense) as an ideology of postindustrial consumer capitalism. Derrida argues that the overconsumption of excess production by one class (Bataille's or Marx's bourgeoisie) remains entirely economistic and cannot be construed as some kind of symbolic potlatch or destruction of energy or meaning. Derrida seems, however, to raise and yet leave unanswered a crucial question. A revolutionary redistribution of material value in the traditional Marxist sense, dedicated to economic justice and "the principle of balanced accounts," could only "redistribute values within the space of meaning." Why, then, does such a revolution remain "rigorously necessary" as "one phase" of the theoretical revolution projected by general economics? Elsewhere Derrida claims that, "in a reading of Bataille, I have attempted to indicate what might come of a rigorous and, in a new sense, 'scientific' *relation* of the 'restricted economy' that takes no part in expenditure without reserve, death, opening itself to nonmeaning, etc., to a general economy that *takes into account* the nonreserve, that keeps in reserve the nonreserve, if it can be put thus" (Derrida "Différance" 19). But can it put thus? How can we grasp this relation other than by means of the displacement I have described?

A possible but ultimately inadequate answer seems already embodied within the classical Marxist teleology, in which capitalism drives through its inner logic toward its own dissolution because its development of the productive forces eventually creates a material plenitude that makes capitalism itself unnecessary. To rephrase this argument in Bataille's terms, Marx views the restricted economy (here, capitalism itself) as always in service of something else, some as-yet-undreamed-of economy or society in which the social tensions inherent in economistic practices have passed away. As Bataille's critique of the Soviet model indicates, one cannot imagine any utopia, communist or otherwise, that would simply "have" or express a general economy as its self-present principle. Yet Marx's own utopian narrative remains curiously bound to capitalism's, in that both assume an originary economistic Subject and a particular historical trajectory to which that Subject is destined.

Although Marx, as far back as the *Theses on Feuerbach,* declares that "the human essence . . . is the ensemble of the social relations" (*Collected Works* 5:4), he would always retain a certain vision of a historically constructed and culturally determinative Subject who represents the product and, perhaps, the fatal flaw of capitalism. Marx's Subject, like capitalism's, is explicitly constituted by means of a restricted economy, both materially and theoretically. Capitalist production requires investments of ever-greater value, a corresponding expansion of material consumption, and hence, also, "the cultivation of all the qualities of the social human being . . . in a form as rich as possible in needs, because rich in qualities and relations." Capital thus produces a "bourgeois" subject and society characterized by what Marx calls "universality"—an instrumentalization of the world through science, exploration, and a "system of general utility." Finally, then, "the universality toward which [Capital] irresistibly strives encounters barriers in its own nature, which will, at a certain stage of its development, allow it to be recognized as being itself the greatest barrier to this tendency, and hence will drive towards its own suspension" (*Grundrisse* 408–9). The subject that Marx describes here exists wholly as a kind of function and effect of economic restriction: it is the mere subjective reflection of material production founded in capital; and it is itself constituted by a process of conservation and expansion in which it grows ever larger, richer, and more complex as capitalism develops the productive forces of society. Yet in Marx's historical narrative, such a subject is supposed, Frankenstein-like, to turn against its maker and denounce the conditions of its own creation.

Therefore, as I suggested in part 1, most varieties of Marxism join with a certain free-market liberalism in assuming that man produces his essence by his work. Capitalism and the market create precisely the situation—man's alienation from his essence—that a certain humanist Marxism seeks to redress. But Marxism sometimes seems to join classical and neoclassical economics in the assumption that such alienation was *imposed on* a human subject who was, by contrast, "given." Thus, it must be grasped, by contrast, that it is capitalism that created, as *its* given, a Subject that comes into being lost, always-already alienated from "itself" and from some hypothetical community of the past. Such Marxism then seeks to heal the rift (between man and "himself") that capitalism assumes and exploits. It asks humanity to make what is then revealed as an essentially moral choice between capitalism and communism, which is also, from another aspect, a choice between the restricted and general economies—capitalism assuming the role of the former by supposing that the rhythm of investment and return will inevitably produce the greatest good for the greatest number; and communism assuming the role of the latter in its assertion of a plenitude that would wrest a realm of freedom from the realm of necessity. Either way, however, this would be an essentially and merely moral debate, one that, on either side, sees a human subject, a human 'nature,' as producing itself through its work. The moral debate itself would be a central part of that work; while, meanwhile and elsewhere, business would be business.

General economics may then be said to enter at precisely this point where a humanist Marxism fails, attempting to take account at once of the (literal and corporeal) surplus repressed by bourgeois culture and the (ontological and epistemological) excess which confounds the very project of economic reason. Further, Bataille's *terms,* whatever the other failures of his thought, prove essential to thinking the historical and theoretical mechanisms of the curious transformation in capitalism's ideological self-presentation. In the early-modern period, capitalism presented itself as a quintessential restricted economy in both the material and the theoretical senses. Materially, capitalism assumed that the world was defined by a scarcity which mandated productive self-interest and that all progress stemmed from an appropriate (and appropriative) return on investments of time, resources, and knowledge. Theoretically, as that last term indicates, capitalism always went hand in hand with the Enlightenment project, so that, as many scholars have documented, empiricism served the empire, and world exploration was always the harbinger and handmaiden of the global marketplace.

But if the first stage of classical economics was characterized by a certain divorce from theology and positive morality precisely in the name of an *abstract* economic calculation, the marginalist focus on consumer *demand*, and hence on a specifically *hedonistic* calculus, made possible a new economic theology in which risk, chance, and reckless expenditure reemerge as primary themes. Vincent Pecora's critique of the nostalgia for the noble *oikos* that permeates a broad tradition of Western thought is once again useful here, for this critique applies equally to the Bataille who sometimes mourns a "lost sovereignty" and to marginalist economists such as Alfred Marshall, who projects a future capitalism in which each man is no longer prevented from becoming "the noble being he might be" (Marshall 16). But then, capitalism's own apparent appropriation of general economics helps us grasp that Weber's capitalist "spirit" of prudence and calculation was always spurious—and not just because, as in the well-known arguments of Daniel Bell and John Kenneth Galbraith, the consumerism that capitalism fosters contradicts its professed moral values of thrift and abstinence. The conventional restricted economy of so much Western economic thought after Adam Smith has never been more than the ideological mask of a system whose basic form of value, capital itself, is forced by a nonnegotiable exigency to preserve itself "only by *constantly multiplying* itself" (Marx *Grundrisse* 270). Capitalism is finally what Immanuel Wallerstein aptly describes as an insane system, in which one makes money so as to make more money, and so on and so on (see Wallerstein). The world, capitalism's object, is assumed to be inexhaustible in a manner that gives the lie to calculation; and that Ben Franklinesque "spirit" of economism is but the ideological mask of a system that, in its own sense, has always been grounded in loss and sacrifice (of the natural environment, of precapitalist communities, of workers and work).[7] Wage labor itself—which exploits the surplus value created by the laborer—denies to most capitalist subjects precisely that proportionate return which capitalist apologists claimed for so long was the moral foundation of the system.

Materially, then, capitalism might be described as a kind of general economy, actually assuming, not scarcity, but an inexhaustible excess and hence merely masquerading as a restricted economy of proportionate return. In the same way, the restricted theoretical economy—that empiricism that takes the knowing subject as capable of grasping the world—has had a problematic relationship to the economic system that fostered it. The actual field of what is now called economics, the discipline with which capitalism strives to know the domain of its own operation, is, despite its intermittent scientific pretensions, a "restricted" economy in a sense opposite to Bataille's. Since Adam Smith at least, economics has been predicated on a process of *division* in which, as Bourdieu argues, "symbolic interests . . . [are] set up in opposition to strictly economic interests" (*Outline* 177). Indeed, capitalism is profoundly divided in its epistemological commitments, as many of the writers discussed in previous chapters indicate. Capitalism says to its Subject, in effect: you absolutely *can* and *cannot* grasp the world. You can sail the seas, chart the heavenly bodies, and imagine socialism, but the economy, the "real world," cannot be remade, for it has an intractability named after you, a "human nature" that makes such things as poverty and injustice inevitable. These things can be seen and understood, in all their multifarious empirical complexity, and they can even be ameliorated; but by definition they cannot be *rectified*. These are the conditions that prevail.

Finitude and Community

At this limit—the very point where apologists of the market can do no more than endlessly declare the impossibility of community itself—a different thought begins; and the oppositions of work and gift, restricted and general economies, both separately and together, reveal themselves from a slightly different aspect as attempts to grasp the *relation* of immanence and transcendence, of being and Being. Let me pause for a moment to review the two examples which I considered at the conclusions of the first two parts of this book: "autonomist" Marxism and the free-market libertarianism of F. A. Hayek. Each of these two systems can be seen as a limit case of their respective traditions of thought that illuminates a particular vision of this ontical-ontological relation.

Hayek grounds his thought in what he asserts is the absolute insufficiency of immanent being relative to any form of transcendent Being. He argues that "the 'data' from which the economic calculus starts are never for the whole society 'given' to a single mind . . . and can never be so given," and "that the spontaneous collaboration of free men often creates things which are greater than their individual minds can ever fully comprehend" (*Individualism and Economic Order* 77, 85, 7). The object of economics is too big to be knowable: mere finite or singular being will never measure up to the economy, the society, and the "civilization," whose creation remains, however, its definitive vocation and the expression of its (individual or collective) essence.

By contrast, contemporary autonomist Marxism, as summed up in Michael Hardt and Antonio Negri's *Empire,* projects a relation of immanence and transcendence that is the symmetrical converse of this free-market model. As we recall, Hardt and Negri envision a Multitude who exist in the form of pure immanence and who face a "transcendent figure of man" that in principle always involves the "imposition of social hierarchy and domination" (*Empire* 91). In this case, immanent being's very vocation is to confront this dominating and hierarchical transcendent Being in the shape of "a radical counterpower, ontologically grounded" in its own productivity and creativity (66). As such formulations indicate, this thought rightly disposes of an ontology grounded in the insufficiency of immanent being relative to its own creations; but it does so only by absolutely conflating immanence and creation and insisting on an impossible "refusal of all transcendence" (91).

In the rest of this chapter, accordingly, I follow Derrida and Nancy in restating this ontical-ontological relation in a different way. The thought to which I thus join mine remains, however, faithful to a certain thread of the Marxist critique of work even as it also pushes the idea of the gift, via general economics, to its conceptual frontiers and beyond. I begin this last movement by returning to Derrida, using this time his well-known essay "Structure, Sign, and Play in the Discourse of the Human Sciences," one of the seminal statements of what would later be somewhat awkwardly known as poststructuralism. Here, Derrida offers an astonishingly simple yet absolutely unanswerable critique of one of the founding gestures of structuralism, Lévi-Strauss's explanation of his analytic method in the "Overture" to *The Raw and the Cooked.* At one moment in Lévi-Strauss's text, he explains why he has not collected every possible version of the basic South American Indian myth he intends to analyze. First, Lévi-Strauss concedes that, "although the book is carefully documented, I have disregarded certain sources of information, and some others have proved inaccessible," and acknowledges that "further information already available or as yet unpublished will affect my interpretations" (6–7). But then he goes on to suggest, with a certain audacity:

If critics reproach me with not having carried out an exhaustive inventory of South American myths before analyzing them, they are making a grave mistake about the nature and function of these documents. The total body of myth belonging to a given community is comparable to its speech. Unless the population dies out physically or morally, this totality is never complete. You might as well criticize a linguist for compiling the grammar of a language without having complete records of the words pronounced since the language came into being, and without knowing what will be said in it during the future part of its existence. Experience proves that a linguist can work out the grammar of a given language from a remarkably small number of sentences, compared to all those he might in theory have collected. (7)

Derrida points out, however, that Lévi-Strauss has here given two distinctly different reasons for his willingness to renounce totalization. On the one hand, he suggests that it has simply not been practical to collect all versions of the myth, for there are too many of them, and there are too many obstacles to their collection. Totalization is possible in principle, but not in practice. On the other hand, he also claims that the many versions of this central myth join into a system like a language which is open-ended and which continues to evolve even as the analysis goes forward. In this case, to collect every version of the myth would be, not just difficult, but impossible in principle. Even more importantly, such totalization would also be quite useless, because one can re-create the mythic system as a whole with only a relatively few examples, the way a linguist can re-create the grammar of a language using only a few of its infinite number of possible utterances. This latter possibility—the attempt to reconstruct what are alleged to be the underlying structural rules or grammars of all signifying practices—is, of course, the fundamental aspiration of structuralism as a projected theoretical project that might unify the human sciences as a whole. But Derrida's point is that, even as Lévi-Strauss glimpses the absolute impossibility or uselessness of totalization within an open-ended structure such as language, he never quite leaves behind a certain classical empiricism—which, by contrast, endlessly strives to grasp (or at least continues to *regret* its failure to grasp) the totality of an object of study. Empiricism grasps its object, not as a field of openness or incompletion, but merely as "a finite richness which it can never master" (Derrida "Structure" 289).

For my purposes here, there is one thing to emphasize in Derrida's justly celebrated critique. In the case of classical empiricism, the finitude of imma-

nent being—that is, quite simply, the material limits of time, energy, or awareness that finite beings inevitably confront—is grasped as a *reproach.* There is
too much, more than we can say or do, no matter how strenuous our efforts or
how praiseworthy our goals. For Lévi-Strauss to collect every myth would be
like counting every grain of sand on the beach—it would be theoretically possible, but only had we world enough and time. In the case of that open-ended
structure whose paradigm is language, by contrast, a finite number of rules
produce an infinite number of utterances. A language has a relatively simple
grammar, which can be reconstructed from just a few sentences; yet the language as a whole could, in principle, never be exhausted. In this case the apparent limits of the system (its finitude) serve precisely as the access to its limitlessness.

Without insisting on a precise correlation, it is also clear that these two
ways of conceiving the limits of totalization correspond broadly to the restricted and general economies. Under the aspect of the restricted economy,
scarcity itself, the finite limits of ontical (mortal) being, are at once a perpetual
reproach and an irresistible goad. Because there might not be enough, we
must each grab what we can, producing an aggregate of selfishness that ensures the endless repetition of the same scarcity and the same response, the
fundamental economic vicious circle. Under the aspect of the general economy, by contrast, the fact that there is always more than I can have, more than
I can say or write, is grasped not as my frailty or my failure but as the very
ground of what Jean-Luc Nancy calls being-in-common: that is, my access to
the open-ended limitlessness whose name is *community.*

Indeed, as Nancy has argued, Bataille's general economics was always inseparable from an attempt to rethink community. Bataille also recognized, in
Nancy's paraphrase, that the idea of community "included, in spite of everything, themes of justice and equality," for "without these themes, regardless of
the way one chooses to transcribe them, the communitarian enterprise can
only be a farce" (Nancy *Inoperative Community* 20). One can thus pose here a
version of the same question I raised above: in what sense could economic justice ever balance the (material) account without betraying its fundamental
connection to the (theoretical) principle of balanced accounts? Attempts to
relate the restricted and general economies seemingly always return to this
dilemma: the necessary restrictedness involved in the project of justice (or, in
the conventional sense, "economics" itself) seemingly also requires, as its
ground and vehicle, a restricted economy of knowledge—empiricism, "rational choice," the Enlightenment project in general. In other words, a commitment to fairness and equality in the mundane world of practical politics some-

times seems to require one to reject a postmodern or "general" theoretical economy. Thus, on the Right, many writers today defend conservative disciplinary and intellectual values in the name of liberal notions of truth, justice, and the American way; and on the Left, Fredric Jameson identifies "late capitalism" as the very truth of postmodernism, its "cultural logic" (see Jameson *Postmodernism*).

The prevailing discourse of economics, however, would here again relegate all such debates to a spiritual or intellectual sphere of experience, which is accordingly sealed off from any real encounter with the practical. In the other sphere, where business is business, another version of the crucial relation between restricted and general economies suggests itself, as I described above. Here, a (spurious) general economy in the material world (the infinite multiplication of consumer choice) links itself to a (spurious) restricted economy of theory and knowledge (e.g., Hayek's "impossibility of socialism"). And precisely because these economies are spurious, this structure is always subject to a displacement where, as we have also seen, the economic restrictedness of material being (in other words, scarcity itself) always *seems* to reassert itself.

In his reading of Bataille, however, Nancy sketches another relation between the two economies, and hence also between the ontic and the ontological. Bataille always acknowledged, as I cited above, that the motion of universal excess becomes apparent only from the point of view of the collective whole. Thus, "community" is the very site of the general economy—but only as a community of all, emerging from "an originary or ontological 'sociality' that in its principle extends far beyond the simple theme of man" (Nancy *Inoperative Community* 28). In an argument that must be followed, as Nancy concedes, partially with Bataille and partially against him, community is not merely a possibility, something added on to being, something that one might have or not have. The singular beings who populate the earth literally exist only *in* common; they have an irreducible finitude, which means their being itself *takes place* only in the form of what might be called, in a phrase that needs to embrace its own paradox, an *inclination outward*. Thus, in the end, community is "space itself, and the spacing of the experience of the outside, of the outside-of-self" (19). Being itself is being-in-common, which means that "singular beings are, present themselves, and appear only to the extent that they are exposed, presented, or offered to one another" (58). Or in Bataille's terms: being itself is constituted by restricted, finite beings who enter into, as their basic condition of possibility, a general economy of exposing, presenting, and offering—a *giving* that is always and only a *sharing*. The relation of the two economies is thus indicated in Nancy's formula: community is formed by *finite* beings who are *infinitely* ex-posed to one another and also by the infinite ex-position of finitude.

The irreducible finitude of singular beings is not something to be subsumed in a larger whole, such as the family, the party, the nation, or the people. By contrast, the atomistic individual is "infinite" precisely because he presupposes a community defining itself as "a transcendence . . . of a being supposedly immanent to community" (Nancy *Inoperative Community* xxxix). This individual subject also reveals himself as the convenient agent of a spurious general economy, because, as Bataille perhaps too often celebrated, he is capable of consuming extravagantly, wastefully, uselessly. The generosity of which the Individual is doubtlessly capable merely enters him into a cycle of exchange—no wonder, then, if a capitalist apologist like George Gilder can perversely reimagine commerce as "a pattern of giving"!

Finitude is bound to a kind of restricted economy in that its very existence is predicated on "return," in that it exists only so far as it is ex-posed. But this very ex-position involves finitude within the general economy of the community, where energy and meaning are limitless. To risk an awkward formulation: the most economically restricted of practices (reaping and sowing, the labor of thought and writing and their circular "return") are at the same time the very conduit and constituting elements of the general economy of community, where we are exposed, given, offered to be shared. "Community is given—or we are given and abandoned to the community: a gift to be renewed and communicated" (Nancy *Inoperative Community* 35). Finite beings sink into the community, the very product of their inclination outward; and the community, constituted by this motion, at the same time returns them to "themselves." But this is not a return to self as to one's essence (in which the subject would produce itself *as* its own essence) but rather the subject offering and surrendering itself as the very possibility of "communication." Here, the restricted economy relates to the general economy *not* as its "truth," and not as the voice of some inescapable practicality that belittles theory, but rather as its shared condition of possibility. If the structure of displacement I described in part 2 might be designated as *loss with return,* the formula for which I argue in closing might be designated *return with loss.* It is the general economy which returns as the unsurpassable frontier of all economic restriction: the non-account of which, as Derrida argues, we must finally take into account. Thus, Nancy's "unworking" community, like Blanchot's "negative" community and like general economics itself, remains faithful in some ultimate sense to Marx's celebrated vision of the irreducible relation between the individual and the collective. The Marxist "economy" is one that, so to speak, employs calcula-tion in order to end calculation. That is, it grasps the limits of mortal (re-stricted) finitude as no more than an opening to the limitlessness of an econ-omy which is "general" precisely because it is no longer bound up in the calculations or appropriations of an individual subject.

Let me conclude by returning, for some final clarification of this argument, to the famous passage from the unfinished third volume of *Capital* where Marx speaks of a "realm of freedom" that "actually begins only where labour which is determined by necessity and mundane conditions ceases" (*Collected Works* 37:807). We must certainly join Nancy in celebrating the "generous ex-uberance" with which these lines project a time or a place "in which surplus work would no longer be an exploitative *work,* but rather art and invention" (*Inoperative Community* 7). But we must also observe here the same paradox-ical attitude toward work that, as we have seen in chapter 1, Hannah Arendt discovers in the Marxist project generally. As Arendt suggests, Marx seems, throughout his long career, to envision work at once as the curse from which humanity must be freed and as the essential and definitive human vocation. Just so, in these famous lines, Marx seems to envision both a freedom *from* work and a freedom *in* work. He first suggests, as strongly and clearly as pos-sible, that the realm of freedom "lies beyond the sphere of actual material pro-duction." This realm of necessity, however, remains forever inescapable and is what Marx calls the "basis" of a realm of freedom:

Just as the savage must wrestle with Nature to satisfy his wants, to maintain and repro-duce life, so must civilized man, and he must do so in all social formations and under all possible modes of production. With his development, this realm of physical neces-sity expands as a result of his wants, but, at the same time, the forces of production which satisfy these wants also increase. (*Collected Works* 37:807)

History therefore takes the shape of a kind of meta-instrumentality, in which an unending struggle for material survival finally produces a broader im-provement in the means of production themselves, which in turn steadily di-minishes the collective burden of that continuing struggle. But freedom itself, Marx goes on to suggest, "can only consist in socialized man, the associated producers, rationally regulating their interchange with Nature, bringing it un-der their common control . . . and achieving this with the least expenditure of energy and under conditions most favourable to, and worthy of, their human nature." Thus, freedom "consist[s]" of a struggle to overcome necessity; yet only "beyond" this necessity, Marx suggests, "begins the development of human energy which is an end in itself, the true realm of freedom" (*Collected Works* 37:807).

In such formulations, the wresting of freedom from necessity seems to take place both synchronically and diachronically: that is, in two temporal frames of reference which themselves, however, are radically inconsistent. On the one hand is a daily struggle against nature for sustenance and survival that can in principle never end; on the other hand is a broad historical struggle to overcome scarcity once and for all. And yet this latter struggle, of course, has not yet even begun; for, as Marx argues in his fundamental critique of political economy, the evident increase of the productive forces that takes place under the regime of capital does *not* release workers from their burden of labor but, rather, merely increases the amount of value exploited from them. Indeed, capitalism discovers a secret ally in necessity's Law of Value, which it uses to justify and perpetuate its own Law of Command. To recognize this is to acknowledge once more the inescapable force and urgency of the many thinkers and writers, some of them discussed elsewhere in this book, who continue today to rethink and reject what Ulrich Beck calls "the value imperialism of work" (125). This is the absolute and irreducibly practical insight to which we must remain faithful above all: that, as Marx argues, the "basic prerequisite" of freedom is to be found, quite simply, in "the reduction of the working day" to its minimum practical limit.

Even after such recognition, however, it remains necessary to think through to its limit the paradoxical doubleness that haunts the Marxist thought of work. In the coming community Marx invites us to imagine, the improvement of the productive forces and consequent reduction of necessary labor will have revealed themselves at last to have always-already been the ultimate *ends* of all human exertions. *All* work, therefore, finally works *on* work. Underlying such hopes, however, at least in one possible reading, would be an anthropological determination of Man grounded in a narrative of origin and progress that Marx indicates above, for example, in his invocation of the "savage" who must wrestle with nature even to fulfill his minimal needs. Indeed, as I suggested above, in this Marxist schema of history, the development of the productive forces would appear to be merely the ground and precondition of an assumed inevitable self-development of the human subject: the same assumption which seemingly unites all the various thinkers and texts considered in this book. And as is even perhaps obliquely indicated in Marx's famous rhetorical invocation of a "realm" or "reign" of freedom, the freedom made possible by our triumph over necessity would itself *be* a necessity, an obligation, something at once grounded in the perpetually unfinished labor of producing itself *and* yet somehow absolutely other to that labor.

One must thus raise a double objection and observe that the goal or end of an instrumental history constituted by work cannot itself *be* a further Work of self-development and that neither the mundane work that pervades history nor the historical Work of liberation can really be thought of as *ends in themselves*. The freedom indicated by this "in itself" cannot be, precisely as such, something to be made present or achieved in some exceeding or overcoming of something else or as the absolute fulfillment of some instrumental process. Nor, as Nancy suggests, can freedom lie in "the autonomy of a subjectivity in charge of itself and its decisions, evolving freely in perfect independence from every obstacle. What would such an independence mean, if not the impossibility in principle of entering into the slightest relation—and therefore of exercising the slightest freedom? (*Experience* 66).

Thus, we must draw out Marx's schema in a slightly different way: still discovering freedom in the acts of "associated producers" but putting the emphasis on the first, rather than the second, word of this phrase. It is only in the commonality that precedes all production and self-production that our mundane or historical wresting of freedom from necessity can take place. This would be a history reconceived as an instrumentality always-already in excess of itself, taking the shape (to do no more than slightly restate the formula stated above) of a process of production intended to undo production.

It is here, too, that what we have seen throughout to be the enigmatic promise of the gift finally reemerges, though only in a radically different relation to work and the Work than that which haunts the discourses surveyed in this book. This time the idea of the gift presents itself quite precisely *in* and *as* relation itself. The "freedom" constituted by the association of singular beings is one "that gives relation by withdrawing being. It is then freedom that gives humanity, and not the inverse. But the gift that freedom gives is never, insofar as it is the gift of *freedom*, a quality, property, or essence on the order of '*humanitas*'" (Nancy *Experience* 73). Or in other words, in Nancy's concise double summary: "Freedom does not come to produce anything, but only comes to produce itself" (78); and therefore, accordingly: "*Freedom gives— freedom*" (73).

To reiterate, then, the reign of freedom is not an achieved presence but an absence; it is not a liberation *of* work but a recognition of *unworking;* it is not the developed substance or expressed essence of singular beings but only what Marx's son-in-law, Paul Lafargue, writing at the turn of the twentieth century, memorably calls a "right to be lazy"—even if, of course, it is not precisely a *right* but rather a gift without return or reserve, a sharing, something inseparable in principle from the relation and association of singular beings with each other.[8] Lafargues's perhaps too-little-known text is admittedly itself pervaded with that same yearning for human self-fashioning that, as I have suggested throughout, always seems to limit the attempt to think an end to work. "When, in our civilized Europe," Lafargue writes, "we would find a trace of the native beauty of man, we must go seek in the nations where economic prejudices have not yet uprooted the hatred of work" (11). It is "work, in the vitiated atmosphere of the capitalist factory" (17) that atrophies and destroys the health of "the primitive animal" (11). And in some imagined future beyond work:

When there are no more lackeys and generals to decorate, no more free and married prostitutes to be covered with laces, no more cannons to bore, no more palaces to build, there will be need of severe laws to compel the working women and working-men who have been employed on embroidered laces, iron workings, buildings, to take the hygienic and calisthenic exercises requisite to re-establish their health and improve their race. (49)

This is one more case where a certain ethos of creative self-development and a certain vision of community as work still cling to the thought of a writer otherwise enthralled with the sovereign possibility of doing *nothing*. Perhaps, then, one might best conclude with one more unworking of a text to draw out its absent presence. In this case I will re-cite and alter a Virgilian epigraph already summoned to prominence by Lafargue. *Deus nobis haec otia fecit,* writes Virgil in the *Bucolics.* "A god has granted us this idleness" (quoted in Lafargue 12). Who could resist or deplore such an image of sun-drenched shepherds under an open sky whose work is none other than the seeing and saying of its lack? But idleness is not quite something to be *granted* and neither arrives from some locus of transcendent possibility nor locates itself in the irrecoverable arcadian past indicated by Virgil's pastoral. Still, with more rigor and yet no less joy, we might indicate the limit and opening of the thought of work and gift one last time by merely stating the obvious.

Which is to say, simply: we ourselves (will) give ourselves—each Other—this idleness.

Introduction

1. This is my transcript from Martin's recording *Let's Get Small* (Warner, 1977). Elsewhere on this record Martin parodies the colloquial expression in which work is construed as a kind of gift. Claiming to be angry at the production staff, Martin says of himself: "You know, I'm out here, and I'm giving, and I keep giving, and I give some more. . . ."

2. I take this crucial formulation from Scott Michaelsen, who employs it in our coauthored essay "Practical Politics at the Limits of Community" (see Michaelsen and Shershow).

Chapter One

1. For observations of such developments, see in particular Aronowitz and DiFazio; Aronowitz and Cutler; Beck; and Schor.

2. For another powerful critique of the prevailing ethos of work, see also the "Manifesto against Labour" by the Gruppe Krisis, a collective of German thinkers, available in English translation as of May 2004 at http://www.giga.or.at/others/krisis/manifesto.against.labor .html. I discovered this text only as I was finishing the present manuscript. Thanks to Neal Larsen for calling my attention to the Krisis Group.

3. See, e.g., the essays collected in Larrabee and Meyersohn's *Mass Leisure* (1958) and in Smigel's *Work and Leisure* (1963).

4. By the addition of "emphasis added" following the page number, I always note when italics in a quotation are mine. Otherwise, italics in quotations are in the original.

5. For a somewhat different critique of Arendt's argument, see Aronowitz and DiFazio 331–34.

6. Marx discusses Aristotle in *Capital* (1:353 n. 6); and see also Marc Shell's discussion in *The Economics of Literature* (94).

7. For the first image, see, e.g., the portrayal of "the Borg" on the television show *Star Trek: The Next Generation* or the hostile insect aliens portrayed in Robert Heinlein's *Starship Troopers* and in Orson Scott Card's *Ender's Game*. For the latter image, see, e.g., Michael Moorcock's *The Dancers at the End of Time*, John Varley's *Steel Beach*, or the portrayal of the "Q Continuum" on *Star Trek: The Next Generation*.

8. The political problems of this passage can be vividly indicated by juxtaposing it to a classic text of American "free-market" thought, Andrew Carnegie's "Gospel of Wealth." Here, Carnegie uses the example of Peter Cooper's founding of the Cooper Institute to argue for the benevolent patriarchal administration of the surplus wealth of the few for the benefit of the many. Had the money expended in founding the institute, Carnegie suggests, been "distributed in small quantities among the people," it "would have been wasted in the indulgence of appetite, some of it in excess" (Carnegie 34–35).

9. Scapp associates the final vision of *Perestroika* with what Derrida, in *Specters of Marx*, calls "messianicity." It appears to me, by contrast, that Kushner's concluding vision actually evokes a community founded in common being and self-present identity, which is quite unlike what Derrida calls "the new international."

10. For example, Joe Pitt, the Reaganite lawyer and self-denying gay man, is pointedly excluded from the final image of community.

Chapter Two

1. As Peter Laslett suggests in his introduction to *Two Treatises of Government*, Locke himself uses the word "property" in a manner that hovers between two meanings: a physical object or place that one "owns" in law, and a kind of immanent quality or intrinsic function ("the property of rain is to wet"). See Locke and Laslett 102.

2. On this point, see also Kaus, who argues for the "end of equality" in a well-known neoliberal (or, more precisely, neoconservative) book, precisely because, he claims, people care more about their relative social dignity than about literal economic equality.

3. Here again, I refer the reader to the exhaustive summaries and powerful critiques of this material in Frank's *One Market under God*.

4. Rifkin 176. In addition to works otherwise cited, see Bond *Going Solo* (1997); Reinhold *Free to Succeed: Designing the Life You Want in the New Free Agent Economy* (2001); Pink *Free-Agent Nation* (2001); and McGovern and Russell *A New Brand of Expertise: How Independent Consultants, Free Agents, and Interim Managers Are Transforming the World of Work* (2001).

5. This discourse also provides a ready-made foundation for another "hot-button" issue of contemporary business management: the idea of "managing diversity." See, e.g., Trompenaars.

6. For full citation of these titles, see the bibliography entries under L. Jones, Murdock, Jonathan Robinson, Secretan, Hawkins, and Larkin. In February 2001, the online book retailer Amazon.com listed eighty-seven titles under the subject heading "Business Life—Inspirational." On the general phenomenon of "spiritual" business books, see also Frank *One Market under God* 3–5.

Chapter Three

1. In the preface to *The Logic of Practice* (2), Bourdieu expresses reservations about the early book Wilson cites here.

2. Heilbroner's famous introduction to classical economics, *The Worldly Philosophers*, was first published in 1958 and is currently in its seventh edition.

3. Such questions invite a parenthetical comment on a passing detail of Heilbroner's exposition. The Yir-Yiront of Australia, one of the groups he mentions as still living in the primitive moment before the birth of work, have, he claims, "the same word for work and play." On this point he again cites Sahlins, but in fact Heilbroner has intensified the latter's point; for Sahlins merely claims that "the Yir Yiront . . . do not discriminate between 'work' and 'play'" (64). Sahlins, in turn, cites as source a 1958 essay by Lauriston R. Sharp, whose thesis is that the Yir-Yiront are a "people without politics," because their only way of naming or understanding any social role or relationship is in terms of kinship. Although the Yir-Yiront do have practices "which an institutional approach would classify as familial, economic, legal, religious, esthetic; yet the native, who does not even distinguish work from play, emphasizes only and always the kinship component of any role" (Sharp 6). This passing reference is the sole source of Heilbroner's rather more striking claim. Further, a recent lexicon of Yir-Yiront compiled by Barry Alpher discusses at length their word *woq*. According to Alpher, this word has the basic meaning "work," and although some have suspected that it is a postcolonial derivation from the English word that it resembles phonetically, it also has an "exact phonological correspondence" with the word *wuku* from another Australian people. Alpher also appends a detailed note on the word's colloquial usage:

> Activities spoken of as **woq** in 1987–8 include making dillybags, nets, spears, coolamons, boomerangs, firesticks, and other manufactures, washing clothes (one's own or others'), cleaning houses, sewing clothes, working as a stockman. Not counted as **woq** are hunting . . . fishing, foraging, shopping at a supermarket, copper- Moariing, performing ceremonies, singing. . . . Activity of any kind done for a boss and/or pay is **woq**. A woman says minding her own children is **woq**, and a man says it isn't. RLS, asking a woman (a not fully traditional Koko-Bera speaker: childless, a schoolteacher) about these matters in 1934, was told that "work" includes digging, getting firewood, making bags, house-building, and cooking, but not minding children. (629–30)

This intricate and gendered set of distinctions—in which, for example, women with children consider child care to be *woq* although men and childless women do not—surely suggests, at least, that the Yir-Yiront indeed distinguish "work" from other practices. But this striking rediscovery of precisely Heilbroner's own uncertainties about this category, at the very heart of the alleged archaic world of nonwork, further suggests that, as Scott Michaelsen argues, anthropology itself tends to be "self-motivated": a projecting of our own longings and desires onto the Other. See Michaelsen "Resketching" 225–26.

4. In part, Marx laughs off this possibility by having an imaginary capitalist justify his profit by asking: "'Have I myself not worked? Have I not performed the labour of superintendence . . . ? And does not this labour, too, create value?' The capitalist's own overseer and manager shrug their shoulders" (*Capital* 300).

Chapter Four

1. My critique of Hardt and Negri's vision of "immanence" and the temporal ambiguity of their vision of history was significantly influenced by conversations with Scott Michaelsen.

Chapter Five

1. Cameron declares: "A rigorous philosophy of absolute correctness permeated every department, from Set Design and Construction through Decorating Props, Wardrobe, Hairdressing and Visual Effects" (xii–xiii).

2. Jack's line is cited as spoken in the film, slightly differently from the line as it appears in the published script.

3. See, e.g., Fumerton; Sebek. For a treatment of gift-giving practices after 1700, see Carrier.

4. See, among other possible examples, Caputo and Scanlon, and the essays collected in Schrift *Logic of the Gift* and in Wyschogrod, Goux, and Boynton *Enigma of Gift*.

5. Just one year before his first important text on the concept of "expenditure," Bataille coauthored (with Raymond Queneau, who went on to edit Alexandre Kojève's *Introduction à la lecture de Hegel* [1947]) an essay entitled "Critique of the Foundations of the Hegelian Dialectic" (1932). The essay argues for freeing the dialectic from its mechanistic application in the late Engels and in classical Marxism generally and reinterpreting it in the light of psychoanalysis and phenomenology (see Bataille *Visions* 260 and see also Surya 521 n. 6).

6. Curiously, this passage appears only in the "mass-market" paperback edition and does not appear in the hardcover edition of this book from the same year.

7. Bataille's *The Accursed Share* will be cited with reference to its three original volumes, although the cited English translation includes Bataille's original volumes 2 and 3 in its second of two volumes.

Chapter Six

1. Cf. Richman's suggestion that "Mauss condemns modern man to a purely symbolic reconstruction of a past irretrievably lost" (15).

2. For a critique of Agnew and other scholars who discuss the connection of market and theater in early-modern England, see Shershow.

3. The idealist underpinning of Fukuyama's thought is evident in his interpretation of Weber, who, he claims, "stood Karl Marx on his head by arguing that it was not underlying economic forces that created cultural products like religion and ideology but rather culture that produced certain forms of economic behavior" (43–44). In fact, as many other commentators have suggested, Weber is scrupulous in attempting to maintain a dialectical balance of materialist and idealist interpretations of historical change.

4. The word "generosity" itself emerges from the Latin word *genus* and thus refers in its root sense to actions "appropriate or natural to one of noble birth" (*Oxford English Dictionary,* s.v. "generous," a:2.a).

5. This phrase is used as the title of two sections of volume 1 of *The Accursed Share*.

Chapter Seven

1. "I think it's fair to say the debate is over," Mr. Clinton said on August 16, 1997. "We know now that welfare reform works" (quoted in Broder).

2. A obvious conflict of structural and agential interpretation is evident in the debate about the so-called social-control thesis, first argued at length by Frances Fox Piven and Richard A. Cloward in their widely cited *Regulating the Poor* (1971; 2nd ed. 1993). These authors contend, in brief, that "relief arrangements are ancillary to economic arrangements" and that "their chief function is to regulate labor"—by alleviating the worst suffering of the unemployed but also by serving to "demean and punish those who do not work" so as "to exalt by contrast even the meanest labor at the meanest wages" (*Regulating the Poor* 3–4). Although Piven and Cloward's analysis is rigorously structural, focusing on the systemic effect of organized welfare programs, their critics often charge that they misrepresent the motives and intentions of people who work with the poor. Thus, John K. Alexander, in an anthology of responses to Piven and Cloward, reproaches them for "dismissing moral considerations entirely" from their analysis (16); and James Leihy, in the same volume, argues that "a professional historian should reconstruct his subjects' situation and ideas with more empathy" (105). Such critiques entirely miss the point, which is, as Piven and Cloward document persuasively, that organized relief programs have the *effect* of regulating labor *regardless* of what may have been the good intentions of some of the people who designed and administered them. Nevertheless, having reframed the debate as one of intentions versus effects, other conservative voices in essence reappropriate the same conceptual structure: arguing that contemporary welfare programs emerged from good intentions but ended up merely fostering "dependency." This is precisely the thesis, as its title suggests, of Marvin Olasky's *Tragedy of American Compassion;* and for a much earlier version, see Irving Kristol's "Welfare, the Best of Intentions, the Worst of Results," a review of the first edition of *Regulating the Poor.*

3. As Joel F. Handler and Yeheskel Hansenfeld summarize, from the early-modern period to the present moment the "theory of welfare and poverty remains the same. It is the indiscriminate giving of aid that destroys the moral fiber. It is soul that the poor need, not soup. . . . The task then of welfare administration is to separate the 'deserving poor'—those who are poor through no fault of their own—from the 'undeserving poor'" (201).

4. Cf. the film *Mrs. Doubtfire* (Twentieth-Century Fox, 1993), in which Robin Williams plays a devoted father whose failures in paid employment cause him to be (temporarily) denied access to his children. The happy ending of this film—in which the protagonist becomes a children's entertainer on television, thus allowing him to employ his parental skills *as* his work—operates by *uniting* the two roles in a fantastic way.

5. This argument is also developed, in slightly different form, in Michaelsen and Shershow.

6. Nearly the same passage appears at the end of *Poverty and Compassion* (389), suggesting its central importance to Himmelfarb's thought.

7. Indeed, in the same brief essay already cited for its frank defense of the workhouse, Himmelfarb also claims that the whole notion of "social insurance" that was adopted in both England and America in the 1930s was a crucial turning point in our alleged contemporary moral decline. Yet she also acknowledges that "I find it difficult to point out where on the slippery slope we should have pulled up short" ("Moral Responsibility" 6).

8. I cite Clinton's speech on November 25, 2000, from CNN.com. The word "large" appears in brackets in the original.

Chapter Eight

1. Himmelfarb cites Bloom's work on the Bible as an instance of what is wrong with contemporary literary criticism; and yet, in the decade following Himmelfarb's paper, Bloom himself emerged as a central public advocate for the traditional canon.

2. Virtually the same passage appears in Pie's *Usuries Spright Conjured*. On how anti-usury texts from the early seventeenth century preserve an otherwise lost manuscript defense of usury, see Jones *God and the Moneylenders* 153.

3. Cf. how Sahlins claims that "Marcel Mauss's famous *Essay on the gift* becomes his own gift to the ages" (149); and Mary Douglas claims, on the back cover of Davis's *The Gift in Sixteenth-Century France,* that "this book itself is the perfect gift."

4. See Haskin for more on Milton's intense interest in the parable of the talents, which he alludes to often, most famously in his "Sonnet on His Blindness."

5. On such practices, see Archer, Barron, and Harding, who define "forestalling" as "going out before the market and buying from those who would otherwise have brought goods to the market themselves"; "engrossing" as "buying up the whole, or a large part of, the stock of a particular commodity, with the implication of selling again at an enhanced price"; and "regrating" as "buying goods in one market for resale in another" (5). The general principle of the early-modern moral economy, they add, is that "the producer should market his own her own produce, without the intervention of middlemen or dealers" (5). On the classical and early Christian distrust of economic "middlemen," see also Viner 35–36.

6. On "spiritual usury," see, e.g., T. Wilson 189–90; Downame 286–89. Mosse's summary is exemplary in its analogy between literal charity and the obligatory development of personal "gifts": "There is an other kind of *usury* which may not unjustly be called *Foenus spirituale, Spiritual usury*. And of that there are two sorts. The first is *giving of alms*"; another is "the profitable employing of the gifts which wee have received from God to the advancing of his glory, and the benefit of men. . . . Of this usury also our *Savior Christ* speaketh in the parable [of the talents]" (13–15).

7. For more on the virtual obsession with beggary in early-modern England, see Carroll; Woodbridge.

8. I have edited quotations from Tyndale and other early-modern writers here and elsewhere by eliminating scribal contractions and modernizing spelling, while retaining archaic diction such as "shalt" or "harboreth."

9. In "The Use of Money," his most famous sermon, Wesley similarly argues: "Money is an excellent gift of God" and "all who fear God [must] know how to employ *this valuable talent*" (2:268; emphasis added)—which can be done, in particular, "by using in your business all the understanding which God has given you" (2:273). This sermon is built around the famous homiletic formula "Gain all you can, save all you can, give all you can," which conveys with remarkable concision how working and giving remain the central points of interest within the moral economy.

10. Strictly speaking, for Hayek, solidarity and altruism are not quite "instincts" in the strict sense; rather, they arose from an *interaction* of "innate instincts" and our "physiological constitution" (*Knowledge, Evolution and Society* 38). But Hayek is not rigorous about maintaining this distinction. For example, in another essay from the same volume, he writes, "Our *instincts* tell us, first, that our duty is to serve the visible needs of our known friends; and, second, that the activity that gives us most satisfaction is to join in a common effort for common ends" (38; emphasis added).

Chapter Nine

1. See Robinson and Godbey for a study based on "time diaries" that questions some of the conclusions of Schor and others. Although the claim that Americans are overworked is often made from the Left, the same claim, as Frank documents, is sometimes used by defenders of contemporary capitalism to claim the essential justice of new working conditions. For example, Frank cites an article in *Wired* magazine asserting proudly: "The rich, the former leisure class, are becoming the new overworked" (*One Market under God* 10).

2. On the connection of Futurism and fascism, see, e.g., Hewitt.

3. E.g., in 1968 the Museum of Modern Art in New York held an exhibit entitled *The Machine, as Seen at the End of the Mechanical Age*. See Hultén.

4. This book is bound in the same volume as Home *Neoist Manifestos*.

5. Critiquing this position, Home also observes: "To undertake [art's] realization and suppression is an attempt to *save* this mental set at the very moment the category is *abolished*. Art disappears from the museums *only* to reappear *everywhere!*" (*Assault on Culture* 43). Black asks, similarly, "What's the difference, practically speaking," between literal art and an art of living (144)?

6. Cited from http://www.illegal-art.org/, September 2003; emphasis added.

7. The receipt books from these ceremonies have been scrupulously preserved as "works" in their own right. And note that the eight "zones" sold according to the ritual are still listed in catalogs of Klein's work by their "owners" (see Charlet 57; and Rice University, Institute for the Arts, *Yves Klein, 1928–1962: A Retrospective*, catalog numbers 101–103).

8. As Restany observes, "Yves Klein's writings . . . swarm with reflections on alchemy" (Restany and Loselle 40).

9. Referring to a different but similar piece, in which viewers are invited to take a piece of paper from a stack which is replenished, the artist told an interviewer that "this 'letting go' of the work, this refusal to make a static form, a monolithic sculpture, in favor of a disappearing, changing, unstable, and fragile form was an attempt on my part to rehearse my fears of having Ross disappear day by day right in front of my eyes" (interview with Tim Rollins; González-Torres 13).

10. "Without the public these works are nothing," the artist writes. "I need the public to complete the work. I ask the public to help me, to take responsibility, to become part of my work, to join in" (Spector 57).

11. "The Shakespeare File" remains available on the ACTA Web site as of May 2004. "De-

fending Civilization" was reissued in February 2002 in a "revised and expanded" version but is now no longer available on the ACTA Web site except by special request.

12. The same critique of Blanchot was repeated yet again by Richard Wolin in *The Seduction of Unreason* (2004), a book published just as this one was going into production.

13. See Holland's introductions to Blanchot *Reader* and to Hill.

14. For Blanchot's own interest in this figure, see *Vicious Circles*.

15. The temptation to read Blanchot this way may be seen, for example, in the prefatory comments of George Quasha in *The Station Hill Blanchot Reader*. Quasha suggests: "To enter a work by Blanchot armed from the start with a critical perspective [i.e., what he identifies as a deconstructive or historical/political one] violates the free and inquiring nature of his self-revolutional text." Therefore, we should read him in a "pure and simple" manner (x). This rhetoric of purity and violation is, in my view, profoundly unfaithful to Blanchot's thought.

16. Blanchot writes of Heidegger's "unforgivable silence" in his essay "'Do Not Forget'" (*Reader* 246–48).

17. The translation of this essay included in *The Station Hill Blanchot Reader* contains a misleading typographical mistake. There, the beginning of the last sentence in the cited passage reads: "The limit does not disappear, but it takes from language the perhaps *not* unlimited meaning that it claims to limit" (459; emphasis added). In the original, the sentence begins: "Le limite ne disparaît pas, mai elle reçoit du langage le sens, peut-être sans limite, qu'elle pretend limiter . . ." (Blanchot *L'entretien infini*).

Chapter Ten

1. The lines cited are from Aristotle, *Politiques, or Discourses of Gouernment* (1598). The original French translator is Le Roy, called Regius; John Dee has been suggested as the English translator, who is identified in this edition only as I.D. There is some ambiguity, in Aristotle himself and in his commentators, about whether "economy" is natural and "chrematistics" unnatural, or whether there are "natural" and "unnatural" modes *of* chrematistics—such as barter and fair exchange versus exchange for financial gain (buying cheap to sell dear); see Shell 94.

2. These phrases are taken from the Geneva Bible, marginal annotation on Matthew 25:27; from Downame 287 and from Mosse 14.

3. An outstanding example is the work of 1999 Nobel laureate Amartya Sen; see, e.g., his *On Ethics and Economics*.

4. I cite the prepared text of Dole's speech as published in the *New York Times,* August 16, 1996.

5. See, e.g., the essays collected in Peffer.

6. Thanks to John Hanlon for bringing a particularly vivid example of this process to my attention: an advertisement for the business magazine *Forbes* in 1998 depicting a crowd of people, carefully portrayed as culturally and racially diverse, holding red flags emblazoned with world currency symbols, under the caption "Capitalists of the World Unite!"

7. A school of "ecological economics" attempts to address this problem by developing new methods of accounting for "natural capital," the value of the physical environment itself. See, e.g., Prugh and Costanza.

8. One last round of thanks goes to Scott Michaelsen here, for calling my attention to Lafargue.

REFERENCES

Alexander, John K. "The Functions of Public Welfare in Late Eighteenth-Century Philadelphia." In Trattner 15–34.

Alpher, Barry. *Yir-Yoront Lexicon: Sketch and Dictionary of an Australian Language*. Berlin: Mouton de Gruyter, 1991.

Althusser, Louis, and Etienne Balibar. *Reading Capital*. New York: Pantheon, 1970.

Anderson, Martin. *Welfare: The Political Economy of Welfare Reform in the United States*. Palo Alto, CA: Hoover Institution Press, 1978.

Apollonio, Umbro. *Futurist Manifestos*. New York: Viking Press, 1973.

Archer, Ian, Caroline Barron, and Vanessa Harding, eds. *Hugh Alley's Caveat: The Markets of London in 1598*. London: London Topographical Society, 1988.

Arendt, Hannah. *The Human Condition*. 2nd ed. Chicago: University of Chicago Press, 1998. (Originally published 1958.)

Aristotle. *Aristotles Politiques, or Discourses of Gouernment*. Trans. I. D. [John Dee?] London, 1598.

Arnold, Matthew. *Culture and Anarchy*. New Haven, CT: Yale University Press, 1994.

Aronowitz, Stanley, et al. "The Post-work Manifesto." In Aronowitz and Cutler 31–80.

Aronowitz, Stanley, and Jonathan Cutler, eds. *Post-work: The Wages of Cybernation*. New York: Routledge, 1998.

Aronowitz, Stanley, and William DiFazio. *The Jobless Future: Sci-Tech and the Dogma of Work*. Minneapolis: University of Minnesota Press, 1994.

Barrow, Isaac. *The Duty and Reward of Bounty to the Poor*. 2nd ed. London, 1677.

Bataille, Georges. *The Accursed Share: An Essay on General Economy*. Trans. Robert Hurley. 3 vols. in 2. New York: Zone Books, 1991.

———. "Celestial Bodies." *October* 36 (1986): 75–78. (Originally published 1939.)

———. "Van Gogh as Prometheus." *October* 36 (1986): 58–60. (Originally published 1937.)

———. *Visions of Excess: Selected Writings, 1927–1939*. Ed. Alan Stoekl. Trans. Allan Stoekl with Carl R. Lovitts and Donald M. Leslie Jr. Theory and History of Literature, vol. 14. Minneapolis: University of Minneapolis Press, 1985.

Beck, Ulrich. *The Brave New World of Work.* Trans. Patrick Camiller. Cambridge, UK: Polity Press, 2000.

Bell, Daniel. *The Coming of Post-industrial Society: A Venture in Social Forecasting.* New York: Basic Books, 1973.

Benjamin, Walter. *Illuminations.* New York: Schocken Books, 1969.

Bernstein, Nina. "As Welfare Comes to an End, So Do the Jobs." *New York Times,* December 17, 2001, A1.

The Bible and Holy Scriptures Conteyned in the Olde and Newer Testament. Geneva, 1560.

Black, Bob. "The Realization and Suppression of Situationism." In *What Is Situationism? A Reader,* ed. Stewart Home, 143–52. Edinburgh: AK Press, 1991.

Blanchot, Maurice. *The Blanchot Reader.* Ed. Michael Holland. Oxford: Blackwell, 1995.

———. *L'entretien infini.* Paris: Gallimard, 1969.

———. *The Infinite Conversation.* Trans. Susan Hanson. Minneapolis: University of Minnesota Press, 1993.

———. *The Instant of My Death.* Trans. Elizabeth Rottenberg. Stanford, CA: Stanford University Press, 2000. (Published with Jacques Derrida, *Demeure: Fiction and Testimony.*)

———. *The Station Hill Blanchot Reader: Fiction and Literary Essays.* Barrytown, NY: Station Hill Press, 1999.

———. *The Unavowable Community.* Barrytown, NY: Station Hill Press, 1988.

———. *Vicious Circles: Two Fictions and "after the Fact."* Barrytown, NY: Station Hill Press, 1985.

Blazwick, Iwona. "Bitter Victory: The Situationist International." In Blazwick *Endless Adventure* 9–16.

———, ed. *An Endless Adventure—An Endless Passion—An Endless Banquet: The Situationist International Selected Documents from 1957 to 1962.* London: Verso, 1989.

Bloch, Marc Léopold Benjamin. *Feudal Society.* Chicago: University of Chicago Press, 1964.

Bloom, Harold. *How to Read and Why.* New York: Scribner, 2000.

———. *Shakespeare: The Invention of the Human.* New York: Riverhead Books, 1998.

Bolman, Lee G., and Terrence E. Deal. *Leading with Soul: An Uncommon Journey of Spirit.* San Francisco: Jossey-Bass Publishers, 1995.

Bond, William J. *Going Solo.* New York: McGraw-Hill, 1997.

Borsook, Paulina. *Cyberselfish: A Critical Romp through the Terribly Libertarian Culture of High Tech.* New York: Public Affairs, 2000.

Botting, Fred, and Scott Wilson, eds. *Bataille: A Critical Reader.* Oxford: Blackwell, 1998.

Bourdieu, Pierre. *Distinction: A Social Critique of the Judgment of Taste.* Trans. Richard Nice. Cambridge: Harvard University Press, 1984.

———. *The Field of Cultural Production.* Ed. Randal Johnson. New York: Columbia University Press, 1993.

———. *The Logic of Practice.* Trans. Richard Nice. Stanford, CA: Stanford University Press, 1990. (Originally published 1980.)

———. "Marginalia—Some Additional Thoughts on the Gift." In Schrift *Logic of the Gift* 231–41.

———. *Outline of a Theory of Practice.* Trans. Richard Nice. Cambridge: Cambridge University Press, 1977.

Bourriaud, Nicolas. "Blue Company; or, Yves Klein Considered as a World-Economy." In Perlein and Corà 35–44.

Bracken, Christopher. *The Potlatch Papers: A Colonial Case History.* Chicago: University of Chicago Press, 1997.

Braverman, Harry. *Labor and Monopoly Capital: The Degradation of Work in the Twentieth Century.* New York: Monthly Review Press, 1975.

Briner, Bob. *The Management Methods of Jesus: Ancient Wisdom for Modern Business.* Nashville, TN: Thomas Nelson, 1996.

Broder, John M. "Keeping Score: Big Social Changes Revive the False God of Numbers." *New York Times,* August 17, 1997, 4.1.

Brook, Chris, ed. *The K Foundation Burn a Million Quid.* London: Ellipsis, 1997.

Brooks, Cleanth, et al. "The Remaking of the Canon." *Partisan Review* 58, no. 2 (1991): 350–70.

Bucer, Martin. *A Treatise, How, by the Worde of God, Christian Mens Almose Ought to Be Distributed.* London, 1577.

Buchloh, B. H. D. *Neo-Avantgarde and Culture Industry: Essays on European and American Art from 1955 to 1975.* Cambridge: MIT Press, 2000.

Bürger, Peter. *Theory of the Avant-Garde.* Minneapolis: University of Minnesota Press, 1984.

Cabanne, Pierre, and Marcel Duchamp. *Dialogues with Marcel Duchamp.* New York: Viking Press, 1971.

Cahill, Holger. "American Resources in the Arts." In O'Connor *Art for the Millions* 33–44.

———. *New Horizons in American Art.* New York: Museum of Modern Art, 1936.

Cameron, James. *Titanic: James Cameron's Illustrated Screenplay.* Ed. Randall Frakes. New York: Harper, 1998.

Caputo, John D., and Michael J. Scanlon. *God, the Gift, and Postmodernism.* Bloomington: Indiana University Press, 1999.

Card, Orson Scott. *Ender's Game.* New York: T. Doherty Associates, 1985.

Carlyle, Thomas. *Past and Present.* New York: A. L. Burt, n.d.

Carnegie, Andrew. *The Gospel of Wealth, and Other Timely Essays.* Cambridge: Harvard University Press, 1962.

Carrier, James G. *Gifts and Commodities: Exchange and Western Capitalism since 1700.* London: Routledge, 1995.

Carroll, William C. *Fat King, Lean Beggar: Representations of Poverty in the Age of Shakespeare.* Ithaca, NY: Cornell University Press, 1996.

Casillo, Robert. *The Genealogy of Demons: Anti-Semitism, Fascism, and the Myths of Ezra Pound.* Evanston, IL: Northwestern University Press, 1988.

Charlet, Nicolas. *Yves Klein.* Paris: Adam Biro, 2000.

Chrysostom, Saint John. *On Repentence and Almsgiving.* Ed. Thomas P. Halton. Trans. Gus George Christo. Fathers of the Church, vol. 96. Washington, DC: Catholic University of America Press, 1998.

Ciulla, Joanne B. *The Working Life: The Promise and Betrayal of Modern Work.* New York: Random House, 2000.

Cleaver, Harry. Interview with Massimo De Angelis. 1993. http://www.geocities.com/CapitolHill/3843/cleaver (accessed November 2001).

———. *Reading Capital Politically.* 2nd ed. Leeds, UK: Anti/theses, 2000.

Conlin Michelle. "Religion in the Workplace: The Growing Presence of Spirituality in Corporate America." *Business Week,* November 1, 1999, 151–58.

Cowen, Tyler. *In Praise of Commercial Culture.* Cambridge: Harvard University Press, 2000.

Darbel, Alain, and Pierre Bourdieu. *Travail et travailleurs en Algérie.* Paris: Mouton, 1963.

Davis, Natalie Zemon. *The Gift in Sixteenth-Century France.* Madison: University of Wisconsin Press, 2000.

Deal, Terrence E., and Allan A. Kennedy. *Corporate Cultures: The Rites and Rituals of Corporate Life.* Reading, MA: Addison-Wesley, 1982.

Debord, Guy. *Comments on the Society of the Spectacle.* London: Verso, 1990.

———. *Society of the Spectacle.* Detroit: Black and Red, 1983.

Deleuze, Gilles, and Félix Guattari. *A Thousand Plateaus: Capitalism and Schizophrenia.* Trans. Brian Massumi. Minneapolis: University of Minnesota Press, 1987.

Derrida, Jacques. *Demeure: Fiction and Testimony.* (Published with Maurice Blanchot's *The Instant of My Death.*) Trans. Elizabeth Rottenberg. Stanford, CA: Stanford University Press, 2000.

———. "Différance." In *Margins of Philosophy,* trans. Alan Bass, 1–28. Chicago: University of Chicago Press, 1982.

———. "From Restricted to General Economy: A Hegelianism without Reserve." In *Writing and Difference,* trans. Alan Bass, 251–77. Chicago: University of Chicago Press, 1978.

———. *The Gift of Death.* Trans. David Wills. Chicago: University of Chicago Press, 1995.

———. *Given Time.* Vol. 1, *Counterfeit Money.* Trans. Peggy Kamuf. Chicago: University of Chicago Press, 1992.

———. *On Cosmopolitanism and Forgiveness.* Trans Mark Dooley and Michael Hughes. London and New York: Routledge, 2001.

———. *Positions.* Trans. Alan Bass. Chicago: University of Chicago Press, 1981.

———. *Specters of Marx: The State of the Debt, the Work of Mourning, and the New International.* Trans. Peggy Kamuf. New York: Routledge, 1994.

———. "Structure, Sign, and Play in the Discourse of the Human Sciences." In *Writing and Difference,* trans. Alan Bass, 278–93. Chicago: University of Chicago Press, 1978.

Derrida, Jacques, and Jaurizio Ferraris. *A Taste for the Secret.* Trans. Giacomo Donis. Ed. Giacomo Donis and David Webb. Cambridge, UK: Polity, 2001.

Dod, John, and Robert Clever [*sic*]. *A Godly Forme of Household Government, for the Ordering of Private Families, According to the Direction of Gods Word.* London, 1630.

Dole, Robert. "Dole's Speech Accepting the G.O.P. Nomination for President." *New York Times,* August 16, 1996, A12.

Downame, George. *Lectures on the XV Psalme . . . Wherein . . . the Question of Usurie Is Plainely and Fully Decided.* London, 1604.

Drucker, Peter. *Post-capitalist Society.* New York: HarperCollins, 1993.

Duchamp, Marcel. "Apropos of 'Readymades.'" In *Salt Seller: The Writings of Marcel Duchamp,* ed. Michel Sanouillet and Elmer Peterson, 141–42. New York: Oxford University Press, 1973.

Dyer-Witheford, Nick. *Cyber-Marx: Cycles and Circuits of Struggle in High-Technology Capitalism.* Urbana: University of Illinois Press, 1999.

Economiste, "Philanthropy in America: The Gospel of Wealth," May 30, 1998, 19–21.

Engels, Frederick. *The Part Played by Labor in the Transition from Ape to Man.* 1876. Repr., New York: International Publishers, 1950.

Erikson, Kai. Introduction to *The Nature of Work: Sociological Perspectives.* Ed. Kai Erikson and Steven Peter Vallas. New Haven, CT: Yale University Press, 1990.

Feuer, Alan. "Hungry, Cold and Stuck in Line: Food Pantries Find Charity Dwindling as Need Grows." *New York Times,* December 27, 2001, D1–D6.

Forrester, Viviane. *The Economic Horror.* Cambridge, UK: Polity Press, 1999.

Frank, Thomas. *One Market under God: Extreme Capitalism, Market Populism, and the End of Economic Democracy.* New York: Doubleday, 2000.

Fraser, Nancy, and Linda Gordon. "'Dependency' Demystified: Inscriptions of Power in a Keyword of the Welfare State." In *Contemporary Political Philosophy: An Anthology,* ed. Robert E. Goodin and Philip Pettit, 618–33. Oxford: Blackwell, 1997. (Originally published 1994.)

Freud, Sigmund. *The Standard Edition of the Complete Psychological Works of Sigmund Freud.* Trans. James Strachey. 22 vols. London: Hogarth Press, 1955.

Fukuyama, Francis. *Trust: The Social Virtues and the Creation of Prosperity.* New York: Free Press, 1995.

Fumerton, Patricia. *Cultural Aesthetics: Renaissance Literature and the Practice of Social Ornament.* Chicago: University of Chicago Press, 1991.

Geis, Deborah R., and Steven F. Kruger, eds. *Approaching the Millennium: Essays on "Angels in America."* Ann Arbor: University of Michigan Press, 1997.

Geremek, Bronislaw. *Poverty: A History.* Oxford: Blackwell, 1994.

Gibson, William. *Burning Chrome.* New York: Arbor House, 1986.

Gilder, George. *Microcosm: The Quantum Revolution in Economics and Technology.* New York: Simon and Schuster, 1989.

———. *Wealth and Poverty.* New York: Bantam, 1981.

Gillespie, Nick, et al. "Book Symposium: Creating Culture." *Reason Magazine,* December 1997.

González-Torres, Félix. *Félix González-Torres.* Interviewed by Tim Rollins. Essay by Susan Cahan. Short story by Jan Avgikos. Los Angeles: A.R.T. Press, 1993. Distributed by Distributed Art Publishers, New York.

Gorky, Maxim. *On Literature.* Seattle: University of Washington Press, 1973.

Gorz, André. *Farewell to the Working Class: An Essay on Post-industrial Socialism.* Trans. Mike Sonenscher. London: Pluto Press, 1982.

———. *Paths to Paradise: On the Liberation from Work.* Trans. Malcolm Imrie. Boston: South End Press, 1985.

———. *Reclaiming Work: Beyond the Wage-Based Society.* Cambridge, UK: Polity Press, 1999.

Gould, Susan B., Kerry J. Weiner, and Barbara R. Levin. *Free Agents: People and Organizations Creating a New Working Community.* San Francisco: Jossey-Bass, 1997.

Goux, Jean-Joseph. "General Economics and Postmodern Capitalism." In Botting and Wilson 196–213.

Granthan, Charles. *The Future of Work: The Promise of the New Digital Society.* New York: McGraw-Hill, 2000.

Greenfield, Karl Taro. "A New Way of Giving." *Time,* July 24, 2000, 49–51.

Guattari, Felix, and Toni Negri. *Communists like Us: New Spaces of Liberty, New Lines of Alliance.* 1985. Trans. Michael Ryan. New York: Semiotext(e), 1990.

Guillory, John. *Cultural Capital: The Problem of Literary Canon Formation.* Chicago: University of Chicago Press, 1993.

Hammacher, Werner. "Working through Working." *Modernism/Modernity* 3, no. 1 (1996): 23–56.

Handler, Joel F., and Yeheskel Hansenfeld. *We the Poor People: Work, Poverty, and Welfare.* New Haven, CT: Yale University Press, 1997.

Handy, Charles B. *The Age of Unreason.* Boston: Harvard Business School Press, 1989.

Hansan, C. John E., and Robert Morris, eds. *Welfare Reform, 1996–2000: Is There a Safety Net?* Westport, CT: Auburn House, 1999.

Hardt, Michael, and Antonio Negri. *Empire.* Cambridge: Harvard University Press, 2000.

Harris, John F. "Clinton Praises Results of Welfare Reform." *Cleveland Plain Dealer,* August 4, 1999, A10.

Hartman, Louis F. *Encyclopedic Dictionary of the Bible: A Translation and Adaptation of A. Van Den Born's "Bijbels Woordenboek."* New York: McGraw-Hill, 1963.

Haskin, Dayton. *Milton's Burden of Interpretation.* Philadelphia: University of Pennsylvania Press, 1994.

Hawkins, Kathleen L. *Spirit Incorporated: How to Follow Your Spiritual Path from 9–5.* Marina del Rey, CA: DeVorss, 1998.

Hayek, Friedrich A. *The Constitution of Liberty.* Chicago: University of Chicago Press, 1960.

———. *The Fatal Conceit: The Errors of Socialism.* Ed. W. W. Bartley. Chicago: University of Chicago Press, 1988.

———. *Individualism and Economic Order.* Chicago: University of Chicago Press, 1948.

———. *Knowledge, Evolution and Society.* London: Adam Smith Institute, 1983.

———. *The Road to Serfdom.* Chicago: University of Chicago Press, 1944.

———. *Studies in Philosophy, Politics, and Economics.* Chicago: University of Chicago Press, 1967.

Hegel, *Phenomenology of the Mind.* Trans. J. B. Baillie. New York: Harper, 1967.

Heidegger, Martin. *Basic Writings.* Rev. ed. Ed. David Farrell Krell. San Francisco: Harper, 1993.

Heilbroner, Robert L. *The Act of Work.* Occasional Papers of the Council of Scholars, vol. 3. Washington, DC: Library of Congress, 1985.

———. *Behind the Veil of Economics: Essays in the Worldly Philosophy.* New York: W. W. Norton, 1988.

———. *Twenty-first Century Capitalism.* New York: Norton, 1993.

———. *The Worldly Philosophers: The Lives, Times, and Ideas of the Great Economic Thinkers.* Rev. 7th ed. New York: Simon and Schuster, 1999.

Heinlein, Robert A. *Starship Troopers.* New York: Putnam, 1959.

Henriques, Diana B., and David Barstow. "A Nation Challenged: The Red Cross." *New York Times,* November 15, 2001, A1.

Herczeg, Yisrael Isser Zvi. *The Torah with Rashi's Commentary.* 5 vols. Brooklyn, NY: Mesorah, 1994–98.

Hess, Deborah M. *Politics and Literature: The Case of Maurice Blanchot.* New York: P. Lang, 1999.

Hewitt, Andrew. *Fascist Modernism: Aesthetics, Politics, and the Avant-Garde.* Stanford, CA: Stanford University Press, 1993.

Hill, Leslie. *Blanchot, Extreme Contemporary.* Warwick Studies in European Philosophy. London: Routledge, 1997.

Himmelfarb, Gertrude. *The De-moralization of Society: From Victorian Virtues to Modern Values.* New York: Knopf, 1995.

———. *The Idea of Poverty: England in the Early Industrial Age.* New York: Knopf, 1984.

———. Introduction to Tocqueville 9–37.

———. "Moral Responsibility: The British Experience." In *Points of Light: New Approaches to Ending Welfare Dependency,* ed. Tamar Ann Mehuron, 1–7. Washington, DC: Ethics and Public Policy Center, 1991.

———. *Poverty and Compassion: The Moral Imagination of the Late Victorians.* New York: Vintage, 1991.

Hollier, Denis. "The Dualist Materialism of Georges Batailles." In Botting and Wilson 59–73.

Home, Stewart. *The Assault on Culture: Utopian Currents from Lettrisme to Class War.* London: Aporia with Unpopular Books, 1988.

———. *Neoism, Plagiarism, and Praxis.* Edinburgh: AK Press, 1995.

———. *Neoist Manifestos.* Stirling, UK: AK Press, 1991.

Howells, Richard Parton. *The Myth of the* Titanic. Basingstoke, Hampshire, UK: Macmillan, 1999.

Hultén, Karl Gunnar Pontus. *The Machine, as Seen at the End of the Mechanical Age.* New York: Museum of Modern Art, 1968. Distributed by New York Graphic Society, Greenwich, CT.

Hyde, Lewis. *The Gift: Imagination and the Erotic Life of Property.* New York: Random House, 1983.

Jameson, Fredric. *Postmodernism; or, the Cultural Logic of Late Capitalism.* Durham, NC: Duke University Press, 1999.

———. "Reification and Utopia in Mass Culture." In *Signatures of the Visible,* 9–34. New York and London: Routledge, 1992.

Jappe, Anselm. *Guy Debord.* Berkeley and Los Angeles: University of California Press, 1999.

Jevons, William Stanley. *The Theory of Political Economy.* London, 1871.

Jones, Laurie Beth. *Jesus C.E.O.: Using Ancient Wisdom for Visionary Leadership.* New York: Hyperion, 1992.

Jones, Norman. *God and the Moneylenders: Usury and Law in Early Modern England.* Oxford: Blackwell, 1989.

Kant, Immanuel. *Groundwork of the Metaphysics of Morals.* Trans. H. J. Paton. New York: Harper and Row, 1964.

Kaus, Mickey. *The End of Equality.* New York: Basic Books, 1992.

Kelley, Robert Earl. *The Gold-Collar Worker: Harnessing the Brainpower of the New Work Force.* Reading, MA: Addison-Wesley, 1985.

Keynes, John Neville. *The Scope and Method of Political Economy*. 4th ed. London: Macmillan, 1930.

Kirsch, Arthur. "Between Bardolatry and Bardicide." *Times Literary Supplement,* April 20–26, 1990, 421–22.

Knabb, Ken, ed. and trans. *Situationist International Anthology*. 3rd ed. Berkeley, CA: Bureau of Public Secrets, 1995.

Kristol, Irving. "A Capitalist Conception of Justice." In *Ideological Voices: An Anthology in Modern Political Ideas,* ed. Paul Schumaker, Dwight C. Kiel, and Thomas W. Heilke, 286–94. New York: McGraw-Hill, 1997.

———. "Welfare, the Best of Intentions, the Worst of Results." *Atlantic Monthly* 228 (August 17, 1971): 45.

Kushner, Tony. *Millennium Approaches*. Pt. 1 of *Angels in America*. New York: Theatre Communications Group, 1993.

———. *Perestroika*. Pt. 2 of *Angels in America*. New York: Theatre Communications Group, 1994.

Lacoue-Labarthe, Philippe. *Heidegger, Art, and Politics: The Fiction of the Political*. Trans. Chris Turner. Oxford: Blackwell. 1990.

Lafargue, Paul. *The Right to Be Lazy, and Other Studies*. Trans. Charles H. Kerr. Chicago: Charles H. Kerr and Co., 1907.

Larkin, Geri. *Building a Business the Buddhist Way*. Berkeley, CA: Celestial Arts, 1999.

Larrabee, Eric, and Rolf Meyersohn. *Mass Leisure*. Glencoe, IL: Free Press, 1958.

Lazzarato, Maurizio. "Immaterial Labor." In Virno and Hardt 132–46.

Leiby, James. "Social Control and Historical Explanation: Historians View the Piven and Cloward Thesis." In Trattner 90–113.

Lenin. Vladimir Illych. *The Lenin Anthology*. Ed. Robert C. Tucker. New York: Norton, 1975.

Levinas, Emmanuel. *Proper Names*. Stanford, CA: Stanford University Press, 1996.

———. "The Trace of the Other." Trans. Alphonso Lingis. In *Deconstruction in Context: Literature and Philosophy,* ed. Mark C. Taylor, 345–59. Chicago: University of Chicago Press, 1986.

Lévi-Strauss, Claude. *The Raw and the Cooked*. New York: Harper and Row, 1969.

Little, Lester K. *Religious Poverty and the Profit Economy in Medieval Europe*. London: P. Elek, 1978.

Locke, John, and Peter Laslett. *Two Treatises of Government*. Cambridge: Cambridge University Press, 1960.

Lowell, Josephine Shaw. *Public Relief and Private Charity*. In *Poverty U.S.A.: The Historical Record,* ed. David J. Rothman. New York: Arno Press, 1971. (Originally published 1884.)

Lubin, David M. *Titanic*. London: BFI Publishing, 1999.

Luther, Martin. *Lectures on Genesis*. Ed. Jaroslav Pelikan. Vols. 1–8 of *Works,* ed. Jaroslav Pelikan et al. 55 vols. Saint Louis: Concordia Publishing House, 1955–86. (Vol. 1, 1958.)

Mandel, Ernest. Introduction to Appendix in Marx *Capital* 943–47.

Mannox, James, et al. *The Art Strike Papers*. Stirling, UK: AK Press, 1991.

Marcus, Greil. *Lipstick Traces: A Secret History of the Twentieth Century*. Cambridge: Harvard University Press, 1990.

Marinetti, Filippo Tommaso, and R. W. Flint. *Selected Writings.* New York: Farrar Straus and Giroux, 1972.

Marsh, Ed W. *James Cameron's "Titanic."* New York: Harper, 1998.

Marshall, Alfred. *Memorials of Alfred Marshall.* Ed. A. C. Pigou. New York: Kelley and Millman, 1956.

Martin, Jerry L., et al. "Defending Civilization: How Our Universities Are Failing America and What Can Be Done about It." American Council of Trustees and Alumni, November 2001. http://www.goacta.org/Reports/defciv.pdf (accessed November 2001).

———. "The Shakespeare File: What English Majors Are Really Studying." American Council of Trustees and Alumni, December 1996. http://www.goacta.org/Reports/shakespeare.pdf (accessed November 2001).

Marx, Karl. *Capital.* Vol. 1. Trans. Ben Fowkes. London: Penguin, 1973.

———. *Grundrisse.* Trans. Martin Nicolaus. London: Penguin, 1973.

———. *Theories of Surplus Value.* Trans. G. A. Bonner and Emile Burns. New York: International Publishers, 1952.

Marx, Karl, and Frederick Engels. *Collected Works.* Trans. Richard Dixon et al. 49 vols. New York: International Publishers, 1975–2001.

Mauss, Marcel. *The Gift: The Form and Reason for Exchange in Archaic Societies.* Trans. W. D. Halls. New York: Norton, 1990.

McGovern, Marion, and Dennis Russell. *A New Brand of Expertise: How Independent Consultants, Free Agents, and Interim Managers Are Transforming the World of Work.* Boston: Butterworth-Heinemann, 2001.

Mead, Lawrence M. *Beyond Entitlement: The Social Obligations of Citizenship.* New York: Free Press, 1986.

———. *The New Politics of Poverty: The Nonworking Poor in America.* New York: Basic Books, 1992.

Mehlman, Jeffrey. *Legacies of Anti-Semitism in France.* Minneapolis: University of Minnesota Press, 1983.

Michaelsen, Scott. "Resketching Anglo-Amerindian Identity Politics." In *Border Theory: The Limits of Cultural Politics,* ed. Scott Michaelsen and David E. Johnson, 221–52. Minneapolis: University of Minnesota Press, 1997.

Michaelsen, Scott, and Scott Cutler Shershow. "Practical Politics at the Limits of Community: The Cases of Affirmative Action and Welfare." *Postmodern Culture* 12, no. 2 (2002), www.iath.virginia.edu/pmc/text-only/issue.102/12.2contents.html.

Mikulski, Barbara A., Senator. "Personal Responsibility and Work Opportunity Reconciliation Act of 1996—Conference Report." S 9387. 142nd Cong., 2nd sess., *Congressional Record* (August 1, 1996). Bethesda, MD: Congressional Information Service. Available from *LexusNexus Congressional U* (online service).

Milton, John. *Complete Poems and Major Prose.* Ed. Merritt Y. Hughes. New York: Odyssey Press, 1957.

———. *Complete Prose Works of John Milton.* Rev. ed. New Haven, CT: Yale University Press, 1980.

Minowitz, Peter. *Profits, Priests, and Princes: Adam Smith's Empancipation of Economics from Politics and Religion.* Stanford, CA: Stanford University Press, 1993.

Mollat, Michel. *The Poor in the Middle Ages: An Essay in Social History.* New Haven, CT: Yale University Press, 1986.

Moorcock, Michael. *The Dancers at the End of Time.* New York: Harper and Row, 1972.

Mosse, Miles. *The Arraignment and Conviction of Usurie.* London, 1595.

Motherwell, Robert. *The Dada Painters and Poets: An Anthology.* 2nd ed. Boston, MA: G. K. Hall, 1981.

Murdock, Mike. *The Leadership Secrets of Jesus: Practical Lessons for Today.* Tulsa, OK: Honor Books, 1997.

Murray, Charles. Preface to Olasky *Tragedy* xi–xvii.

Nancy, Jean-Luc. *The Experience of Freedom.* Trans. Bridget McDonald. Stanford, CA: Stanford University Press, 1993.

——. *The Inoperative Community.* Trans. Peter Connor et al. Minneapolis: University of Minnesota Press, 1991.

——. *The Muses.* Trans. Peggy Kamuf. Stanford, CA: Stanford University Press, 1996.

——. *The Sense of the World.* Trans. Jeffrey S. Librett. Minneapolis: University of Minnesota Press, 1997.

Negativland. *Fair Use: The Story of the Letter U and the Numeral 2.* Concord, CA: Seeland, 1995.

Negri, Antonio. *Marx beyond Marx: Lessons on the "Grundrisse."* Trans. Harry Cleaver, Michael Ryan, and Maurizio Viano. Ed. Jim Fleming. New York: Autonomedia, 1991.

Neusner, Jacob. *The Economics of the Mishnah.* Atlanta, GA: Scholars Press, 1998.

Norman, Geoffrey. "The Development of American Mural Painting." In O'Connor *Art for the Millions* 50–55.

Novak, Michael. *Business as a Calling: Work and the Examined Life.* New York: Free Press, 1996.

O'Connor, Francis V. Introduction to O'Connor *Art for the Millions* 13–32.

——, ed. *Art for the Millions: Essays from the 1930s by Artists and Administrators of the WPA Federal Art Project.* Boston: New York Graphic Society, 1975.

Olasen, Jens. *Cobra My Passion: Copenhagen, Brussels, Amsterdam.* São Paolo, Brazil: J. Olsen, 1999.

Olasky, Marvin. *Renewing American Compassion.* New York: Free Press, 1996.

——. *The Tragedy of American Compassion.* Washington, DC: Regnery Publishing, 1992.

Origen. *Homilies on Genesis and Exodus.* Trans. Ronald E. Heine. Fathers of the Church, vol. 71. Washington, DC: Catholic University of America Press, 1982.

Park, Marlene, and Gerald E. Markowitz. *Democratic Vistas: Post Offices and Public Art in the New Deal.* Philadelphia: Temple University Press, 1984.

Paulet, William, Marquis of Winchester. *The Lord Marques Idlenes: Conteining Manifold Matters of Acceptable Devise.* London, 1586.

Pecora, Vincent P. *Households of the Soul.* Baltimore: Johns Hopkins University Press, 1997.

Peffer, R. G., ed. *Marxism, Morality, and Social Justice.* Princeton, NJ: Princeton University Press, 1990.

Pelikan, Jaroslav. "Commandment or Curse? The Paradox of Work in the Judeo-Christian Tradition." In *Comparative Work Ethics: Judeo-Christian, Islamic, and Eastern,* by

Jaroslav Pelikan, Joseph Kitagawa, and Seyyed Hossein Nasr, 7–24. Occasional Papers of the Council of Scholars, vol. 4. Washington, DC: Library of Congress, 1985.

Penty, Arthur J. *Old Worlds for New: A Study of the Post-industrial State.* London: Allen and Unwin, 1918.

Perkins, William. *The Workes of That Famous and Worthy Minister of Christ in the Universitie of Cambridge, Mr. William Perkins.* Vol. 1. London, 1612.

Perlein, Gilbert, and Bruno Corà. *Yves Klein: Long Live the Immaterial.* New York: Delano Greenidge Editions, 2000.

Pie, Thomas. *Usuries Spright Conjured, or a Scholastiall Determination of Usury.* London, 1604.

Pilzer, Paul Zane. *God Wants You to Be Rich: The Theology of Economics.* New York: Simon and Schuster, 1995.

Pinchot, Gifford. *Intrapreneuring: Why You Don't Have to Leave the Corporation to Become an Entrepreneur.* New York: Harper and Row, 1985.

Pink, Daniel H. *Free Agent Nation: How America's New Independent Workers Are Transforming the Way We Live.* New York: Warner Books, 2001.

Piven, Frances Fox, and Richard A. Cloward. "Humanitarianism in History: A Response to the Critics." In Trattner 114–27.

———. *Regulating the Poor: The Functions of Public Welfare.* 2nd ed. New York: Vintage, 1993.

Plotnitsky, Arkady. *Reconfigurations: Critical Theory and General Economy.* Gainesville, FL: University Press of Florida. 1993.

Poppendieck, Janet. *Sweet Charity? Emergency Food and the End of Entitlement.* New York: Viking, 1998.

Prugh, Thomas, and Robert Costanza. *Natural Capital and Human Economic Survival.* 2nd ed. Solomons, MD: Lewis Publishers, 1999.

Reinhold, Barbara Bailey. *Free to Succeed: Designing the Life You Want in the New Free Agent Economy.* New York: Plume, 2001.

Restany, Pierre, and Andrea Loselle. *Yves Klein: Fire at the Heart of the Void.* New York: Journal of Contemporary Art, 1992.

Rice University, Institute for the Arts. *Yves Klein, 1928–1962: A Retrospective.* Houston: Rice University; New York: Arts Publisher, 1982.

Richman, Michele H. *Reading Georges Bataille: Beyond the Gift.* Baltimore: Johns Hopkins University Press, 1982.

Rifkin, Jeremy. *The End of Work: The Decline of the Global Labor Force and the Dawn of the Post-market Era.* New York: G. P. Putnam's Sons, 1995.

Robinson, John P., and Geoffrey Godbey. *Time for Life: The Surprising Ways Americans Use Their Time.* University Park: Pennsylvania State University Press, 1997.

Robinson, Jonathan. *Real Wealth: A Spiritual Approach to Money and Work.* Carlsbad, CA: Hay House, 1998.

Rose, Nikolas S. *Governing the Soul: The Shaping of the Private Self.* London and New York: Routledge, 1990.

Ross, Andrew. *No Respect: Intellectuals and Popular Culture.* New York: Routledge, 1989.

Rubin, William Stanley. *Dada and Surrealist Art.* New York: H. N. Abrams, 1968.

———. *Dada, Surrealism, and Their Heritage.* New York: Museum of Modern Art; Greenwich, CT: New York Graphic Society, 1968.

The Ruinate Fall of the Pope Usury, Derived from the Pope Idolatrie Reveled by a Saxon of Antiquitie. London, [c. 1580].

Ryan, Michael. "Epilogue." In Negri 191–221.

Sahlins, Marshall David. *Stone Age Economics.* New York: Aldine, 1972.

Samuelson, Paul Anthony, William D. Nordhaus, and Michael J. Mandel. *Economics.* 15th ed. New York: McGraw-Hill, 1995.

Samuelson, Robert J. "Down-sizing for Growth." *Newsweek,* March 25, 1996.

Savran, David. "Ambivalence, Utopia, and a Queer Sort of Materialism: How *Angels in America* Reconstructs the Nation." In Geis and Kruger 13–39.

Scapp, Ron. "The Vehicle of Democracy: Fantasies toward a (Queer) Nation." In Geis and Kruger 90–100.

Schein, Edgar H. *The Corporate Culture Survival Guide.* San Francisco: Jossey-Bass, 1999.

Schor, Juliet. *The Overworked American: The Unexpected Decline of Leisure.* New York: Basic Books, 1991.

Schrift, Alan D. "Introduction: Why Gift?" In Shrift *Logic of the Gift* 1–22.

———, ed. *The Logic of the Gift: Toward an Ethic of Generosity.* New York: Routledge, 1997.

Sebek, Barbara. "Good Turns and the Art of Merchandizing: Conceptualizing Exchange in Early Modern England" (draft version). *Early Modern Culture.* http://eserver.org/emc/1-2/issue2.html.

Secretan, Lance H. K. *Reclaiming Higher Ground: Creating Organizations That Inspire the Soul.* New York: McGraw-Hill, 1998.

Sen, Amartya. *On Ethics and Economics.* Oxford: Blackwell, 1987.

Sennett, Richard. *The Corrosion of Character: The Personal Consequences of Work in the New Capitalism.* New York: Norton, 1998.

Shapiro, Marc. *James Cameron: An Unauthorized Biography.* Los Angeles: Renaissance Books, 2000.

Sharp, Lauriston R. "People without Politics." In *Systems of Political Control and Bureaucracy in Human Societies: Proceedings of the 1958 Annual Spring Meeting of the American Ethnological Society,* ed. Verne F. Ray, 1–7. Seattle: American Ethnological Society, 1958.

Shaviro, Steven. *Passion and Excess: Blanchot, Bataille, and Literary Theory.* Tallahassee: Florida State University Press, 1990.

Shaw, George Bernard. *Complete Plays with Prefaces.* 6 vols. New York: Dodd, Mead, 1963.

Shell, Marc. *The Economics of Literature.* Baltimore: Johns Hopkins University Press, 1978.

Shershow, Scott Cutler. "Idols of the Marketplace: Rethinking the Economic Determination of Renaissance Drama." *Renaissance Drama,* n.s., 26 (1995; published 1997): 1–27.

Shklar, Judith N. *American Citizenship: The Quest for Inclusion.* Cambridge, MA: Harvard University Press, 1991.

Smigel, Erwin Orson, ed. *Work and Leisure: A Contemporary Social Problem.* New Haven, CT: College and University Press, 1963.

Smith, Adam. *An Inquiry into the Nature and Causes of the Wealth of Nations.* Ed. Edwin Cannan. New York: Modern Library, 1994.

Smith, Henrie. *The Poore Mans Teares, Opened in a Sermon.* London, 1592.

Smith, Henry. *The Sermons of Master Henry Smith*. London, 1622.

Smith, Joan, Immanuel Maurice Wallerstein, and Hans-Dieter Evers. *Households and the World Economy*. Beverly Hills, CA: Sage Publications, 1984.

Sontage, Deborah. "Who Brought Bernadine Healy Down? The Red Cross: A Disaster Story without Any Heroes." *New York Times Magazine*, December 23, 2001, 32–55.

Specter, Michael. "The Dangerous Philosopher." *New Yorker* 75, no. 25 (September 6, 1999): 46–55.

Spector, Nancy. *Felix González-Torres*. New York: Guggenheim Museum/H. N. Abrams, 1995.

Stockl, Allan. "Bataille, Gift Giving, and the Cold War." In Schrift *Logic of the Gift* 245–55.

Strauss, Neil. "Spreading by the Web, Pop's Bootleg Remix." *New York Times*, May 9, 2002, Business and Financial Desk.

Streisand, Betsy. "The New Philanthropy." *U.S. News and World Report* 130, no. 23 (June 11, 2001): 40.

Surya, Michel. *Georges Bataille: An Intellectual Biography*. Trans. Krzystof Fijalkowski and Michael Richardson. London: Verso, 2002.

Taylor, Mark C. *Altarity*. Chicago: University of Chicago Press, 1987.

Theobald, Robert. Preface to *The Guaranteed Income: Next Step in Economic Evolution?* Ed. Robert Theobald. Garden City, NY: Doubleday, 1966.

Thompson, E. P. "The Moral Economy of the English Crowd in the Eighteenth Century." In *Customs in Common*, by E. P. Thompson, 185–258. New York: New Press, 1993.

———. "Time, Word Discipline, and Industrial Capitalism." In *Customs in Common*, by E. P. Thompson, 352–403. New York: New Press, 1993.

Tilgher, Adriano. *Homo Faber: Work through the Ages*. Trans. Dorothy Canfield Fisher. 1930. Repr., Chicago: Henry Regnery, 1958.

Tocqueville, Alexis de. *Memoir on Pauperism*. Trans. Seymour Drescher. Ed. Gertrude Himmelfarb. Chicago: Ivan R. Dee, 1997.

Toffler, Alvin. *Powershift: Knowledge, Wealth, and Violence at the Edge of the 21st Century*. New York: Bantam Books, 1990.

———. *The Third Wave*. New York: Morrow, 1980.

Trattner, Walter I., ed. *Social Welfare or Social Control: Some Historical Reflections on Regulating the Poor*. Knoxville: University of Tennessee Press, 1983.

Trompenaars, Fons. *Riding the Waves of Culture: Understanding Diversity in Global Business*. New York: Irwin, 1994.

Tucker, Robert C. *The Marx-Engels Reader*. 2nd ed. New York: Norton, 1978.

Turan, Kenneth. "'Titanic' Sinks Again (Spectacularly)." *Los Angeles Times*, December 19, 1997. Accessed on Latimes.com, http://www.calendarlive.com/top/1,1419,L-LATimes-Movies-X!ArticleDetail-4625,00.html.

Tyndale, William. *A Path Way I[n]to the Holy Scripture*. London, 1536.

Ungar, Steven. *Scandal and Aftereffect: Blanchot and France since 1930*. Minneapolis: University of Minnesota Press, 1995.

U.S. Congress. *Personal Responsibility and Work Opportunity Reconciliation Act*. HR 3734. 104th Congress, 2nd sess., 1996.

Varley, John. *Steel Beach*. New York: G. P. Putnam's Sons, 1992.

Vaughan, W. *The Golden Grove, Moralized in Three Books.* London, 1600.

Veblen, Thorstein. *The Theory of the Leisure Class: An Economic Study of Institutions.* 1899. Repr., New York: Modern Library, 1934.

Vickers, Brian. *Appropriating Shakespeare: Contemporary Critical Quarrels.* New Haven, CT: Yale University Press, 1993.

Viner, Jacob. *Religious Thought and Economic Society.* Durham, NC: Duke University Press, 1978.

Virno, Paolo. "Virtuosity and Revolution: The Political Theory of Exodus." In Virno and Hardt *Radical Thought in Italy* 189–212.

Virno, Paolo, and Michael Hardt, eds. *Radical Thought in Italy: A Potential Politics.* Minneapolis: University of Minnesota Press, 1996.

Wallerstein, Immanuel Maurice. *Historical Capitalism.* London: Verso, 1983.

Weber, Max. *The Protestant Ethic and the Spirit of Capitalism.* Trans. Talcott Parsons. London: George Allen and Unwin, 1930.

Wesley, John. *The Works of John Wesley: Sermons.* 4 vols. Ed. Albert C. Outler. Nashville, TN: Abingdon Press, 1984–87.

Whitney, Geffrey. *A Choice of Emblemes, and Other Devises.* Leyden, 1586.

Williams, Raymond. *The Country and the City.* New York: Oxford University Press, 1973.

———. *Keywords: A Vocabulary of Culture and Society.* Rev. ed. New York: Oxford University Press, 1985.

Wilson, Thomas. *A Discourse Upon Usury.* 1572. Repr., ed. R. H. Tawney. New York: Harcourt Brace, n.d.

Wilson, William Julius. *When Work Disappears: The World of the New Urban Poor.* New York: Random House, 1996.

Wolin, Richard, ed. *The Heidegger Controversy: A Critical Reader.* Cambridge, MA: MIT Press, 1993.

———. *The Seduction of Unreason: The Intellectual Romance with Fascism from Nietzsche to Postmodernism.* Princeton, NJ: Princeton University Press, 2004.

Woodbridge, Linda. *Vagrancy, Homelessness, and English Renaissance Literature.* Urbana: University of Illinois Press, 2001.

Wyschogrod, Edith, Jean-Joseph Goux, and Eric Boynton, eds. *The Enigma of Gift and Sacrifice.* New York: Fordham University Press, 2002.

Yeats, William Butler. *The Collected Poems of W. B. Yeats.* New York: Macmillan, 1956.

INDEX